THE HOLOCAUST IN THE SOVIET UNION

THE HOLOCAUST IN THE SOVIET UNION

Studies and Sources on the Destruction of the Jews in the Nazi-Occupied Territories of the USSR, 1941-1945

Edited by
Lucjan Dobroszycki and Jeffrey S. Gurock
With a foreword by Richard Pipes

M.E. Sharpe
Armonk, New York
London, England

Photo: "Mass execution of Jews in Vinnitsa, Ukraine, 1941."
Photo courtesy of YIVO Institute.

Library of Congress Cataloging-in-Publication Data

The Holocaust in the Soviet Union : studies and sources on the destruction of the Jews
in the Nazi-occupied territories of the USSR. 1941–1945 / edited by Lucjan
Dobroszycki and Jeffrey Gurock.
p.   cm.
Includes index
ISBN 1-56324-173-0.—ISBN 1-56324-174-9 (pbk)
1. Jews—Soviet Union—Persecutions—Congresses
2. Holocaust, Jewish (1939–1945)—Soviet Union—Congresses.
3. Soviet Union—Ethnic Relations—Congresses.
I. Dobroszycki, Lucjan.
II. Gurock, Jeffrey S., 1949–
DS135.R92h64   1993
940.53'18'0947—dc20
93-415567
CIP

Printed in the United States of America

The paper used in this publication meets the minimum requirements of
American National Standard for Information Sciences—
Permanence of Paper for Printed Library Materials,
ANSI Z 39.48-1984.

∞

BM (c) 10   9   8   7   6   5   4   3   2   1

BM (p) 10   9   8   7   6   5   4   3   2   1

Contents

Part 3. REGIONAL STUDIES

Part 4:   SOURCES FOR STUDY OF THE HOLOCAUST
          IN THE SOVIET UNION

Foreword

Communist regimes always had a problem with the "Jewish Question." Neither Marx nor Lenin acknowledged Jews to be a nation, preferring to treat them as a socioeconomic caste (in the case of Marx, of a uniquely pernicious kind). Its destiny was to assimilate and vanish. The fact that they stubbornly clung to their ways even after the advent of the Communist regime proved perplexing and difficult to explain. The problem was compounded by the fact that the unpopular Communist regime in Russia employed Jews in positions of authority which they had never held before; this led many Russians to blame their miseries on Jews and to identify Communism with them.

To counteract this development, the Communists did all they could to destroy the religious and cultural institutions of Russian Jews, making communal worship all but impossible and outlawing the teaching of Hebrew and the propagation of Zionism. In the 1930s, Jews were systematically eliminated from the government. According to what Hitler told his closest associates, Stalin promised Ribbentrop that as soon as he had enough gentile cadres at his disposal, he would eliminate Jews altogether from his government. As is well known, Stalin intended to have all Soviet Jews deported to Siberia and Central Asia.

The intensification of anti-Semitism in the Soviet Union in the 1920s and especially the 1930s left Soviet Jews entirely unprepared for what was to come. Like all East European Jews, they regarded the Germans with awe and admiration; so much so that during World War I the tsarist authorities had expelled them by the thousands from the combat zone on suspicion of pro-German sympathies. The Soviet press passed over in silence the anti-Semitic excesses in Nazi Germany, pretending that "Fascism" was a reactionary movement directed exclusively against the "proletariat." The mass of Russian, Belorussian, and Ukrainian Jews had, therefore, no inkling that the German invaders came with the express intention of slaughtering them along with the "Communists," and in fact drew no distinction between them.

In the wake of the Holocaust, the Soviet authorities did their best to conceal all evidence of the Nazi war against the Jews in order to maintain the myth of a "Fascist" war on the "proletariat." When the undersigned first visited the USSR in 1957 he found even well-intentioned persons to have been quite unaware of the Nazi obsession with Jews and the systematic nature of their extermination campaign against them.

The present volume gives the fullest available treatment of a subject which until now has received scanty attention from scholars: the deliberate massacre of an estimated one million peaceful citizens inhabiting the USSR and its recently conquered territories by a barbarian horde let loose by the best educated and industrially most advanced country in Europe.

Richard Pipes
Harvard University

Acknowledgments

The convening of the Conference on the Holocaust in the Soviet Union and the preparation of papers from the conference for publication was supported by several distinguished friends of the Holocaust Studies program at Yeshiva University. The editors of this volume would like to acknowledge the encouragement of Dr. Norman Lamm, president of Yeshiva University, Dr. Egon Brenner, Executive Vice President of the university, and Rabbi Robert S. Hirt, Vice President for Administration and Professional Education at the university-affiliated Rabbi Isaac Elchanan Theological Seminary, in the development of the academic parameters of this scholarly gathering. We are likewise grateful to Eli and Diana Zborowski for their continued dedication to the scholarly study of the Holocaust, to Lawrence Newman for his loyal interest in our work, and to Dr. Laszlo N. Tauber for his commitment to the research and publication of quality works on the history of Eastern European Jewry. The editors would also like to thank the fourteen authors who shared their research and perspectives with the Yeshiva University community.

Finally, the editors would like to thank Patricia Kolb and her associates at M. E. Sharpe, Inc., for their able assistance in readying this volume for publication.

J.S.G.

Preface

During the final years of the Soviet Union, new vistas were opened to scholars concerned with objective, scholarly documentation and analysis of the history of the destruction of Jews and Jewish communities during the Nazi occupation of 1941–45. Beginning with perestroika and glasnost, the gates of the Soviet archives, which had been closed to scholars of Holocaust studies for over half a century, were unlocked and then opened wide. The materials in these archives are destined to open a new chapter in the study of the destruction of Jews, not only in the Nazi-occupied territories of the Soviet Union, but in all of Nazi Europe. As it cleared the occupier from Eastern Europe and captured Berlin, Königsberg, and Vienna (the capitals of the Reich, East Prussia, and Austria), in addition to the territories of eastern Germany, the Soviet Army took over a large, if not the largest, portion of German records. Today, we have access to microfilms of selected documents from almost all the former Soviet central and local archives, including those of the Communist Party (now called the Center for the Preservation and Study of Documents of Contemporary History) and the Committee for State Security (KGB). Teams of researchers from Yad Vashem, the Hoover Institute for War, Peace, and Revolution, the United States Holocaust Memorial Museum, the U.S. National Archives, and other institutions in Great Britain, France, Germany, and Poland have filmed during the last two years tens of thousands of documents. The availability of sources from the former Soviet Union combined with the possibility of unrestricted travel to the collections has significantly expanded the field of Holocaust research.

In October 1981, the Eli and Diana Zborowski Chair in Interdisciplinary Holocaust Studies at Yeshiva University, sensitive to this changed atmosphere conducive to research, convened the first international gathering of scholars working in this field in the post-Soviet era to report on their new research initiatives. This conference took place at a most appropriate moment, as it coincided with the fiftieth anniversary of the German invasion of the Soviet Union and the beginning of mass slaughter of millions of Jews. To be sure, the papers given by specialists from Israel, Great Britain, Poland, and the United States reflect the initial stages of the accessibility of primary sources in the archives of the Soviet Union. Many of the papers make use of published sources and interviews with survivors who now reside outside of the former Soviet Union. What they offer are model expositions into underexplored historical territories, and a basis and guide for future investigators.

At the opening session, the keynote address was delivered by Professor Richard Pipes of Harvard University, one of the leading scholars of Russian and Soviet history. Professor Pipes drew attention to the Jewish personalities in the Communist leadership, characterizing them as very visible but, at the same time, completely alienated from the Jewish masses as well as Jewish history, culture, and customs. His analysis of the state of mind of the Jews under the Soviet regime set the stage for a better understanding of their initial reaction to the Nazi occupation.

Three major areas of inquiry are examined in the papers. Mordechai Altshuler, David Engel, Zvi Gitelman, Lukasz Hirszowicz, William Korey, and Rafael Medoff consider a wide range of problems related to Soviet government policies toward the Jews during the Holocaust and the subsequent treatment of the Holocaust in Soviet historiography, belles lettres, the mass media, commemorations, and so on.

Jan Gross, Zvi Kolitz, Dalia Ofer, Gertrude Schneider, and Andrzej Zbikowski focus on the actual destruction of Jewish communities on the territory of the Soviet Union, including areas that had been incorporated into the USSR after September 17, 1939. Sergei Maksudov makes an attempt to quantify the Jewish losses in the Soviet Union during the Holocaust, using census data.

Also examining the question of sources for future research into the history of the Holocaust in the Soviet Union is the contribution by Lucjan Dobroszycki, which characterizes the captured Nazi documents relating to destruction of Jewish communities. Simon Schochet uses newly accessible sources to uncover more of the story of Katyn, while Robert M. Shapiro considers the value of *yizker-bikher* (memorial books) as sources for the study of this tragic period in Jewish history.

L.D.

Part 1

The Holocaust in
the Soviet Union

Soviet Reactions to the Holocaust, 1945–1991

ZVI GITELMAN

The Holocaust in the Soviet Union

About one-third of all the Jews killed in the Holocaust had been living under Soviet rule in 1940. Most estimates, necessarily based on fragmentary information, are that about one and a half million Soviet Jewish citizens who lived in the pre-1939 borders of the USSR were murdered by the Nazis and that 200,000 more died in combat.[1] The rest of the victims were Jews who came under Soviet rule in 1939–40, in the wake of the Hitler–Stalin pact.

The Soviet treatment of the Holocaust, and most notably of the Holocaust within its borders, has been very different from that in the West. William Korey, in the September 1991 issue of *Hadassah* magazine, writes of "the Kremlin's suppression of all reference to the Holocaust until now" (p. 10). This is somewhat exaggerated. While not denying the Holocaust, most Soviet writers have either ignored it or submerged it in more general accounts of the period. A preliminary survey of Soviet writings reveals that they vary significantly in the prominence and interpretations given to the Holocaust. Most Soviet works either pass over it in silence or blur it by universalizing it. Western assertions to the contrary, there seems to be no consistent Soviet "party line" on the Holocaust. Some works do acknowledge and describe the Holocaust, while others discuss only some aspects of it. One can only speculate regarding Soviet motivations, but we can point with greater certainty to some consequences, intended and unintended, of the general Soviet tendency to ignore or downplay the Holocaust. In any case, as the Soviet Union and its dominating party broke up, the treatment of the Holocaust began to change radically.

Soviet treatment of the Holocaust has had profound, if subtle, effects on both Jews and non-Jews in the USSR. On the one hand, it denied Jews any particular sympathy on the part of non-Jews. Unlike in the West, Soviet non-Jews, for the most part, did not feel a need to "make up" to the Jews, as it were, for any of the wrongs done to them. On the other hand, Soviet treatment aroused Jewish consciousness. But it also engendered first puzzlement, and then bitterness, when Jews, especially younger ones, realized that a vital part of their recent history was being denied them. Their worth and importance had been denigrated, their particular history and culture dismissed, and their claims of discrimination rejected. Soviet treatment—or lack of it—of the Holocaust was a significant factor in the reemergence of Jewish national consciousness in the former Soviet Union. It will be not only interesting from an academic point of view, but also important socially and politically, to see how and to what extent the current reexamination of Soviet history, which began as part of *glasnost'*, will reopen the pages of the Holocaust and will permit this chapter to be written in full. Early indications are that this is beginning to occur.

After briefly identifying the main outlines of how the Holocaust was perpetrated in the USSR, we shall discuss how it has been treated in Soviet writings, offer some suggestions as to why it was been accorded such a treatment, and examine the consequences of that treatment.

The War Against Soviet Jewry

Around a quarter of a million of the Jews from the territories annexed by the Soviet Union in 1939–40 either fled to the interior beyond the Nazi grasp or were inadvertently saved by the Soviets from Nazi annihilation when the former deported them to Siberia and Central Asia.[2]

The Soviet occupation of the western territories brought with it a tragic, fateful divergence in the perceptions and interests of Jews and non-Jews. In all of those territories anti-Semitic regimes in the 1930s had made life increasingly uncomfortable—in many cases intolerable—for Jews. America and Palestine were closed to immigration, and Jews in Poland, Romania, Latvia, and Lithuania had little hope of improving their lot. The entry of the Red Army, with its Jewish officers and men, its promises of national equality and social justice, gave hope to some of the younger and more radically inclined Jews. Despite misgivings about the Bolsheviks' militant atheism, their persecution of Zionism, and nationalization of property, many Jews welcomed the Red Army as a liberator. A resident of eastern Poland recalled that when the Red Army came, "There was a holiday atmosphere. Things changed overnight. . . . The Germans would not come in and that was the most important thing."[3] Others saw the Soviets as the lesser of two evils. Another survivor from the same area comments, "when the Russians came in we were a little afraid, but not as afraid as we were of the Germans in the western part of Poland."[4]

By contrast, the Poles, Baltic peoples, and Romanians saw the Red Army as an invader, not a liberator, one that was depriving them of their hard-won and all too brief political independence. Jews who welcomed the Red Army were seen as traitors, and all Jews were assumed to be Bolshevik sympathizers and betrayers of the lands of their birth. Little wonder, then, that in 1941 when the Germans drove the Red Army out, many non-Jews greeted the Germans as liberators from Soviet oppression and took the opportunity to wreak harsh vengeance on the traitorous Jews. In the first few days of the German occupation of Lithuania, for example, Lithuanian groups murdered 5,000 Jews.

Three million German troops invaded the USSR from the west, quickly encircling the main centers of Jewish population. The Nazis had long been explicit about their consuming hatred for both Bolsheviks and Jews, whom they equated with each other. Adolf Hitler wrote in 1930, "The Nordic race has a right to rule the world. . . . Any cooperation with Russia is out of the question, for there on a Slavic-Tatar body is set a Jewish head."[5] German General von Reichenau issued an order stating, "The most essential aim of war against the Jewish-Bolshevistic system is a complete destruction of their . . . power. . . . Therefore, the soldier must have full understanding for the necessity of severe but just revenge on subhuman Jewry." General von Manstein wrote, "More strongly than in Europe, [Jewry] holds all the key positions in the political leadership and administration. . . . The Jewish-Bolshevist system must be exterminated once and for all. The soldier must appreciate the necessity for harsh punishment of Jewry, the spiritual bearer of the Bolshevist terror."[6]

Though the Nazis could not have been more explicit about their intentions, following the Nazi-Soviet pact of August 1939 the Soviet media had draped a blanket of silence over Nazi atrocities. Together with older people's memories of the Germans of World War I as "decent people," this may have left many Soviet Jews unprepared for the mass murder campaign conducted by four *Einsatzgruppen*, or mobile killing squads, who liquidated much of Soviet Jewry by machine gunning them in or near their home towns. Others were placed in ghettos, most of which were liquidated, along with their inhabitants, by 1941–42. Within five months, the *Einsatzgruppen*—whose officers were largely intellectuals and professionals, as Raul Hilberg observes—had killed about half a million Jews. Needless to say, these killings were often preceded by extensive torture.[7] By war's end, perhaps two or three million Jewish civilians had been killed, singled out from the rest of the population for "special handling."

Soviet Historiography of the Holocaust

Some Western observers charge that it was Soviet policy to suppress any public discussion of the Holocaust. William Korey writes of "the Soviet attempt to obliterate the Holocaust in the memories of Jews as well as non-Jews."[8] Writing in 1970, Mordechai Altshuler asserts that "The wall of silence regarding the Holocaust still stands in the Soviet Union, though here and there small cracks were observed. . . . The paucity of publications on the Holocaust of Soviet Jewry . . . and the attacks on Yevtushenko's 'Babi Yar' . . . testify to a purposeful policy of the regime to suppress the Holocaust in the Soviet Union."[9] This policy is sometimes explained as a consequence of Soviet anti-Semitism and hostility toward Jewish history and culture. Korey's explanation is more sophisticated: "Expunging the Holocaust from the record of the past was hardly a simple matter, but unless it were done the profound anguish of the memory was certain to stir a throbbing national consciousness. Martyrdom, after all, is a powerful stimulus to a group's sense of its own identity."[10] In his study of Lithuanian Jewry's resistance to the Nazis, Dov Levin points out that Soviet writing on World War II generally downplays the role of the Jews in the war, and does so regarding Lithuanian Jewry as well. He reasons that this is in order not to diminish the already marginal role of the Lithuanians in the resistance against the Nazis.[11]

A closer examination of Soviet writings on World War II reveals that if there existed a policy of repressing the Holocaust, it was applied unevenly at best. Nevertheless, it remains true that the overall thrust of the Soviet literature was to assign the Holocaust far less significance than it has been given in the West. One cannot entirely dismiss the possibility that this is the consequence of having large, articulate, nationally conscious Jewish populations in the West where they are mostly free to explore Jewish history and draw whatever conclusions they wish, whereas conditions in the Soviet Union until now permitted neither such exploration nor such expression. Moreover, no country in the West lost as many of its non-Jewish citizens in the war against Nazism as did the USSR, so that the fate of the Jews in France, Holland, Germany, or Belgium stands in sharper contrast to that of their conationals or coreligionists than it does in the East. On the other hand, in Yugoslavia and Poland, where civilian populations were decimated in no less a proportion than they were in the USSR, greater public attention has been paid to the specifically Jewish tragedy of the war period. Thus, the Soviet Union did treat the issue differently from most other countries, whether socialist or not, though this treatment was not uniform.

In striking contrast to the way it has been treated in the West, in the Soviet Union the Holocaust was not presented as a unique, separate phenomenon. It was not denied that six million Jews were killed, among them many Soviet citizens, nor that Jews were singled out for annihilation. But the Holocaust was seen as an integral part of a larger phenomenon—the murder of civilians, whether Russians, Ukrainians, Belorussians, Gypsies, or other nationalities. It was said to be a natural consequence of racist fascism. The Holocaust, in other words, was but one of several reflexes of fascism, which is, in turn, the ultimate expression of capitalism. Thus, the roots of the Holocaust lie in capitalism, expressed in its most degenerate form. Armed with the theory of "scientific socialism," the Soviets were able to explain in a facile way how so many were murdered. For them there was no mystery about the Holocaust. In the West, by contrast, there is a vast literature which seeks to understand how it happened. There are cultural explanations, psychological and sociological ones, political and bureaucratic ones. There is an extensive theological literature which seeks to confront God with the Holocaust. My impression is that not a single book published in the USSR sought to explain the Holocaust as *sui generis*. In fact, the term "Holocaust" is completely unknown in the Soviet literature. When discussing the destruction of the Jews, the terms "annihilation" *(unichtozhenie)* or "catastrophe," and more recently, "Holocaust" (transliterated from English) have been used. The *Black Book* of Soviet Jewry, containing documentation gathered from all over the country by the writers Ilya Ehrenburg, Vassily Grossman, and others, had 1,200 typescript pages by 1944, and was printed in 1946. But every single copy was sent to storage warehouses where they were destroyed in 1948, along with the type from which they were set. Only one copy, which had been sent abroad, survived, and now additional materials from Ehrenburg's archives have been brought to Israel. Thus, the major work on the Soviet Holocaust was never published in the USSR, though there are Hebrew, English, and even Russian (published in Jerusalem) editions. The Holocaust was treated as regrettable, but merely as one small part of the larger phenomenon which, according to the Soviets, resulted in the death of over 20 million of their citizens. If the Nazis gave the Jews "special treatment," the Soviets did not.

This premise translated into a policy of bypassing the Holocaust for most general audiences, and addressing it in a highly ideological way for certain specialized ones. William Korey's survey has shown that Soviet elementary school history textbooks contain no reference to Jews at all, and a 30-page chapter on World War II in one of them has not a single reference to either Jews or anti-Semitism. The same is true of secondary school texts and syllabi, except for a single reference to "terrible Jewish pogroms."[12] The controversy over the construction of a monument at Babi Yar, the site in Kiev where over 35,000 of the city's Jews were shot in the course of two days, is well known. For years, no monument was placed there, and the site was prepared for housing, a park, and other uses. In 1959 the writer Viktor Nekrasov protested plans to turn the site into a park and soccer stadium, and momentum began to build for the construction of a memorial monument. When this was finally done, the inscription referred only to "Soviet citizens," and not to Jews specifically. Similarly, when Yevgeny Yevtushenko published his poem "Babi Yar," whose first line reads "Over Babi Yar there are no monuments," he was roundly criticized by conservative writers who charged him with slandering the "Russian crew-cut lads" who had fought the Nazis. The writer Dmitri Starikov asserted that "the anti-Semitism of the Fascists is only part of their misanthropic policy of genocide. . . the destruction of the 'lower races' including the Slavs."[13] When Dmitri Shostakovich included

"Babi Yar" in his thirteenth symphony, Yevtushenko was forced to make two additions to the text. One line reads: "Here, together with Russians and Ukrainians, lie Jews," and the other is, "I am proud of the Russia which stood in the path of the bandits." Again, the point is not that others suffered along with Jews, which no one would dispute, but that there was nothing unique about the quality and quantity of Jewish suffering, a far more dubious assertion.

The same issue arose in regard to Anatoly Kuznetsov's novel, *Babi Yar*. Public controversy arose over whether Jewish travails should have been singled out from among those of all others. Kuznetsov's novel and *Heavy Sand* (1978), by the Jewish writer Anatoly Rybakov, are among the very few Russian-language novels which acknowledge— even assert—a special fate for the Jews during the war.

The issue arises not only in regard to novels and monuments, but even in connection with museum displays. For example, despite the testimony of her uncle and several others, the seventeen-year-old Jew-ish partisan Masha Bruskina, hung by the Nazis in Minsk, is still identified as an "unknown partisan" in the Minsk Museum of the History of the Great Patriotic War. Significantly, the authorities' refusal to identify her name and nationality was seen by some Jews as a deliberate insult and a refusal to acknowledge Jewish heroism. A highly decorated war veteran, Lev Ovsishcher, commented, "This story explains why Jews who understand what is happening in this country feel the only correct decision is to leave." He subsequently emigrated to Israel, after a long struggle.[14]

Examining strictly historical treatments of the period 1941–45, whether popular or scholarly, reveals a more complex picture. The overall tendency remains to downplay, even ignore, the Holocaust, but some striking contrasts appear. While some works that should logically discuss the Holocaust ignore it completely, and others touch only on selected aspects of it, still others present a relatively straightforward and well-rounded account.

A fairly close examination of the six-volume official Soviet history of the war reveals not a single reference to Jews. Nor do the terms "anti-Semitism" or "Holocaust" appear in the index. In the third volume, the occupation is referred to as "a regime of terror and occupation." Einsatzgruppen are mentioned, as is Babi Yar, but the word "Jew" does not appear in any of these connections.[15] A large history of Ukraine, published in 1982, does not mention Jews once, not even in connection with the Holocaust, despite the fact that Jews have lived in Ukraine for centuries, played a major role in the economy and culture, and died there in the hundreds of thousands during the Holocaust.[16] In striking—almost ludicrous—contrast is a study of wartime Estonia. In 1939 there were over 1.5 million Jews living in Soviet Ukraine, and only 5,000 in "bourgeois" Estonia. Yet, while at least two histories of Ukraine pass over Jewish history and the Holocaust in silence, the study of Estonia presents a sympathetic account of Jewish suffering during the Holocaust and an undistorted account of Jewish participation in the armed struggle against the Nazis. The Germans' robbery of art and other treasures in private Jewish hands is mentioned explicitly. German documents are quoted which report "the total liquidation of the Jews. . . . At the present time there are no more Jews in Estonia." The editors comment, "Implementing their monstrous racial theories, the German fascists and their collaborators in Estonia exterminated each and every Jew and Gypsy."[17] Collaboration by Estonians with the Nazis in the murder of Jews is discussed frankly.[18] The authors acknowledge that Estonian collaborators "boasted to their bosses that they had outdone the others in annihilating the Jews," and that the groundwork had been laid before the war by anti-Semites, one of whom is quoted as saying to an audience of the Estonian military academy, "We should be happy that we have few Jews among us. We took in a good number from Tsarist Russia, but we look down on the Jews."[19] Unlike other studies, this one prominently features Red Army men and partisans of obviously Jewish extraction.[20]

A documentary collection on Belorussia includes, among other items, the order establishing the ghetto in Minsk; descriptions of Germans killing Jews wantonly, mass murders of Jews in the Brest-Litovsk area, and the extermination of the Jews in Pinsk, including a German report on the resistance of one of the condemned men; and a photograph of Jews being herded into the Grodno ghetto. The historical origins of ghettos are explained, concluding with the observation that "the Hitlerites revived ghettos in territories occupied by them, turning them into camps for the mass annihilation of the Jewish population."[21] A pamphlet on the Ninth Fort in Lithuania, where thousands of Jews were killed, mentions several Nazi "Aktions" against the Jews. Here, however, there is a greater attempt to blur the specifically Jewish tragedy. It is said that Einsatzgruppe A entered Kaunas with "the special task of exterminating the local party and Soviet *aktiv*, eliminating the resistance by Soviet patriots, exterminating the Jews." The order in which the victims are listed here may be significant. Even clearer is the contrast between the reproduction of a German document reporting on the "special handling" of 4,000 Jews in the Ponary death camp and the Russian caption, which says, "the Hitlerite security police report: another 4,000 *people* have been killed."[22]

One of the most popular Soviet books on the war treats the Holocaust most curiously. S.S. Smirnov's three-volume work appeared in an edition of 100,000, and Smirnov was a popular guest in media features on the war. In the three volumes Smirnov refers several times to the suffering of the Jews, but he seems to go out of his way to avoid references to Jews as fighters and resisters.

> For the Hitlerites, all peoples, aside from the Germans, all nations aside from the Germanic ones, were inferior and superfluous inhabitants of this earth. . . . The first among these "inferior" nations that would have to disappear were the Jews. The Germans left them no choice—this nation was to be completely exterminated. In all countries captured by the Hitlerite armies the extermination of the Jews was carried out on an unprecedented scale, with typical German planning and organization. Millions of people of Jewish nationality or with a tinge of Jewish blood became victims of mass shootings, were burned in crematoria or asphyxiated in the gas chambers and trucks. Whole neighborhoods were turned into Jewish ghettos and were burned to the ground with their thousands of inhabitants who wore the yellow six-pointed star, the compulsory badge for Jews in lands occupied by the Germans.[23]

Smirnov goes on to say that Kievans "remember how, hour after hour, endless columns of Jews passed on the way to being shot at Babi Yar. Prisoners at Auschwitz, Maidanek, Treblinka remember how thousands of groups of Jews from Poland and Hungary, the Soviet Union, and Czechoslovakia, from France and Holland, passed through the gas chambers in an endless convoy of death and how piles of bodies lay at the ovens of the crematoria."[24] He speaks of "the terrible fate of those who lived behind the barbed wire of innumerable ghettos." His generalizations are exemplified in the story of Roman Levin: "The ten-year-old Roman, who until then had been simply a Soviet boy, a Pioneer and school boy, suddenly learned that he was a Jew, and because of that they could insult him with impunity, beat him or even kill him." Levin escaped the Brest ghetto and was hidden by a devout

Polish Catholic woman who was later shot when the Gestapo discovered her ties to the partisans.[25]

In subsequent volumes, Smirnov discusses the persecution of Jews in Ukraine and in Hungary. In Ukraine, "often they marched groups of people, condemned to being shot, along the streets. . . on their way out of town. At first they shot groups of communists, Soviet officials, and people active in civic affairs. After that along the same route they began to take Jews, whole families, young and old. After that came columns of Gypsies who were also considered an inferior nation."[26] He reports that the Germans used a slogan: "Germans—*gut;* Jews—*kaput;* Russians—also *(tozhe);* Ukrainians—later *(pozzhe)."* Smirnov also describes the huge concentration of Jews in the Budapest ghetto and their deportation.[27] At the same time, he assiduously avoids identifying fighters as Jews. Describing the defenders of the Brest fortress, he mentions "the Russians Anatoly Vinogradov and Raisa Abakumova, the Armenian Samvel Matevosian, the Ukrainian Aleksandr Semenenko, the Belorussian Aleksandr Makhnach, . . . the Tatar Petr Gavrilov," and even "the German Viacheslav Meyer." The one hero whose nationality is not mentioned is Efim Moiseevich Fomin. Lest there be any doubt about his nationality, he is described as "short . . . dark-haired, with intelligent and mournful eyes," a political commissar from a small town in the Vitebsk area, the son of a smith and a seamstress—all characteristics that are stereotypically Jewish. Yet, Fomin is identified only as "the renowned commissar of the Brest fortress, a hero and a true son of the Communist Party, one of the chief organizers and leaders of the legendary defense."[28] When other heroes are described, their nationality is pointed out (Gavrilov, the Kazan Tatar; Matevosian, "of a poor Armenian family"; and Kizhevator, "the son of a Mordvin peasant").[29] The same pattern is followed in Smirnov's description of Soviet partisans in Italy.[30] Why did Smirnov describe Jewish martyrdom in detail yet assiduously ignore Jewish heroism? Was this in line with an official directive? Was it the compromise he reached with himself, or, more likely, with a censor? We cannot tell, of course, but the pattern is too consistent to be accidental. Another book, published one year earlier, presents Jews in a heroic light as partisans: Sarah Khatskelevna Levin and her Yiddish-speaking daughter meet "remarkable people who have not lost their courage and their human dignity" even in the Minsk ghetto. They "refused to give in without a struggle" and formed a fighting organization.[31]

The sharp contrast between treatments of the Holocaust in Ukraine, Belorussia, Lithuania, and Estonia raises several possibilities. The variance may be explained by the choices made by writers themselves, or, less likely, by republic-level policies that differ from one republic to another or by the caprice of censors in different places. It should be noted that the Holocaust is treated most openly in the Estonian volume and is avoided in the Ukrainian literature. In Estonia there is no tradition of anti-Semitism, whereas in Ukraine there is a substantial one. But whatever the reasons, the different treatments of the Holocaust clearly indicate the absence of a uniform, universally applied party line on the issue, though there is an overall thrust toward downplaying it or generalizing it to include many peoples.

Thus, a Soviet study of Nazi propaganda mentions Nazi views of Poles, Gypsies, and Jews as inferior races and the fact that the Nazis played up "the Jewish origins" of the leaders of the Russian revolution. The author does refer to the Nazis' "pathological anti-Semitism" and their claim that in the Soviet Union those who could not show Jewish origins were considered class enemies. This foreshadowed the "fate that the German racists prepared for the Jews."[32] But further details are not given, and it should be noted that this is an academic monograph, published in a relatively small edition. A documentary history of the Soviet Union which devotes an entire chapter to World War II includes no references to the Nazis' racial policy. The excerpt from the diary of Masha Rolnikaite, a Jewish girl in the Vilnius ghetto, does not mention the word "Jew."[33] The *Great Soviet Encyclopedia* notes that anti-Semitism "found its most extreme expression in fascist Germany," and states succinctly that "The Nazis carried out a policy of mass extermination of the Jews; about 6 million Jews were murdered in World War II."[34] In short, Soviet audiences are generally not exposed to even the most elementary details of the Holocaust. In the 1960s, a few volumes were published which did provide more information. Significantly, at least some were translations from other languages.[35] It is therefore all the more striking that *Sovietish haimland,* the Soviet Yiddish monthly appearing since 1961 (originally in an edition of 25,000, later reduced to 7,000), has material on the Holocaust in almost every single issue— stories, poems, memoirs, factual information. But a reading of the journal shows that certain themes appear consistently and serve a didactic political purpose. These are that: (1) Gentiles frequently saved Jews in occupied territories; (2) the Jews who resisted did so for universal, not parochial, reasons; (3) there was much cooperation among all nationalities against the Nazis; (4) the only collaborators with the Nazis were fascists, and nearly all of them now live in the West. The first theme is illustrated by a letter from a woman, now living in New York, who describes how the Lithuanian couple Ruzgis and the Polish doctor Hrabowiecka saved her daughter, and how the Russian family Iakubovskii did so later. Short stories show Russians, especially workers, saving Jews, and wealthy Jews serving on *Judenraten*.[36]

The theme of *druzhba narodov* (friendship of peoples) is emphasized throughout. Even an account of the Warsaw ghetto uprising praises Soviet Yiddish writing on it because

> The heroic uprising. . . is presented as a national event, . . . but it would really be an act of national narrowness and a demeaning of the heroes of the Warsaw battles if only their national impulses and national defense were described. . . . [This was] not only an act of national struggle, but in the main a struggle against the dark forces of fascism. . . . The Warsaw ghetto uprising should be seen as an important contribution of the Jewish masses to the international struggle of the progressive forces of all peoples, led by the Soviet Union, against fascism and international reaction.[37]

Of course, the role of Communists in the uprising is emphasized, and there are fictional accounts of Red Army men sneaking into the ghetto to help the resisting Jews.[38]

A description of how Bulgarians saved Jews concludes that "the struggle of the Bulgarian people to save the Jews, under the leadership of the communists, can in no way be separated from the general struggle of the Bulgarian people against fascism." The struggle against anti-Semitism can be successfully conducted "only in close alliance with the progressive and democratic forces of the world."[39] The other side of this coin is seen in the resistance of Soviet authorities to the publication of Peretz Markish's novel *Trot fun doires*, on the grounds that its hero was a "Zionist." The portrayal of him dying wrapped in a prayer shawl was also objectionable. The objections to publishing the novel were overridden by special authorization of the Soviet Writers' Union.[40] Thus, resistance to the Holocaust and to anti-Semitism must be universalized. They have to be portrayed as part of larger progressive struggles, led by communists.

A third theme appearing frequently is the cooperation of all nation-alities in the struggle against the Nazis. "One of the main sources of the world-historical victory. . . was the friendship among the Soviet peoples. Against the. . . enemy, Russians, Ukrainians, Belorussians, Jews, Georgians, Armenians—the sons and daughters of all the peo-ples of the Soviet Union—fought shoulder to shoulder."[41] A story about a Jewish Hero of the Soviet Union, Chaim Tevelevich Diskin, points out the heroism of his two Russian comrades, and another re-lates how Russians in Taganrog saved Jews.[42] In discussing the pro-posal to put up a monument in Kiev, it is stressed that "people of different nationalities—Russians, Ukrainians, Jews—were attracted by the idea of putting up a monument in Babi Yar."[43]

The well-known writer Boris Polevoi claims that Gentiles "stub-bornly opposed the murderers of the Jews, and Jewish families were hidden."[44] An editorial comment asserts that "in the days of the Great Patriotic War, friendship among peoples, among nations, was the most powerful weapon in the struggle with the fascists."[45] Writing about the sculptor Elmar Rivosh, whose entire family was killed in Riga, Misha Lev points out that Rivosh saved himself only because of the assis-tance of "his friends, identified and anonymous Latvians and Russians, Jews and Poles." A Russian woman on the "Aryan side" fed him, a Russian doctor healed him, a Latvian friend helped him find a hiding place.[46] This is the pattern emphasized throughout the literature, whether in Russian or in Yiddish.

How then can one explain collaboration with the Nazis on the part of hundreds of thousands? The answer is simple. They were all ideo-logically deformed. "Petty bourgeois are the same all over. Whoever has might, is right, they feel."[47] All the collaborators—whether Lat-vian, Polish, Ukrainian or Russian—were "bourgeois nationalists" or marginal elements, "the refuse of the Latvian people," as one article puts it.[48] Many of them, it is claimed, are now leading anti-Soviet agitators in the West. The Soviets had long written off anti-Soviet émigrés as collaborators with the Nazis, and there is no doubt that the label fits many. Sometimes it is acknowledged that these people "par-ticipated in the annihilation of the Jewish population." Recently, some have called for a reassessment of Soviet émigrés. "Our compatriots abroad—until just recently we pretended they did not exist (and if there were some abroad, they were all former Vlasovites, traitors to the homeland one and all). And yet millions of our fellow countrymen—

Russians, Ukrainians, Belorussians, Armenians, Jews—live far from their native land and many of them were scarcely burdened with inexpiable guilt."[49] But the more usual pattern is to omit the Jews. "It is precisely in the West. . . that traitors on whose hands the blood of Latvians, Lithuanians, and Estonians will never dry have taken refuge."[50]

Of course, these discussions avoid the fundamental problem of explaining how such large numbers of people could have been so infected with anti-Semitism—or so hostile to the Soviet regime—that they participated in the Nazis' work.[51]

Other problems that were swept under the rug and not mentioned were anti-Semitism in the Red Army and among the partisan groups.[52] In fact, the existence of separate Jewish partisan groups was completely unacknowledged. The role of Jews in the armed struggle against the German invaders was generally downplayed, as we have seen in the works of S.S. Smirnov. Writing about Hero of the Soviet Union Chaim Tevelevich Diskin, Marshal V. Kazakov never mentions Diskin's very obvious Jewish nationality.[53] Even partisan leader Col. Dmitri Medvedev, who accepted Jewish survivors, including women and children, into his group, never mentions the nationality of three Jewish heroes he describes, "although in his two books Medvedev rarely forgot to tell his readers whether his heroes were Russians, Ukrainians, Belorussians, Poles or Kazakhs."[54] He also does not mention how he saved 150 Jewish women, children, and old people. The assumption is that the censors or editors deliberately omitted these items.[55] Jewish combatants are mentioned in general discussions of the armed forces[56] and there are a few pamphlets or books published about Jewish war heroes, though the total number of this genre is very large.[57] Again, *Sovietish haimland* is different from the literature in Russian. In this Yiddish journal there is considerable fictional and nonfiction material about Jewish fighters. Jewish partisans are described in positive terms,[58] memoirs of Jewish generals and soldiers of lesser rank are often published,[59] and many Jewish soldiers, including those who gave their lives, are portrayed.[60] But the overwhelming majority of Soviet readers, even Jewish ones, have no access at all to this literature. The role of the Jews as combatants, even more than as victims, was largely ignored—and in most cases, it would seem, deliberately.

For many years it was assumed that anything published in the Soviet Union, since it had to pass official censorship, reflected policy at some level. Our examination of the literature on the Holocaust casts some doubt on this assumption. Nevertheless, the published literature remains almost the only source on reactions to the Holocaust, since to date there have been no other instruments for gauging public reaction to it. Thus far, there have been no surveys of people's reactions to the fate of the Jews during the war, nor are there any measures of their knowledge of the Holocaust. However, a survey conducted among over 300 Soviet Jewish immigrants in Detroit, within half a year of their arrival in 1989–90, reveals that few knew the approximate number of Soviet Jews killed in the Holocaust, though a majority cited the figure of six million for the total number of Jews who died. When asked whether they had read about the Holocaust in the USSR, a majority of those over the age of thirty had read some literature on the subject. The most frequently cited works were Rybakov's novel *Heavy Sand,* Yevtushenko's poem "Babi Yar," and Kuznetsov's novel of the same name. The most frequently cited source of information on the Holocaust is discussions among family and friends. Almost no non-fictional, historical, sources of information are cited. One can presume that if Jews were not aware of any other sources of information on the Holocaust, non-Jewish Soviets are even less so.

The Holocaust and the Soviet Political Calculus

Why was the Holocaust generally glossed over, suppressed, or universalized in the Soviet literature on the subject? Several possible explanations present themselves. One is that this is the result simply of anti-Semitism. The Soviets were incapable of showing sympathy for the Jews and refused to acknowledge the national tragedy. This may be too simplistic. As we have seen, there is considerable variation in the treatment of the Holocaust in Soviet works on the subject.

Another approach is to see the origins of this policy in Stalin's postwar anti-Semitism. A different kind of Holocaust was being prepared after the war, as foreshadowed by mass arrests in 1948, the "anticosmopolitan campaign," the execution of the Yiddish writers in 1952, the "doctors' plot," and the building of large barracks in Siberia. To admit that Jews had just been so terribly prosecuted and to signal to the Soviet public that their suffering was a matter of concern might have impeded this policy.

A third explanation has to do with the shift in the Soviet "political formula." The basis of legitimation of the Soviet regime, the legitimating myth, had moved from the Revolution to World War II. After all, only a tiny minority of Soviet people remember the Revolution, but a far greater number can identify with the Great Patriotic War. Moreover, while the outcome of the Revolution might not be welcomed by all, no Soviet citizen could wish for a different outcome of World War II. For several decades there was a virtual cult of World War II in literature, movies, art, and television. To emphasize the Jewish role and fate might have diminished from the all-union effort and experience.

It is bad enough, some would argue, that the Revolution was identified with the Jews. To "give the war to the Jews" would not only be a gross distortion of history but would erode the legitimating power of the experience and would arouse great resentment by other nationalities. Of course, this does not explain why such strenuous efforts were made to diminish artificially the Jewish fate. After all, straightforward treatment would not in any way have diminished from the overall Soviet sacrifice or effort. Soviet authorities no doubt were aware that knowledge of the Holocaust raises Jewish consciousness and retards assimilation. It is no accident that Jewish educators in the United States emphasize the Holocaust in curricula for children and adults, especially for audiences that have less than intensive exposure to other Jewish experiences. The Holocaust is so recent, so devastating, that few can remain untouched or unmoved by it. The most assimilated Jew—whether in the United States or the former USSR—must be in some way affected by it. The Soviets, who saw assimilation as the solution to "the Jewish question," were opposed to anything that would "artificially" raise Jewish consciousness. Moreover, the Holocaust raises the troublesome question of what the non-Jews were doing during mass murder of Jews. An "incorrect" understanding can lead one to draw equally "incorrect" conclusions about the prospects for assimilation. Indeed, in the Detroit survey, when asked what was the attitude of most non-Jews to the murder of Jews during the war, most respondents thought they had been hostile or indifferent. The conclusion the respondents drew from that was that "there is no place for me in the Soviet Union," as many of them put it. Zionists have used the Holocaust to justify the "negation of the diaspora," to argue that the world is inherently anti-Semitic, and that, therefore, there is no other solution to the Jewish problem but a Jewish state and emigration to it. Since the Soviets opposed this conclusion, they were wary of even dealing with the premise as raised by the Holocaust.

Finally, the Holocaust raises the troublesome issue of collaboration and betrayal of the USSR, an issue with which Soviet historiography was not yet comfortable and which continues to trouble the successor states. Indeed, the matter has not been thoroughly investigated in the West and remains a major source of tension between Jewish and East European communities there.

Some Consequences of the Soviet Treatment of the Holocaust

The ultimate universalization of the Holocaust is the Soviet equation of fascism with Zionism and the charge of collaboration between the two. As one Soviet writer put it, "Many facts have convincingly demonstrated the fascist nature of the ideology and policies of Zionism. Fascism is disgusting in any of its guises—its Zionist version is no better than its Hitlerite one."[61] In 1975–78 there were at least twenty-three articles in the Soviet press claiming that Zionists collaborated actively with the Nazis. A 1983 pamphlet explained alleged Zionist collaboration with the Nazis, manifested in the presence of Zionists on Judenraten, in Zionist attempts to negotiate with Nazis in order to save Jews, and in their alleged defense of war criminals.[62] In another pamphlet, published a year later, Zionism is said to be "a bourgeois-nationalistic ideology, suffused with the poison of racism and chauvinism, militarism and extremism, representing a threat to all of humanity"— precisely the characteristics generally attributed to Nazism.[63]

In the late 1980s criticism was voiced of some anti-Zionist works for their "inexact formulations and even incorrect assertions," including exaggerations of the linkages between Zionism and Nazism and the claim that Zionists attempted to form a "united anti-Soviet front of Hitlerism, West European and American capitalism at the end of World War II." But there was no rejection of the Nazism-Zionism link, only an admonition to "evaluate properly the real dimensions of the cooperation among various elements in the course of historic events."[64] The legitimacy of making the association between Nazism and Zionism remained unchallenged. One can make such arguments if one argues that ideology and class, not ethnicity, were what determined the behavior of the Nazis and the fate of the Jews. Nazis and Zionists were said to share class-based interests, strategies, tactics, and goals.

One of the great ironies in this is that in 1947 Soviet diplomat

Andrei Gromyko told the United Nations: "During the last war, the Jewish people underwent exceptional sorrow and suffering. . . . The time has come to help these people not by word but by deeds."[65] This was his explanation for the Soviet vote to partition Palestine and create a Jewish state. Forty years ago, then, Zionism was a justified consequence of fascism. Later it became but a variant of it. The equation of Zionism with fascism may have made Zionism comprehensible to Soviet citizens, but it was deeply insulting to Soviet Jews. In fact, even the universalization or suppression of the Holocaust deeply injured them, because a traumatic part of their recent history was denied. Not surprisingly, it led them to ask questions about a system that does such a thing, about their neighbors, about their own fate as Jews, as the Detroit study makes clear. Many came to precisely the Zionist conclusions the regime wished to avoid.

A less important, but not trivial, consequence of the Soviet downplaying of the Holocaust is that it was perceived in the West as further evidence of Soviet anti-Semitism. Moreover, the issue of collaboration by the Jews with Bolsheviks, and by Balts, Poles, and Ukrainians with the Nazis, remains an extremely controversial and touchy point in the relations between Jews and those communities and has become even more sensitive with the achievement of political independence by Ukraine and the Baltic states.

The dominant Soviet approach to the Holocaust, criticized by most Westerners who are aware of it, raises an interesting question. It is obviously a malicious distortion to pass over the Holocaust in silence. It robs people of an important part of their history, desecrates the memory of millions, and signals that Jewish lives are not worth remarking on. But what about the other Soviet strategy of embedding the Holocaust in the larger "struggle against fascism"? Disregarding the question of historical accuracy for the moment, and concentrating on the question of using knowledge of the Holocaust to prevent future such occurrences, one wonders whether the latter aim is best served by emphasizing the Jewish catastrophe's uniqueness. Especially in a country with some anti-Semitic traditions, assigning the Holocaust to a marginal minority, despised by some, may allow many to dismiss it as either irrelevant to their concerns or something Jews might have "deserved." In the Soviet Union and elsewhere some people with very partial knowledge expressed contempt for the Jews who suffered much, but who "did not fight back," and this is an image that one could easily derive from the Soviet literature. Perhaps the approach of some Soviet writers—discussing the Holocaust in the context of the overall Soviet struggle, but pointing out those features which set the Jews apart from others—might be most effective in the Soviet Union and other Slavic countries in simultaneously alerting others to the dangers that face *all* people while not diminishing the Jewish tragedy. Western Gentiles did not suffer nearly as much from the Nazis—and American noncombatants not at all—as the people of Eastern Europe. For Westerners the Jewish tragedy stands out more starkly than for East Europeans who witnessed the totality of the Nazi occupation. The Jewish experience is not so easily shoved off in Western societies where Jews are more accepted than in the former USSR. In Eastern Europe and the USSR, the Holocaust must be embedded in a larger mosaic of palpable, immediate suffering, though its unique configurations should not be submerged in that mosaic, for even in the experience of those regions the unspeakable tragedy of the Jews remains unique.

During the period of glasnost' the time seemed ripe for a Soviet reassessment of the war, and we were told that a new ten-volume history of the Great Fatherland War was in preparation. The previous history "no longer meets the present-day requirements of our society, in which an expansion of openness and democracy is now under way."[66] As part of glasnost' and perestroika there was a major reexamination of Soviet history in the Soviet Union. As *Izvestiia* put it: "The creation of an honest school course in USSR history is a task of paramount state importance."[67] Another article noted that "The public's growing interest in history is an indisputable fact. . . . Only by not concealing facts, but subjecting them to public scrutiny, thorough examination, objective analysis and impartial assessments can our historical scholarship restore its reputation."[68]

Not surprisingly, the new ten-volume history of the war that was supposed to be published in 1991, the fiftieth anniversary of the Nazi invasion, became embroiled in political controversy. The chief of a team of editors, Colonel-General Dmitrii Volkogonov, was dismissed and also left his post as director of the Military History Institute. He was attacked from two sides. In November 1990 three historians charged that the team was not properly trained, had not reviewed non-Soviet literature on the subject, and did not have access to the necessary documents.[69] Thus, the new work would be no improvement over its predecessor published in 1973–82. The new edition, the critics said, was under the supervision of Marshal Yazov and others selected on the basis of their posts, not their abilities or knowledge, and so it was "doomed to be a repetition of its predecessors."

On the other hand, the late Marshal Sergei Akhromeev accused Volkogonov of being "clever and glib," of having a "deep antipathy for socialism," after having hypocritically espoused communism in the past. Thus, it was no wonder that the draft of the first volume "makes it seem that Stalinism was the dominant, distinguishing feature of the prewar decades" and "relates almost nothing of the Soviet people's dedication and heroic efforts in building socialism during those years."[70]

Even after the first volume draft had been re-edited, Marshal Yazov accused Volkogonov of "giving a tendentious, anticommunist interpretation of the events preceding the start of the war." Volkogonov replied that, working in the archives, he realized that "a great deal that people ought to know is kept shrouded in secrecy." He observed that it might be possible to compile a true history of the war in twenty or thirty years, after the last of the participants had died.

In 1989–90 several articles on the Holocaust appeared in the Soviet press, particularly in Ukraine. The massacre at Babi Yar and its specifically Jewish aspects were commemorated in public ceremonies. A Kiev newspaper devoted an entire page to an excerpt from Ehrenburg and Grossman's *Black Book*, referring to an earlier article in a Moscow evening newspaper which had revealed to Soviet readers the existence and fate of that documentary study.[71] In September 1988 a large gathering in Moscow commemorated the slaughter at Babi Yar, while the event was marked publicly at Babi Yar itself. Not only did police not interfere, as they had in earlier years, but scenes from the meetings were shown on television. In Minsk, Lvov, and Vilnius memorial sculptures commemorating the Jewish Holocaust were commissioned or planned.[72] In 1989 an agreement was reached between Soviet archivists and the Yad Vashem Institute in Jerusalem which permitted researchers from Jerusalem to go through several Soviet archives and microfilm German and Soviet documents pertaining to the Holocaust. At an April 1990 international congress of historians in Moscow, Dr. Yitzhak Arad, director of Yad Vashem, and one or two others delivered papers on the Holocaust period. It is highly significant that there are several groups of amateur historians—in Moscow, Leningrad, Minsk, Odessa, and elsewhere—who have been studying the Holocaust, conducting taped interviews with survivors and with non-Jews who observed aspects of the mass murder of the Jews. The great majority of these researchers appear to be people who were themselves born after the war. In fall 1989 several of them were invited to Israel to participate in a training seminar for Holocaust researchers, and this was done again in subsequent years.

The politization of the Holocaust has continued since the breakup of the USSR. In September 1991, the Lithuanian government, having just achieved Soviet recognition of its declaration of independence, pardoned about 1,000 Lithuanians who had been convicted by Soviet tribunals of collaborating with the Nazis. Jewish and Israeli circles immediately protested. Clearly, the Lithuanian motivation was political: having achieved independence, they are inclined to say everything Soviet was bad. If a Soviet tribunal adjudged a man guilty, he must have been innocent. This was not only *prima facie* absurd, but also a foolish move politically. The Lithuanians modified their position, suspending the rehabilitations in October and set up a Lithuanian-Israeli-American commission of experts to review rehabilitation requests.

The incidents points up several things: (1) the continued sensitivity of the collaboration issue; (2) the tendency to politicize the issue and give it contemporary significance; (3) the very different perceptions of Jews and other peoples.

In Ukraine the issue is at least as sensitive as in the Baltic. In September 1991 Ukrainian and Jewish groups, with the sponsorship of the Ukrainian government as well, organized a large-scale commemoration of the massacre at Babi Yar that had taken place half a century earlier. The main streets of Kiev were lined with photographs of Kievan Jews who had been murdered at Babi Yar. Several days of conferences, meetings, exhibitions, concerts and speeches were devoted to the commemoration, and a *Book of Memory* was published in 75,000 copies. The media reported these events extensively, and the subject of the Holocaust generally achieved a prominence unknown in the Soviet period.

The collapse of the USSR means that its former constituent parts will now have to face the issue of the Holocaust individually. As they rewrite their histories, the Holocaust will again become a major issue between the Ukrainians, Latvians, Lithuanians, Belorussians, Moldavians, Russians, and others, on one hand, and the Jews, on the other. Revisions of history may be politicized and tendentious at first.

One would hope that these might be only infantile disorders of newly won independence, though they may turn out to be symptoms of a more chronic illness of longer duration.

Notes

This chapter is an abbreviated version of an original essay commissioned by the Holocaust Memorial Center of West Bloomfield, Michigan, for publication in a critical assessment of how countries from around the world have reacted to the Holocaust since 1945. I am also grateful to the Office of the Vice-President for Research at the University of Michigan for its financial support and to Yury Polsky and Scott Tarry for their assistance in research. Much of the material in this essay has also appeared in *Holocaust and Genocide Studies,* vol. 5, no.1 (1990).

  *For more information on this period, see Zvi Gitelman, *A Century of Ambivalence: The Jews of Russia and the Soviet Union from 1881 to the Present* (New York: Schocken, 1988); Salo Baron, *The Russian Jew Under Tsars and Soviets* (New York: Macmillan, 1964).

  1. Mordechai Altshuler asserts that "Estimates of the number of Jewish Holocaust victims in the Soviet Union fluctuate between 2.5 million and 3.3 million." See *Soviet Jewry Since the Second World War* (New York: Greenwood Press, 1987), p. 4.

  2. On this population movement, see B.Z. Pinchuk, *Yehudai BrithaMoetsot mool pnai haShoah* (Tel Aviv: Tel Aviv University, 1979); Mordechai Altshuler, "Hapinui veham'nusah shel yehudim miBelorussiya haMizrakhit bitkufat haShoah (Yuni-August 1941)," in *Yahadut Zmaneinu,* vol. 3 (Jerusalem: Hebrew University, 1986); and Solomon Schwarz, *Evrei v Sovetskom Soiuze* (New York: American Jewish committee, 1966).

  3. Z. Segalowicz, *Gebrente trit* (Buenos Aires, 1947), p. 96.

  4. Interview with Allen Small, Video Archive for Holocaust Testimonies at Yale University, Interview no. T–833, 14 December 1986.

  5. Quoted in Alexander Dallin, *German Rule in Soviet Russia, 1941–1945,* 2nd ed. (London: Macmillan, 1981), p. 9.

  6. Quoted in Matthew Cooper, *The Phantom War* (London: Macdonald and James, 1979), pp. 171–73.

  7. Many accounts can be found in Ilya Ehrenburg and Vasily Grossman, *The Black Book* (New York: Holocaust Library, 1981).

  8. "Down History's Memory Hole: Soviet Treatment of the Holocaust," *Present Tense* (Winter, 1983), p. 53.

  9. M. Altshuler, "Pirsumim Russiyim biVrit haMoetsot al nosiim Yehudiyim bashanim 1917-1967," in Altshuler, ed., *Pirsumim Russiyim biVrit haMoetsot al Yehudim veYahadut* (Jerusalem: Society for Research on Jewish Communities and the Historical Society of Israel, 1970), p. lxvi. See also "Seventy years of Soviet Jewry," *Insight* (London), November 1987, p.6.

  10. William Korey, *The Soviet Cage* (New York: Viking, 1973), p. 90.

  11. Dov Levin, *Fighting Back: Lithuanian Jewry's Armed Resistance to the Nazis, 1941-1945* (New York: Holmes and Meier, 1985), p. xii.

12. "Down History's Memory Hole."

13. Quoted in Korey, "No Monument over Babi Yar," in *The Soviet Cage*, p. 109.

14. Bill Keller, "Echo of '41 in Minsk: Was the Heroine a Jew?" *New York Times*, 15 September 1987.

15. *Istoriia velikoi otechestvennoi voine Sovetskogo Soiuza, 1941–1945 gg.* (Moscow: Voenizdat, 1962–1965). See vol. 3 (1962), pp. 438, 442, 443, 446.

16. Iu.Iu. Kondufor, et al., *Istoriia Ukrainskoi SSR* (Kiev: Naukova dumka, 1982).

17. L.N. Lentzmann, et al., *Estonskii narod v velikoi otechestvennoi voine Sovetskogo Soiuza 1941–1945* (Tallin: Eesti Raamat, 1973), p. 437.

18. Ibid., pp. 440, 449.

19. Ibid., p. 452.

20. See, for example, p. 330, and the pictures between pp. 448 and 449.

21. P.P. Lipilo and V.F. Romanovskii, eds., *Prestuplenia nemetsko-fashistkikh okkupantov v Belorussii 1941–1944* (Minsk: Belarus, 1965), pp. 24–25, 28, 56–58, 231, 397.

22. O. Kaplanas, *Deviaty fort obvinaet* (Vilnius: Mintis, 1964), pp. 37–38, 40.

23. S.S. Smirnov, *Sobranie sochinenii* (Moscow: Molodaia gvardiia, 1973), vol. 1 *(Brestskaia krepost', krepost' nad Bugom)*, pp. 331–32. .

24. Ibid.

25. Ibid.

26. Smirnov, vol. 3 *(Stalingrad na Dnepre; Na poliakh Vengrii; Liudi, kotorykh ia videl)*, p. 23.

27. Ibid., pp. 32, 274.

28. Ibid., vol. 1, pp. 227, 187, 194.

29. Ibid., pp. 157, 44, 235.

30. Ibid., vol. 2, pp. 131, 214–15.

31. N. Matveev, *Parol'—"Brusnika"* (Moscow: Molodaia gvardiia, 1972). This book was published in an edition of 100,000 by a publishing house that has issued several books considered anti-Semitic by many. Yet this volume favorably presents heroes of obvious Jewish nationality, such as Captain David Keimach (whose pseudonym was Dima Korneenko), a Red Army officer who worked behind the German lines; Rafael Monusovich Bromberg; and Sarah Levin. Thus, the portrayal of Jews is not consistent.

32. Iu. Ia. Orlov, *Krakh nemetsko-fashistkoi propagandy v period voiny protiv SSSR* (Moscow: Moscow State University, 1985), pp. 95, 61.

33. V.I. Vinogradov, *Istoriia SSSR v dokumentakh i illustratsiiakh* (Moscow: Prosveshcheniia, 1981).

34. *Great Soviet Encyclopedia*, vol. 9, p. 293. There is no "holocaust" entry in the encyclopedia.

35. For example, F. Kral's *Prestuplenie protiv Evropy* (1963) and *SS v deistvii*.

36. See, for example, Henrik Hoffman, "Dos iz geshen in Taganrog," *Sovietish haimland*, 1966, no. 2; Hirsh Dobin, "Der koiech fun lebn," *Sovietish haimland*, 1966, no. 3; Yekhiel Falikman, "Der shvartser vint," *Sovietish haimland*, 1967, no. 8.

37. Hersh Remenik, "Der ufshtand in Varshever getto in der Yidisher Sovetisher literatur," *Sovietish haimland*, 1963, no. 2, p. 150.

38. Ibid., p. 153. In a poem by Shmuel Halkin, the Soviet warrior Bereza comes to the ghetto to help the fighters. The Jewish fighter Ratnitsky says, "Let the people be blessed and the land from which this man came to participate in our struggle as an equal." A major study of the Warsaw ghetto mentions no such episode and points out that the Soviet Union, like the other allies, "did not come to the aid of the fighters in the ghettos." Ironically, spokesmen of the Polish Home Army believed that "the ghetto is no more than a base for Soviet Russia. . . . The Russians were the ones who prepared the revolt in the Warsaw ghetto." See Yisrael Gutman, *The Jews of Warsaw, 1939–1943* (Bloomington: Indiana University Press, 1982) pp. 408, 409, 417. A Polish Communist historian also does not mention Red Army men in the two versions of his history of the Warsaw ghetto uprising. See B. Mark, *Powstanie w getcie Warszawskim* (Warsaw: Zydowski Instytut Historyczny, 1953; Idisz buch, 1963).

39. Israel Meyer, "Dos Bulgarishe Folk hot geratevet di Yidn fun fashistisher oisrotung," *Sovietish haimland*, 1967, no. 6, p. 124.

40. See Esther Markish, *The Long Return* (New York: Ballantine, 1978), p. 152.

41. *Sovietish haimland*, 1963, no. 2, p. 158.

42. Yudl Pertsovsky, "Er hot farteidikt Moskve," *Sovietish haimland*, 1966, no. 2; Henrik Hoffman, "Dos iz geshen in Taganrog," in ibid. See also Hirsh Dobin, "Der koiech fun lebn," *Sovietish haimland*, 1966, no. 3, 1966.

43. *Sovietish haimland*, 1966, no. 3, p. 158. The Ukrainian writer Ivan Khomenko described how his mother hid a Jewish teenage girl for nine months. He published a poem, "Di Yidishke," about the incident (*Sovietish haimland*, 1966, no. 10). Other items emphasize the friendship among nationalities in the ranks of the partisans (*Sovietish haimland*, 1963, no. 6, p. 122) and the sympathy of Gentiles for the massacred Jews (*Sovietish haimland*, 1964, no. 3, pp. 156–157).

44. Boris Polevoi, "Doktor Vera," *Sovietish haimland*, 1967, no. 3, p. 46.

45. *Sovietish haimland*, 1965, no. 5.

46. *Sovietish haimland*, 1962, no. 5, p. 37.

47. See Iosif Yuzovsky, *Sovietish haimland*, 1967, no. 3, p. 132.

48. M. Vesterman, *Sovietish haimland*, 1963, no. 2, p. 155.

49. "There's No Turning Back," *Pravda*, 24 August 1987, translated in *Current Digest of the Soviet Press (CDSP)*, vol. 39, no. 34 (23 September 1987) p. 1.

50. Gennady Vasilev, "Journey to Russian America," *Pravda*, 16 November 1987, translated in *CDSP*, vol. 39, no. 46 (16 December 1987), p. 21–22.

51. Yu. Kirilchenko, " 'Touchstone of Ill Will,' " *Pravda*, 23 August 1987, in ibid., p. 2.

52. One result of the policy of *glasnost'* is the possibility of opening up this issue. As one article puts it, "Ignorance of history is kindling wood for the bonfire of fervent nationalism. But one has to admit that in the Baltic republics textbooks. . . suffer from a lack of objectivity and, with incomprehensible diffidence, pass over in silence, to put it bluntly, tragic periods in the life of Latvia, Lithuania and Estonia. . . . Anti-Soviet propaganda takes skillful advantage of this, filling the blank spots in the textbooks with malicious fabrications and fanning national enmity." O. Meshkov, et al., "In a Foreign Voice," *Pravda*, 1 September 1987, translated in *CDSP*, vol. 39, no. 34 (23 September 1987), p. 7.

53. "Der goirl fun a held," *Sovietish haimland,* 1966, no. 12, p. 12, translated from *Sovetskaia Rossiia,* 24 September 1966.

54. Reuben Ainsztein, *Jewish Resistance in Nazi-Occupied Europe* (London: Paul Elek, 1974), p. 373.

55. Ibid.

56. See, for example, *Istochniki pobedy Sovetskogo naroda v velikoi otechestvennoi voine 1941–1945* (Moscow: Nauka, 1985), pp. 187, 194, 197.

57. Among the biographies listed in one Western bibliography are four on Jewish heroes. At least one other biography, a second one of General David Dragunsky, has appeared since. See Michael Parrish, *The USSR in World War Two* (New York and London: Garland Publishing, 1981), vol. 2. The later biography of Dragunsky is V.Z. Krivulin and Iu. I. Pivovar, *I eto vse v odnoi sud'be* (Moscow: Izdatel'stvo politicheskoi literatury, 1986).

58. *Sovietish haimland,* 1963, no. 2, p. 145: "The Jewish fellows distinguished themselves by their discipline, courage, steadfastness."

59. For example, Guards Lt. Gen. Hirsh Plaskov, "Frontovnikes," *Sovietish haimland,* 1966, no. 5. Plaskov writes elsewhere of his traditional Jewish upbringing, and here he writes about several Jewish heroic soldiers.

60. For example, Shire Gorshman, "Zol feln a hor," in ibid.

61. *Nash otvet klevetnikam* (Kiev: Prapor, 1976).

62. R.M. Brodskii and O. Ia. Krasivskii, *Istinnoe litso sionizma* (Lvov: Kameniar, 1983), pp. 34–39.

63. L.E. Bernshtein, *Antikommunisticheskaia sushchnost' ideologicheskikh kontseptsii sionizma* (Kiev: Politicheskaia literatury Ukrainy, 1984), p. 33.

64. L. Ia. Dadiani, S.I. Mokshin, and E.V. Tadevosian, "O nekotorykh voprosakh istoriografii proletarskogo internatsionalizma," *Voprosy istorii KPSS* (January 1987), p. 76.

65. Quoted in Yaacov Ro'i, *Soviet Decision Making in Practice* (New Brunswick: Transaction Books, 1980), p. 70.

66. S. Bugayev, "History Covered with Glory," *Krasnaia Zvezda,* 15 August 1987, translated in *CDSP,* vol. 39, no. 33, 16 September 1987, p. 18. See also Yury Perechnev, "Ten Volumes on the War," *Moscow News,* 20 September 1987, in *CDSP,* vol. 39, no. 50 (13 January 1988), p. 7.

67. V. Svirsky, "History Passes Over in Silence," *Izvestiia,* 21 July 1987, translated in *CDSP,* vol. 39, no. 29, 19 August 1987, p. 6.

68. Yury Orlik, "Treat History with Respect," *Izvestiia,* 8 August 1987, translated in *CDSP,* vol. 39, no. 32 (9 September 1987) pp. 9–10.

69. *Izvestia,* 19 November 1990, translated in *CDSP,* vol. 42, no. 46, 19 (December 1990), p. 27.

70. Interview with Major-General V.I. Filatov, *Voenno-Istoricheski Zhurnal,* 1991, no. 4 (April), translated in *CDSP,* vol. 43, no. 17 (29 May 1991), p. 17.

71. " 'Chernaia Kniga' sushchesvuet," *Vechernii Kiev,* 29 September 1989.

72. See Mordechai Altshuler, "Changes in Soviet Jewry," *Jews and Jewish Topics in the Soviet Union and Eastern Europe* (Summer 1989), p. 28.

The Holocaust in the Soviet Mirror

LUKASZ HIRSZOWICZ

Introduction

The subject of how the Holocaust was reflected in the "official" Soviet Union encompasses many levels—public commemorations such as the erection of monuments, observance of anniversaries, exhibitions, public meetings, and so forth, as well as treatment of the Holocaust in textbooks, academic publications, and the media, in literature, in the theater, and in film. There is a general feeling among Jews both in the USSR and abroad that in the USSR the Holocaust is a kind of non-event. One is reminded of an old formula which very well characterized the official Soviet position with regard to the Jewish question: "There are Jews, but there is no Jewish question." With regard to the Holocaust the position is that, indeed, many Jews were killed by the fascists, but there was no special Holocaust. Yet a different view of the Holocaust is implied in the definition of genocide given by the eminent Soviet Jewish lawyer A. Trainin after the war: "The aim of genocide is the destruction of a racial, national group. Outside these groups there are no victims of genocide. Within the group, every individual is a victim, so that the whole people, the whole nation perishes" *(Izvestiia,* 4 May 1948).

The Jewish position was authoritatively expressed in D.A. Taubkin's inaugural address to the Founding Congress of Jewish Inmates of Ghettos and Concentration Camps in Odessa on 3 June 1991. The statement compared unfavorably the situation in the USSR with respect to commemoration of the Holocaust with the situation in the West. The speaker said:

To the present day, most of the sites of mass executions of Jews and death camps remain in a state of neglect. The names of those who perished are unknown as even the collected information on the martyrs was not published. There is no exact knowledge of the general number of victims. . . . Up to the present there is no specialist research in Soviet historiography devoted to the genocide of the Jews. School and university textbooks say nothing about it and authors of monographs on the period of the 1941–45 war keep silent. Articles on the subject started to appear in the press only recently. Among a part of Soviet people, even Jews who survived the genocide, there is no understanding that everybody . . . was a victim of . . . the fascist totalitarian regime.

The speaker went on to say that the perpetuation of the memory of the innocent victims was a moral duty of the reviving Jewish movement, and it was also important for the democratization of the Soviet society at large.

Indeed, the concealment of the Holocaust in the USSR has no analogy in Europe or America. As hinted above, there is no denial that the Nazis treated the Jews in a most brutal way. But it is asserted that this happened to everybody else in the occupied parts of the USSR. Jews who wanted to mourn their dead were frowned upon. Hence the Holocaust was reflected in the Soviet mirror in a peculiar way, in line with Soviet ideological percepts and desired cultural attitudes and with the existing policies, both internal and foreign. My research leads to the conclusion that on various levels there existed different reflections of the Holocaust in the Soviet mirror. One is to forbid or sabotage the erection of a monument, shape entries in textbooks and encyclopedias in the spirit of concealment, and the like. This is done almost within the bureaucracy. Then there is management of the media, which must reflect current events and serve immediate political needs, and control over literary and artistic creativity. While the former is done under the directives the ideological authorities, the creative pursuits have had to be managed on a longer rope.

There existed circumstances in the USSR which favored the blurring of the singularity of the Holocaust. It was already mentioned that it went against the ideological grain. But it must be kept in mind that under the Soviet regime, before the war, repressions against groups characterized by social or ethnic status, including mass exile and execution, were a well-known phenomenon. Another major factor has been the great number of Nazi victims from among the non-Jewish population, incomparably larger than in Western Europe, and in certain areas of the USSR even much larger than in Poland. Moreover, the main extermination camps in which the Jews were killed *en masse* by gassing were outside Soviet territory.

What Did the Soviets Report About the Holocaust?

As mentioned above, no special publications on the Shoah appeared in the USSR. The publication of Ehrenburg's and Grossman's *Black Book,* which was intended to be exactly such a work, was aborted. However, a considerable amount of material about the Holocaust (obviously without using this or any similar description) appeared in the Soviet Union during the war and in its immediate aftermath. In particular, the Soviet note of 6 January 1942 must be remembered as an important document by a major Allied power which emphasized the Nazi treatment of the Jewish population. It mentioned the killing of Jews and Poles in Lvov, the mass execution of Jews in Kiev, and "the bloodbath murders especially directed against unarmed and defenseless Jews," and listed the numbers of victims in several Ukrainian cities. During the war and in 1945–46 the reports of the Extraordinary State Commissions for Establishing and Investigating the Crimes of the German Fascist Occupiers were published, and much of this material is available in English as well. Gromyko's celebrated declaration at the United Nations in which he linked the USSR support for Jewish aims in Palestine with the special sufferings of the Jewish people under the Nazis was also made in this period.

Three volumes about *Odessa in the Great Patriotic War of the Soviet Union* appeared in 1948, 1949, and 1951. But the materials of the Nuremberg trials appeared only in the late 1950s and the 1960s. Several more volumes of relevant documents were published in the 1960s, for instance, *The Crimes of the German Fascist Occupiers in Belorussia, 1941–1944* (Minsk, 1965), and *The Kharkov Region in the Years of the Great Patriotic War, 1941–43* (Kharkov, 1965), which includes a chapter on the German occupation regime. Volumes of documents on the crimes of the Nazis and their accomplices appeared also in the Baltic countries in the 1960s. In 1987 *Nazi Crimes in the Ukraine, 1941–1944, Documents and Materials* appeared—a new, revised edition in English translation of a volume of documents which appeared shortly after the war. The way the fate of the Jews under the Nazis is reflected in these publications will be discussed below. These materials, except perhaps the wartime reports on German atrocities, were destined for a limited and specialized audience, and this was reflected in their print-runs. But many references to the events of the Holocaust did appear in the Soviet mass media, included in reports on war criminals and war crime trials. This was an issue in which the USSR was strongly interested in connection with the policies of the Western powers vis-à-vis Germany and former Nazi cadres as well as the Soviets' own battle against anti-Soviet nationalism in the Baltic, Ukraine, and elsewhere. However, as we shall see, the reporting of war crime trials, whether those held abroad or those held in the USSR, did not automatically mean that crimes committed against the Jews were discussed.

The Soviet media reported the Nuremberg trials, and they would become a recurring subject in Soviet journalism. Among those who wrote about the trials in later years, perhaps Lev Bezymensky and Boris Polevoi are the best known, and they usually inserted some Jewish references in their articles. The Soviet media gave much space to the Eichmann case, a Jewish case par excellence, from the moment of Eichmann's capture in 1960 to his execution two years later. Subsequently the Soviet media wrote about the hunt for major Nazi criminals such as Bormann, Mengele, Stangl, Rauff, and others, and in this context even found a few good words for Simon Wiesenthal (see, for example, V. Cherniavskii, "The Root of Evil," *Literaturnaia gazeta*, 15 July 1965; and reports about the hunt for Martin Bormann in *Pravda Ukrainy,* 5 April 1967, and *Komsomolskaia pravda,* 14 May 1967). The Soviet media reported the numerous trials abroad, first and foremost in West Germany. Many of these trials dealt directly, and sometimes mainly, with crimes committed in the occupied territories of the USSR against the Jews and members of other Soviet nationalities, mainly Belorussians, Ukrainians, and Russians.

Virtual Silence Under Stalin

From 1949 until Stalin's death, mention of the Jewishness of Nazi victims was rather avoided. In the reports on Mannstein's trial, the murder of Jews and Gypsies was quoted from the indictment *(Pravda* and *Izvestiia,* 11 September 1949, and *Pravda* 14 September 1949). Not a word was uttered about the Jews when the arrest of Koch was reported (*Novoe vremia*, 1949, no. 24). During the so-called Kravchenko *(I Chose Freedom)* case, the Soviets strongly protested against calling as witnesses three Ukrainian displaced persons whom they accused of mass killings of "peaceful inhabitants, former employees of Soviet institutions, and Stakhanovites" *(Pravda* and *Izvestiia,* 23 February 1949); no mention of killing of Jews was made. There were exceptions to this rule. For instance *Novoe vremia,* in issue no. 13 of 1952 and no. 2 of 1953 mentioned the destruction of over 5 million Jews. The Jews were even put at the head of the list of nations who suffered from Nazi extermination policies, contrary to the often repeated, almost canonical assertion that the Slav peoples were the main target of the Nazi policy of enslavement and extermination. Bearing in mind the timing of the mentioned publications, just on the eve of the Slansky trial and the Doctors' Plot, one is inclined to suspect that they might have been part of a disinformation operation.

Later on there was no such complete or virtually complete silence about the Jewish victims of Nazi extermination policies. But a variety of other gimmicks was employed to distort the true scope of the genocide against the Jews.

Methods of Distortion—Silence Continued

What were these gimmicks? Sometimes an old method was used, and nothing was said of the nationality of the victims, particularly when practically all were Jewish. For instance, in a report of a trial in Graz of SS-Untersturmführer Friedrich Lex, accused of participating in the killing of 70,000 people in Ternopil (an oblast capital in western Ukraine), *Sovetskaia Rossiia* (17 March 1965) did not mention that the overwhelming majority of these 70,000 victims were Jewish. In the part of the collection of documents entitled *Kharkovshchina v gody Velikoi Otechestvennoi voiny,* which deals with the occupation regime in the Kharkiv region, there is no direct mention whatever of the extermination of Jews. In Document 85, dated 9 March 1943, which includes excerpts from a statement by a commission of the city soviet on the atrocities and crimes of the Nazis in Kharkiv, it is said that on 15 December 1941 the German commandant of Kharkiv ordered that the inhabitants of the central streets move out into barracks of Kharkiv enterprises and that in January 1942 the Nazis machine-gunned them in Drobnitskii yar. In a description of the occupation of Rybnitsa in

Moldavia *(Sovetskaia Moldaviia,* 31 March 1984) it is reported that "expulsion and resettlement of inhabitants according to nationality was widely practiced." Many other examples could be quoted of "forgetting" the identity of Nazism's main victims.

Methods of Distortion—Jews Last in the Pecking Order

In many cases several nationalities to which the victims belonged were enumerated and the pecking order was chosen according to circumstances, mainly geographical. For example, Belorussians were mentioned first when the crime was perpetrated in a Belorussian locality, and Ukrainians when a place in Ukraine was involved. Russians were put first also in descriptions of a more general character. And so on. The Jews were put in the last place, or just before "and others." For instance, in a comparatively recent article in *Pravda* (24 April 1985), the rector of Erevan University, S. Ambartsumian, wrote about the killing by the Nazis of Russians, Ukrainians, Belorussians, Jews, and others. In a 1987 documentary publication titled *Nazi Crimes in the Ukraine 1941–1944,* the introduction says that "Ukrainians, Russians, Belorussians, Jews, and representatives of many other nationalities of the Soviet Union were submitted to such inhuman treatment" (p. 9). Nonetheless, the documents reproduced in this publication pay considerable attention to the fate of the Jewish population of Ukraine.

Another method, often used when crimes of specific individual Nazis or their collaborators in a definite place or area were described, was to add one or two sentences in which certain crimes against Jews are mentioned specifically, as if the other crimes discussed were directed against other categories of people. For instance, in a TASS dispatch from Bonn of 20 June 1966, I. Iakovlev writes about the Nazi war criminal Fritz Hildebrand, who commanded an operation of extermination of old people, women, and children in the regions of Przemysl and Drogobycz in 1942–44. He goes on to report that the same individual led an "action" of extermination of many hundreds of peaceful citizens in 1943. He adds that in October 1942 Hildebrand led an "action" of exterminating Jews in the neighborhood of Przemysl and in March 1944 in Drogobycz. The informed reader will of course guess who the old people, women, and children were, but it seems clear enough what were the constraints under which the reporter worked and what kind of impression he was supposed to create.

Sometimes the evidence of Jewish witnesses to a Nazi crime supplied the only clue to the nationality of the victims or a great part of them. For instance, in connection with the trial in Koblenz of Georg Heuser and others directly involved in the Holocaust in Minsk and other places in Belorussia the Soviets called a press conference. *Pravda* (31 January 1963) gave excerpts from the statement of the Belorussian State Commission on Nazi Crimes and statements made at the press conference by Berta Gindelevich and Lazar Goldin. There were of course many Belorussian victims and potential Belorussian witnesses, but it was probably deemed opportune to make an appropriate hint for the benefit of foreign public opinion.

Methods of Distortion—The Special Jewish Cases

In some cases, notably that of Treblinka, the fact that this was a special camp whose purpose was the extermination of Jews was mentioned quite often, and this also applies to Sobibor and Belzec (see, for example, *Novoe vremia*, 1967, no. 20, and *Rabochaia gazeta*, 2 July 1967; but Jews were not mentioned in *Za rubezhom*, 1962, no. 18, or *Pravda Ukrainy*, 27 June 1962). But the rising in Sobibor has been presented as carried out by Soviet POWs, and their Jewishness was either heavily blurred or completely forgotten—a method often employed in Soviet descriptions and analyses of anti-Nazi resistance. The 1987 volume of *God za godom* prints an item by Aleksandr Pecherskii, the leader of the uprising; this is introduced by excerpts from a textbook on USSR history (Moscow, 1963, p. 711) and a German report on the uprising of 15 October 1943. The Soviet textbook says that a Soviet officer, A.A. Pecherskii, and other Soviet citizens transferred to the labor camp, together with the Polish Communist Sh. Leytman, organized an underground group and on 14 October 1943 killed the camp's staff and led the inmates out of the camp. The name of the camp is not mentioned. The German report says that on the above-mentioned day at 5 P.M. a Jewish uprising occurred in Sobibor. The juxtaposition of these two presentations is a significant statement on the way the Holocaust is reflected in the Soviet mirror. A similar juxtaposition can be made with respect to documents published in the documentary volume *Prestupleniia nemetsko-fashistskikh okkupantov v Belorussii, 1941–1944* (Minsk, 1965). While the German documents reproduced in this collection are quite clear in identifying the object of their murderous

deeds or intents—Belorussian villages, partisans, or Jews—the reproduced Soviet documents, or excerpts from them, intentionally omit
mention of the fate of the Jews.

In connection with the extermination of the Jews, publications
sometimes refer to the Wannsee conference. But then it is *de rigeur* to
emphasize that the Jews were by no means the sole target of the Nazis.
It is said that at the same time the extermination of the "inferior" Slavs
was intensified and there is reference to the General Plan Ost. For
instance, *New Times* (1985, no. 15) reported in connection with
Mengele and Auschwitz: "One of the components of the genocide
program was the Wannsee plan envisaging the annihilation of the Jewish population of Europe. But there were even more far-reaching plans:
. . . General Plan Ost, which provided for the liquidation of the Slav
peoples. . . . 30–50 million people were to be killed."

All this is done in the name of the general principle of not separating the Jewish tragedy from the general calamities visited on the
USSR, the Slavs, and Europe. But the real result has been the blurring
of the Jewish tragedy, its being subsumed in the general picture to the
point of complete disappearance. Especially in Belorussia one discerns
an intensive effort to omit explicit references to Jewish victims and
heroes in propagandist, popular, and even academic publications, but
not in *belles lettres*. For instance, in the book *Stolbtsy* (Minsk, 1981)
there is not a word about the ghetto in this town or about its liquidation
in 1942; there is only information that the Nazis killed 300 persons in
the town on the second day of the occupation and 3,500 in October
1941. In another brochure on my home city, Grodno (in French because Grodno is twinned with Limoges), there is also no mention of
the ghetto and its liquidation: the inhabitants of the city were said to
have been taken to several camps such as Kolbasino and Lososna, but
Treblinka and Auschwitz—camps with a strong Jewish connotation in
the public mind and where the great majority of Grodno's Jews were
taken—are not mentioned.

Some of the true reasons for these practices came to light in the
attacks on Yevtushenko's Babi Yar poem and Shostakovich's Thirteenth Symphony. Ariadna Ladygina, for example, explained ("Lis-
tening to the Thirteenth Symphony," *Sovetskaia Belorussiia,* 2 April
1963) that the Jewish question was dead and should not be revived;
"history denies the unity of the class-inequality-ridden Jewish people; and one should not look to the Jewish question for material

about fascist atrocities, because anti-Semitism is neither the sole nor the really important feature of fascism. And, in general, raising the problem of Jewish suffering under fascism is evidence of loss of civil tact." Which means: you should write about your own, not about aliens.

The Anti-Zionist Campaign

In the framework of the official anti-Zionist campaign, the above arguments were, at least in part, put aside. Rather, the Nazis' hostility to the Jews and extermination policies were emphasized, and the Zionists presented as accomplices. This subject has been widely discussed by publicists and academics in Israel and the West, and recently also in the Soviet Union. At the same time, the need for propaganda countering Jewish grievances over the treatment of Jews and Jewish problems by the Soviets, including the Holocaust, became more pressing. In this context, the Zionists and other Western anti-Soviets were accused of attempting to impose the opinion on the world that only the Jews were victims of fascism. This line was taken, for instance, by *Radianska Ukraina* (27 September 1981) in reply to Jewish dissatisfaction about the treatment of the Babi Yar massacre, and in a more general way by the eminent political analyst Igor Beliaev in *Literaturnaia gazeta* (10 April 1985). The *Radianska Ukraina* author, Dmytro Donskoi (probably a pen-name, after the hero of Kulikovoe pole), accused the Zionists of the desire to separate the Jewish tragedy from the tragedy of other nations, which proved they were interested in fanning anti-Semitism; indeed they had helped the Nazis in the past while at present they honor such individuals as Axel Springer and Otto Skorzeny.

On 9 April 1985 the Anti-Zionist Committee of the Soviet Public called a press conference to refute Jewish accusations. The main Zionist accusation was presented as contending that the saving of concentration camp inmates was not part of the intentions of the Soviet command and that the truth about genocide against the Jews was being silenced in the USSR. This was emphatically denied. The spokesmen stressed that the Jews who perished were citizens of the USSR, Poland, France, and other countries, and they included 200,000 Jewish soldiers of the Red Army. The Zionists have no relation to "our victims."

Extreme Politicization

Another characteristic of Soviet dealing with war crimes in general, including the Holocaust, appears to be of the greatest importance from their point of view. A usual Soviet discussion of Nazi atrocities, including the usual report of a war crime trial, is very rarely limited to the description of the act in question, the culprits, the evidence, the court proceedings. There is a tendency to discuss these matters in the wider context of fascism in general, which is seen as a legitimate outgrowth of capitalism, not only Nazi policies and behavior. Hence the responsibility for Nazism and its crimes is widened to accuse practically the whole German political, military, economic, and administrative establishment. The Federal Republic of Germany is from this point of view a direct continuation of the Nazi state, and its use of personnel of the former Nazi state is seen as the embodiment of this continuity. Furthermore, the responsibility for this state of affairs is put on individuals, political forces, and governments of the West who provided these Germans tainted with Nazism and its crimes with the opportunity to continue operating in public life. Moreover, Nazi crimes are said to have their continuation in the policies and actions of the USSR's cold war rivals, especially the United States, which is also the main culprit in the revival of German militarism and expansionism. Other members of NATO and Israel are also among the culprits. The actions of the American military in Korea and Vietnam, and in the last decades also those of Israel, are branded as a direct continuation of the crimes of the Nazis.

This is how all war crime trials held in the West were reported, and the classic example is the reporting of the Eichmann case in 1960–62. While the role of Eichmann in the Holocaust was admitted, the reports diluted the story of Nazi atrocities in a flood of propaganda against the West German establishment, the United States and other Western powers, Israel, and Zionism. If Eichmann is on trial, then how is it that Globke, the competent drafter and interpreter of the Nuremberg laws, is not only not on trial but occupies an important post in the West German government? The same question was also asked with regard to other German military and economic figures. Why was Eichmann not brought to justice earlier, though he was quite high on the list of war criminals? Was not his escape and finding a safe haven part and parcel of a Western policy of enabling the criminals to escape and using many of them against the USSR, a policy that is being continued? Does not Israel cooperate with the Western powers and West Germany and does it not pay for their favors by limiting the scope of the trial, keeping out references to other German dignitaries including those who like Globke were directly involved in the *Endlösung*? And is not the Israeli Zionist establishment itself interested in keeping silent about Zionist dealings with the Nazis, for instance those dealings which had come to light in the Kastner affair a few years ago? The writers often drew a parallel between the military operations in Korea and Vietnam and Western defense policies ("war preparations against the USSR") on the one hand and Nazi crimes during World War II on the other hand. All this was a steady companion to reports about the Nazi war crimes in general and the Holocaust in particular, with the anti-Zionist and anti-Israeli ingredient much more in evidence after the Six-Day War.

Hence, as far as the media were concerned, the reflection of the Holocaust and Nazi crimes in general in the Soviet mirror was highly politicized. The terrible events of the Nazi era were as if veiled and drowned out by political diatribes—often irrelevant to the problem, but very much relevant to Soviet political objectives. It happened very rarely that a discussion of the Holocaust and of war crime trials appeared in the media without such political references or with only a small dose of this ingredient.

War Crime Trials in the USSR

The media also paid attention to war crime trials held in the USSR. The Eichmann case seems to be a landmark with regard to the reporting of Soviet war crime trials. Before 1960, with the notable exception of trials of well-known collaborators with the enemy in the immediate postwar years, there was little if any reporting in the accessible media of such trials held in the USSR. But there is every reason to believe that under Stalin many people who had had any contacts with the occupiers, including war criminals and participants in the Holocaust, were prosecuted and sentenced, and that there were such trials after 1953 as well. I came across reports of depositions by people accused of war crimes in 1949 and 1959 (see *Czerwony Sztandar*, 1 February 1961 and 29 July 1967) and a report of a war crimes trial in 1957, the latter without any Jewish connotations *(Komsomolskaia pravda*, 21 and 22 March 1957; *Izvestiia*, 23 March 1957; and *Pravda*, 24 March 1957). The amnesty decree of the USSR Supreme Soviet of 17 September 1955 "for Soviet citizens who collaborated with occupiers during the Great Patriotic War, 1941–45" should be mentioned in this context. The amnesty applied to a very wide group of offenders, with the explicit exception of individuals guilty of murder and torture of Soviet citizens (*Izvestiia*, 18 September 1955; for amnesty in Lithuania see *Sovetskaia Litva*, 22 March 1956). The amnesty must have signified a certain relaxation with regard to people under the cloud of accusations of collaborating and sympathizing with the enemy. Hence, the reasons for the lack, or the extreme paucity, of reports about war crime trials must have been complex, and the unwillingness to bring the fate of the Jewish population to general attention could have been only one of them.

After 1960 we find in the media a considerable number of reports of war crime trials in the USSR, in the Baltic republics, in Ukraine, and Belorussia, as well as in the RSFSR. In the course of the trials the Nazi crimes against the Jewish population were discussed, in most cases in the same way as described above with regard to trials held abroad. Naturally, there are no attacks on the leniency of the courts or on the way the trial is conducted.

The more important trials were reported at greater length in the press of the republic where the trial was held, and there was also reporting in the central press, though less frequent and shorter. We know very little about the way of reporting the trials in the local press.

Trials in the Baltic Countries

Thus, for instance, the Estonian trial in March 1961 of Mere, Gerrets, and Vix, accused of killing Estonian Jews and Jews from other occupied countries in the Yagala and Kalvi-Layva camps, was reported in *Sovetskaia Estoniia*, in the republican papers *Sovetskaia Belorussiia* and *Zaria Vostoka*, as well as in the central *Izvestiia, Krasnaia zvezda, Literaturnaia gazeta, Ogonek*, and others. The story of their crimes had been repeatedly told since the end of 1960. In this context, the journalist Erwin Martinson, who wrote on the Holocaust and other crimes committed in Estonia by the Nazis and their accomplices, should be mentioned. His writings were seen as deserving appraisal in the prestigious thick literary journal *Neva* (1964, no. 5, S. Pevzner, "We Shall

Not Forget Either the Good Or the Bad"). A volume of materials and documents entitled *Maski sorvany* (The Disguises Thrown Off) was published in Tallinn. During and after the trial accusations of war crimes, sometimes accompanied by documents, were published. For instance, *Sovetskaia Estoniia,* 19 May 1961, published names of individuals living in Australia, the United States, Canada, Iceland, and Sweden whom it accused of participating in the Holocaust in Tartu. Demands for extradition, with accompanying photostats of documentary materials, were publicized *(Sovetskaia Estoniia* 21 April and 17 May 1961).

In Latvia a trial was held of nine Latvians accused of participation in the Holocaust in Slonim and in executions in villages in the region of Korelichi and Kopyl, where many Belorussians perished. This was reported in the Latvian press *(Sovetskaia Latviia,* 9 and 12 March 1961) and in the Belorussian press *(Zviazda,* 11 March 1961).

The major trial of Latvian war criminals was held in October 1965. It was reported at length in the Latvian press: *Sovetskaia Latviia* wrote about it almost every day from 12 to 31 October. The sentence was given in *Pravda* (31 October 1965). The Holocaust in Rezekne and the region occupied an important place in the proceedings and also in the documents published at that time. In the wake of the trial a volume entitled *Ne zabyvai Audrini* (Riga, 1965) was published which was mainly devoted to the scores of Audrini villagers killed by the Nazis' Latvian accomplices. This volume gave considerable attention to anti-Semitism in bourgeois (i.e., independent) Latvia and to the participation of Latvian collaborators in the Holocaust. Directly linked to the trial were the notes sent by the Soviet Foreign Ministry to the governments of West Germany, the United States, and Canada demanding extradition of persons whose crimes were established during the trial. In 1984 a documentary film, *They Hide from Retribution. . . ,* was made in which the sheltering of war criminals by "U.S. ruling circles" was condemned and the crimes of Boleslav Majkovskis, who was accused *in absentia* in the October 1965 trial, and the units he commanded were exposed, including their participation "in the killing of 12,000 people in Riga" *(Sovetskaia Latviia,* 12 April 1984)—that is, the Holocaust in the Latvian capital.

War crime trials were held in Lithuania in the 1960s. A trial of three war criminals, all of them sentenced to death by shooting, was reported in the local and central press *(Sovetskaia Litva,* 25 February 1961, and *Trud,* 1 March 1961). Two large trials were held—in Kaunas on 26 September 1962 and in Vilnius on 10 October 1962—and they were widely reported in the local and central press. The killings in the Kaunas IX Fort in October 1941 constituted an important part of the indictment. The trial of five Lithuanians, held apparently in September 1967, seems to have been reported only in the republican press *(Sovetskaia Litva,* 27 September 1967). They were accused of mass killings at the Jewish and the nondenominational cemeteries.

Other activities in Lithuania with regard to war crimes included the publication at the turn of 1960 and 1961 of the collection *Facts Accuse: Documents About the Crimes of Lithuanian Bourgeois Nationalists.* Brochures about the killings in the IX Fort were published in 1961, and items on this subject appeared from time to time in the press. As a rule these publications referred to Communists and members of the underground in Lithuania and only marginally mentioned the ghetto (see for example Z. Kondrates, *IX Fort* [Kaunas, 1961], and *Sovetskaia Litva,* 26 December 1968). In 1984 a book by V. Zeymantas, *Justice Demands,* appeared which is strongly preoccupied with Lithuanians accused of war crimes living abroad, particularly in the United States. This subject was raised in Lithuania as early as the 1960s. *Sovetskaia Litva* (7 March 1961) published an article about the Holocaust in Ukmerge and accused an émigré named Macis Paskavicius of participating in the murders. A few days later a mass meeting was held in Ukmerge demanding retribution for the murders *(Czerwony Sztandar,* 15 March 1961). In 1962 *Novoe vremia* (no. 18) wrote about Lithuanians involved in the Holocaust and other war crimes who live in the United States and *Sovetskaia Litva* (6 July 1962) wrote about the mass murders, primarily of Jews, perpetrated in the first months of the German occupation mainly by pro-Nazi nationalist elements. In connection with these crimes one Antanas Impolavicius, living in Philadelphia, was mentioned, and a note from the Soviet Foreign Ministry demanded his extradition. He was also accused of participation in the killings in the Kaunas IX Fort *(Sovetskaia Litva,* 25 July 1962) and in Lithuanian murder squads in Belorussia *(Komsomolskaia pravda,* 10 August 1962). The issue of the war criminals living in the United States and Great Britain was raised again in the 1980s.

Trials in Belorussia and Ukraine

There were also war crime trials in Belorussia. Thirteen Nazi collaborators, members of Dirlewangers SS special battalion, were tried in Minsk in October 1961 *(Sovetskaia Belorussiia*, 5, 6, 7, and 14 October 1961). In March 1962 four collaborators accused of operating in the camp in Koldychev were tried in Baranovichi. In August 1963 there was a trial in Khoyniki of Belorussian policemen accused among other things of participation in the extermination of Jews and Gypsies in Khoyniki, Gomel, and other places. Here too accusations were made against individuals living in Germany and France. In April 1966 there was a trial in Vitebsk of four Soviet POWs who were involved with a detachment of the Geheime Feldpolizei and participated in the execution of "Soviet citizens" in Nevel in 1941, in Polotsk, Smolensk, and Shumilino (Vitebsk oblast), in 1942 *(Pravda*, 12 and 24 April 1966). Another trial against ten Geheime Feldpolizei members was held in Gomel in November and December 1967. In these cases accusations were made against German officers involved in these crimes, and it was alleged that they were living in West Germany *(Pravda*, 16 November and 4 December 1967). In November 1971 a great trial of six members of the 57th Police Battalion was held. Ninety-four witnesses appeared, and names of German officers involved in the crimes were mentioned *(Izvestiia*, 11 November 1971). Another trial of seven members of the same battalion was held in 1973. There was no explicit mention of crimes against Jews; the defendants were accused of having "exterminated peaceful Soviet citizens" *(Pravda*, 11 August 1973), and the scarcity of details in the reports makes it difficult to ascertain what kind of crimes were committed.

There were many war crime trials in Ukraine, and the events of the Holocaust in various localities played a considerable, sometimes central role in them. The heroic Aleksandr Pecherskii appeared in the 1963 trial of "eleven traitors," apparently guards in the Sobibor death camp *(Krasnaia zvezda* 13 April 1963) and a Babi Yar survivor, Dina Pronicheva, gave evidence in trials held in the USSR and abroad. In 1967 there was a trial in Lviv of six Ukrainians involved in the operation of and murders in the Ianov camp *(Pravda*, 15 and 25 December 1966). The parallel trial of seventeen SS-men in Stuttgart was also reported *(Zhovten*, 1967, no. 4). The reports of a 1967 trial in Nikolaev of eleven members of Selbstschutz units made no mention of crimes against Jews in any form whatever. A report in *Pravda* (25 February 1967) of a two-week trial in Dnepropetrovsk of five defendants accused of participation in extermination of people in Belzec and other concentration camps contains no reference to Jewish victims. The same applies to *Pravda* reports about killings in a concentration camp in the Crimea *(Pravda,* 26 December 1970 and 12 July 1972). In the 1983 trial of three Red Army deserters who served in the Nazi police in Mirgorod the accusation was of crimes "against Soviet citizens of Jewish nationality, Soviet POWs, and Soviet activists" *(Radianska Ukraina,* 21 October 1983).

As in the case of war criminals in the Baltic countries, the issue of Ukrainians accused of war crimes who live abroad was raised in the 1960s and Holocaust-related information appeared in reports about them. One case which kept returning in press reports over several years deserves mentioning. At the end of 1963, *Trud* (8 December 1963) reported that the brothers Sergei and Mykola Kovalchuk from Kremenets live in Philadelphia (the exact address was given) and that there is evidence that they operated in the ghetto of Lyubomla, as witnessed by B. Trakhtenberg, a survivor. In 1981 there appeared in *Lyteraturna Ukraina* (28 August 1981) a long item about what happened in the Lyubomla ghetto and the Holocaust in general, the occasion apparently being the arrival in Ukraine of an America team of investigators. Sergei Kovalchuk, who was deputy chief of police in Lyubomla, was again discussed in *Pravda Ukrainy* (17 November 1984), and the evidence deposited by (then deceased) B. Trakhtenberg with the Ukrainian writer Shafeta was quoted. Both in 1981 and in 1984 several names of alleged Ukrainian collaborators living in the United States were mentioned. In the 1960s and 1980s several individuals accused of collaboration with the Nazis were reported, with details of their alleged crimes and of crimes perpetrated in the respective places in general. The individuals in question were reported as living in France, Canada, the United States, and Great Britain.

Trials in the RSFSR

A great part of these war crime trials were held in the North Caucasus region. But the trial of nine "Gestapo accomplices accused of mass extermination of the peaceful population" held in Krasnodar in 1963 dealt with crimes committed in a wide area "from Simferopol to Rostov, from Krasnodar to Belorussia and Lublin" *(Pravda,* 25 October 1963). The trial held in Krasnodar in 1965 of six Red Army soldiers who surrendered and were trained in Trawniki dealt also with their crimes committed in the Belzec, Sobibor, and Ianov camps *(Pravda,* 2 and 9 June 1965). In January–February 1966 in Mineralnye Vody, Stavropol krai, six defendants were tried who had worked for the Nazi police. The report of the first day of the trial *(Pravda,* 1 February 1966) said that within one week, 2–8 September 1942, the entire Jewish population of Piatigorsk, Kislovodsk, Essentuki, and Mineralnye Vody was exterminated, including prominent members of the Soviet intelligentsia. It added that an obelisk was erected for the 60,000 Soviet citizens exterminated in the Stavropol territory. Also, the report of the sentence *(Pravda,* 14 February 1966) mentioned "the systematic extermination of the Jewish population," a close reference to the Holocaust. A further trial was held in Krasnodar of individuals who operated under Einsatzgruppe D who shot and killed in *dushegubki* (motor cars converted into gas chambers) 4,000 Soviet citizens in Maikop, Armavir, Simferopol, Stavropol, and other places *(Pravda,* 22 December 1967). In May 1968 a trial in Stavropol of "six traitors" accused of shooting "peaceful Soviet people" was reported *(Pravda,* 14 May 1968), and in June 1972 a trial of ten former police agents accused of mass atrocities in Piatigorsk against "innocent Soviet citizens, including old men, women, and children" *(Izvestiia,* 9 June 1972).

In 1966 *(Pravda,* 1 March 1966; *Izvestiia,* 30 August 1966) and in 1967 *(Pravda,* 7 and 15 December 1967), trials against individuals were held in Leningrad oblast. *Krasnaia zvezda* (15 December 1970) reported a trial in Leningrad of five individuals who joined the Geheime Feldpolizei. Two trials in Pskov, in November 1972 *(Izvestiia,* 23 November 1972) and June 1973 *(Pravda,* 14 June 1973), of individuals who served in punitive detachments were reported, as were two in Novgorod in March 1976 *(Izvestiia,* 26 March 1976) and December 1978 *(Pravda,* 29 December 1978) of participants in punitive expeditions, and a trial in Orel in December 1978 of two members of Geheime Feldpolizei whose crimes included the shooting of inmates of prisons in Briansk and Orel and apparently other mass executions *(Sovetskaia Rossiia,* 22 December 1978).

In the accessible reports of all these trials only the reports about the trial in Mineralnye Vody mentioned the extermination of Jews. In other reports there is no reference whatever to the Shoah, though in many of the trials the killing of Jews ought to have been among the accusations.

"Bourgeois Nationalism" a Major Target

There was a trial in the RSFSR in which there were clear references to the nationalist and religious orientation of the defendants: this was a trial against a group of Kalmyks accused of mass atrocities *(Pravda,* 11 January 1968). But the main political target of reports of trials held in Ukraine and in the Baltic were anti-Soviet nationalists. Not only individuals were accused but the nationalist movement in general was blamed in newspaper articles, in books, and in brochures. The Ukrainian leader Stecko was accused of involvement in the July pogrom in Lviv, Ukrainian nationalists were said to have participated in the Babi Yar executions, SS–Galizien was accused of participation in the *Endlösung.* The political aim of the accusations does not make them automatically untrue. Although the reasons that triggered them may seem questionable, the accusations may nevertheless be substantiated. For instance, the accusations against the Kovalchuks seem to have appeared as a result of the parcels they sent to their old parents in Kremenets. Accusations against one Ivan Stebelsky of participation in "actions" in Boryslaw and Drohobycz were probably the result of his activity in the Denver Committee for the Defense of Human Rights in the Ukraine *(Radianska Ukraina,* 3 July 1984), and so on and so forth.

With the onset of the anti-Zionist campaign, the crimes of Ukrainian collaborators against the Jews were mentioned in the context of alleged collaboration of Zionism and Ukrainian bourgeois nationalism. The nationalists were said to look for new breadgivers, and to have found them in the person of the Zionists (e.g., *Visti z Ukrainy,* 17 July 1975); they were also trying to present themselves as engaged in armed resistance to the Germans and to repudiate their anti-Semitic past *(Molod Ukrainy,* 25 January 1984).

In the Baltic countries the prewar record of the anti-Soviet nationalists of support to right-wing governments and their anti-Semitism were often mentioned in the reports of war crime trials.

The cases and reports enumerated above are far from exhaustive. But they show what information about the Holocaust reached the wider

Soviet public, the method of silence, and the political aims of the publications. It should be realized that holding war crime trials and reporting them are two different issues. We mentioned the scarcity and sometimes complete absence of war crime trial reports from 1949 to 1960. We also have information that many war crime trials were held in the course of the 1980s. In a meeting held 28 January 1988 with the British all-party war crime group, Natalia Kolesnikova, who represented the Soviet Procuracy, gave the figure of sixty-seven war crime trials "in the last five years" *(Izvestiia,* 30 January and 10 February 1988; *Soviet Weekly,* 6 February 1988). Soviet Procurator General Rekunkov quoted the figure of sixty members of punitive Nazi units tried and sentenced in 1981–86 *(TASS,* 30 September 1986, according to *BBC Summary of World Broadcasts,* 3 October 1986). Of all these trials there were only a few short reports in the press.

The Holocaust in Soviet Literature

The study of the reflection of the Holocaust in Soviet literature must cover literary works which appeared in book form, items in newspapers, weeklies, and thick literary journals. We found that the treatment of the fate of the Jews by writers and poets is different from that in media reports of war crimes and war criminals.

Though the war is a major subject of Soviet literary works, there are very few works devoted to the Shoah, but many more in which the fate of the Jews is discussed in a few paragraphs or on a few pages. Max Hayward remarked *(Bulletin of Soviet and East European Jewish Affairs,* December 1969) that a virtual taboo on being offensive to the Jews existed in Soviet *belles lettres.* This changed in later years and several offensive anti-Zionist works appeared which included material showing the pernicious role of the Jews/Zionists in the Holocaust.

Among the few early works in which the Holocaust occupied a substantial place are Ilya Ehrenburg's *The Storm* (1946) and Vassily Grossman's *For a Just Cause* (1952). Both authors were very assimilated Jews who became involved in Jewish affairs during the war, initiated and compiled the celebrated *Black Book,* and planned further collections on the Jews in the Great Fatherland War. The fate of the *Black Book* is well known. According to Natan Rapoport's testimony (quoted by Ewa Berard-Zarzycka in "Ilya Erenburg in Stalin's Post-

War Russia," *Soviet Jewish Affairs*, vol. 17, no. 1, p. 32), Ehrenburg told him in 1945 that he was forced to abandon his idea of writing a novel about the fate of the Jews. *The Storm* would therefore appear to be a deformed offspring of this project. The novel has many pages about the fate of the Jews under the Nazis both in the East and in the West. The reasons why this novel was accepted and earned Ehrenburg the Stalin Prize are aptly discussed in Ewa Berard-Zarzycka's article mentioned above, which is part of a book on Ehrenburg that appeared recently in French. Vasily Grossman was less lucky: his novel, which also includes considerable material on the Jews and the Holocaust, was severely criticized. In very ominous days for the Soviet Jewish minority, *Pravda* (13 February 1953) printed an article by Mikhail Bubennov, "Concerning Grossman's novel *Za pravoe delo*," in which the Jewish family described by Grossman was said to be a narrow, mediocre family, with petty passions, and the heroes of Stalingrad presented in a completely unacceptable way as individuals permeated by a sense of doom and sacrifice, instead of despising death.

The publication in 1961 of a Russian translation of *The Diary of Anne Frank* with an introduction by Ilya Ehrenburg was an important event. This was not the only translated work on the Holocaust which appeared in the USSR. There appeared some others—a few translations of Polish, Czech, and East German works. Anne Frank's *Diary* deserves a special mention because it found a wide response in reviews and original works by Soviet writers. Its publication probably paved the way for Masha Rolnikaite's *I Must Tell*. This is a diary by a survivor, a Jewish school girl in Lithuania, telling about her experiences in the years of war. It was first published in Lithuanian with an introduction by the leading poet Eduardas Mezelaitis. In 1965, under Brezhnev, it was translated into Russian and then into other languages of Soviet nationalities. The book was widely reviewed, and the introduction was often quoted and was reprinted in full in *Pravda Ukrainy* (24 March 1965). In the near future we may learn more about the politics behind this publication. Our general impression is of slight changes for the better in the position of the Jewish minority during the first years after Khrushchev, a tendency that was reversed after the Six-Day War.

There also was a wide echo to the documentary novel by Anatoly Kuznetsov, *Babi Yar*, which appeared in *Iunost* (1966, nos. 8, 9, and 10) and then in book form in 1967. A full, uncensored text appeared in the West (published by Posev, Frankfurt) in 1970 after the author defected from the USSR. He told about the many difficulties he encountered, and one cannot but agree with his assessment that the novel could not have appeared a year later.

Though the most outspoken, *Babi Yar* was not the only novel on the Holocaust which appeared in the USSR at that time. In a note by L. Zhuk *(V mire knig,* 1967, no. 5), "People, Be Vigilant," it is said that three noteworthy books "on the antifascist theme" had appeared recently: Ilya Konstantinovskii's *Srok davnosti* (Period of Prescription), *Na chem derzhitsia mir* (What Keeps the World Going) by Itskhokas Meras, and Kuznetsov's *Babi Yar.* Konstantinovskii's is a story of a Polish Jewish woman who perished in the Holocaust and of her son who had been taken by a gentile Polish-German couple now living in West Germany. It turns out that the child is by the German partner to this marriage, who was encouraged to have sexual intercourse with the hiding Jewess by his childless wife, who then chucks the Jewish woman out, sending her to a certain death. Meras is a Jewish Lithuanian writer who went to Israel in the early 1970s. His volume is in two parts: one is about a Lithuanian peasant woman who during the war cares for several abandoned children of various nationalities, including a German and a Jewish child; the second part is a requiem for the Vilnius ghetto and its heroes. In 1963 Meras published a children's book, *The Yellow Star,* about a Jewish child surviving the German occupation. In a way, taking into account the Soviet context, it is amazing that three books with a noticeable Jewish and Holocaust context appeared within a relatively short time.

After the Six-Day War many years passed until another major book on Jews and the Holocaust saw the light of day and, if only for that reason, acquired wide resonance in the USSR and considerable publicity in the West. Anatolii Rybakov's *Tiazhelyi pesok* (Heavy Sand) was published first in the thick literary monthly *Oktiabr* (1978, nos. 7, 8, and 9) and then in book form. There is an English translation by Harry Shukman. The book is a saga of a Jewish family: the story starts around the period of World War I, and its last part is devoted to the German occupation and the Holocaust.

There appeared several smaller items on the Holocaust, some of them of major importance. First of all, Yevtushenko's "Babi Yar" must be mentioned, along with the controversy to which it gave rise. Another poem that acquired wide publicity is Andrei Voznesenskii's "The

Call of the Lake" (1966). Twenty years later Voznesenskii published another poem *(Iunost,* 1986, no. 7) about Jews shot near Simferopol and about the looting of their mass grave. But there were some, though not many, more. To mind comes a document printed in *Neva* (1962, no. 2), "A Letter from the Camp," written by Zalmen Grodovsky, a member of the Auschwitz Sonderkommando; a poem by Boris Slutsky, "How They Murdered My Grandmother" *(Iunost,* 1963, no. 12), a poem by Rimma Kazakova, "Thoughts at the Grave of My Grandfather in Sevastopol" *(Iunost,* 1965, no. 3), and a poem by V.I. Lifshits, "Detskaia legenda" (Novyi mir, 1967, no. 4), about the yellow star worn by the king in Copenhagen.

Most of these works devoted mainly or in a great part to the Jews and the Holocaust are by writers with some ethnic Jewish connections. Also the novel about the Holocaust in Lvov by Yuly Shulmeyster, *Tsena svobody* (The Price of Freedom), published in Lviv in 1981, is in this class. Shulmeyster is an anti-Zionist propagandist, but the novel, based on a great mass of factual material and *bona fide* sources, cannot be regarded as obnoxious propaganda (see the review by Victor Swoboda in *Soviet Jewish Affairs,* vol. 12, no. 3, pp. 66–69). It is of interest that in Belorussia there appeared a few works on the Holocaust written by Belorussian writers in Belorussian, and so not widely available to the Soviet reader unless translated. Two novels—*Sparks in the Ashes* by Lidzija Arabiej (1969) and *The Bloody Banks of Niamikha* by Vladzimir Karpau (1962 journal publication, 1972 book edition)—are assessed by Vera Rich in her essay in *The Image of the Jew in Soviet Literature* (IJA, 1984) as two major novels on the Holocaust. She also points to a novella by Ivan Samiakin, *The Market Woman and the Poet* (1976 and 1979), as a work which discusses the attitude of a common Belorussian woman to the unfolding tragedy of the Jews.

In the works of most non-Jewish writers the problem of the Jewish fate during World War II and Jewish characters appear only incidentally. Thus, the Belorussian writer Vasil Bykov has a Jewish character in his novel *Sotnikov,* also published in Russian: he shows a courageous very young Jewish girl and the sympathy she receives from her Belorussian partners in misery. The Ukrainian warrior and writer Petro Vershihora, author of the celebrated *People with Clear Consciences,* includes in a story "Pereprava" (The Crossing, *Dnipro,* 1961, no. 1) a scene in which Germans and local collaborators discuss the killing of Jews. Ilya Vergasov in "Yalta" *(Druzhba narodov,* 1967, nos. 4 and 5) includes pages on the Holocaust in the Crimea, and V. Taras, in "Euthanasia" (*Neman*, 1967, no. 7), writes about the fate of the Jews in Minsk under German occupation. A documentary war crime story by Lina Glebova, "The Case of Kolesnikov" *(Oktiabr*, 1968, no. 10) includes pages on the fate of the Jews in Piatigorsk. Kolesnikov is directly involved in organizing the Holocaust in Piatigorsk and derives direct advantage from his actions. Others talk with detached sympathy about the predicament of the Jews. Vladlena Fedorova, the wife of a local Gestapo employee, reports a conversation about anti-Jewish measures and says: "So did we talk in a town where we made merry and danced when close by the *dushegubka* traveled in the streets, when others were dying here opposite in the Gestapo building. . . . I understand that now, but at that time. . . ."

The Holocaust in Soviet Yiddish Literature

Naturally, the Holocaust, the Jewish fate, occupies an important place in Soviet Yiddish literature, though care is taken by writers and censors that "nationalist" feelings should not come to the surface. It is significant that an article by the Yiddish writer Ilya Gordon, "In a United Family: On Yiddish Literature in the USSR" *(Literaturnaia gazeta*, 8 December 1976), mentions writings about the Civil War and socialist construction as well as the participation of Yiddish writers in the war, but omits any mention of the Holocaust except for an indirect reference, namely to the Yiddish newspaper of the Resistance in the ghetto of Kaunas. This article was an important ideological and political statement, a reaction to the cultural symposium convened in Moscow by the Jewish activists and to the worldwide demands for cultural rights for Soviet Jewry. Those who solicited the article and its author clearly did not regard writings about the Holocaust as a welcome and representative feature of Soviet Jewish literature. However, unlike in 1946–49, there were no direct public attacks on Yiddish and Jewish writers for being preoccupied with Jewish martyrology and the Holocaust.

Nevertheless, works about the Holocaust or with strong references to the Holocaust are an important part of Soviet Yiddish literature. As long as the works are in Yiddish their print-runs are small and their reading public is steadily shrinking. But some of the Yiddish works are translated into Russian and other Soviet languages. They then appear in many more copies than in Yiddish, and sometimes the publication of the translation precedes that of the original.

Some of the authors combine writing about the Holocaust in the strict sense of the word with writing about resistance. One such writer is Hirsh Dobin. Most of his translated short stories deal with partisan warfare in Belorussia and Jewish participation in the partisan movement. He also has a major novel on the Minsk ghetto, but I do not know of a Russian translation. Among his novels about the Holocaust *sensu stricto* is one entitled *In the Workshop (Rasskazy,* Moscow, 1973), about a group of Jewish artisans who manage to survive for the time being because their work still saves their lives: Dobin shows the development of their attitudes from passivity to resistance.

The problem of passivity appears in Samuil Gordon's *Vechnaia mera* (Eternal Measure) (Moscow, 1981), which is set in postwar Soviet life but is full of reminiscences of that war and the Holocaust and presents situations that are a direct outgrowth of that period. Also, the above-mentioned Belorussian novel by Lidzija Arabiej deals with the issue: she finds it was the Jewish way to stick to the end with family. L. Glebova's mentioned war crime story also refers briefly to the problem of Jewish behavior in the face of German policies.

Another writer who integrates Holocaust and resistance is Misha Lev, who wrote about the Sobibor camp and the uprising there. The Soviet Jewish critic Uran Guralnik regards his book *Trial After the Sentence* (reviewed by Josephine Woll in *Soviet Jewish Affairs,* vol. 13, no. 2, pp. 73–76) as "one of the most distinguished Yiddish works on the experience of the Great Patriotic War" *(Literaturnaia gazeta* and *Sovetskaia kultura,* 26 August 1981).

Another novel which Uran Guralnik mentions in this context is *Ogon i pepel* (Fire and Ashes) (Moscow, 1977) by Yehiel Falikman, which also exists in a Russian translation. Falikman's novel, like his other works on Holocaust themes, is an interesting work. It is a tale of the life and fate and private relationships of several individuals against a wide panorama of the war in 1942–43. The memory of the Babi Yar massacre and the Holocaust in Liubach, the Ukrainian hometown of many of the characters, and the description of the last stage of Babi Yar before the liberation of Kiev bind together the narrative. The author takes us from the front line at Stalingrad and the everyday life of the fighting army to occupied Liubach and Kiev, to a partisan unit and the Kiev resistance. Alongside people who wholeheartedly hate the

Nazis and fight them the author presents defeatists, traitors, and anti-Semites. The author gives vent to his thoughts about Jewish history, the place of the Jews in the anti-Nazi camp, and the necessity of remembering the Holocaust and its many victims. The issue of memory returns explicitly and in the form of hints and allegories in several works by Yiddish writers and in their Russian translation.

Another important Holocaust novel is *Ia vizhu tebia, Vilnius* (I See You, Vilnius) (Moscow, 1975), by Iosif Rabin, a volume in a series of novels about Jewish life in Lithuania–Belorussia in the nineteenth and twentieth centuries. The author subtitled it "A Poem." The author's thoughts and recollections lead him to associations with people and events of 1905–1943, the central element in them being the Vilnius ghetto and its heroes, Itsik Vitenberg, Sonya Madeysker, and Hirsh Glik. Iosif Rabin also wrote Holocaust short stories and a few that present the results of the Holocaust many years after the war. For instance, the short story "Letter to a Friend" (1961) is about a boy and a girl who are brought up as brother and sister by a woman who rescued them, but they fall in love. Another short story, "Seven Days in the Week" (1960), is about a girl, a Holocaust survivor in a Polish small town who is rejected by her love's mother. In a review of this story, *Literaturnaia Rossiia* (1961, no. 22) hints that such things happen in the USSR as well. An interesting feature of the story is the description of how the situation leads to the girl's quest to discover her ancestry, in which she is helped by her gentile boyfriend. Again, the issue of memory, of continuity with the past appears.

Khaim Melamud, in *Merilo zhizni* (The Criterion of Life) (Moscow, 1982), writes about the Holocaust in small localities in the Ivano-Frankivsk (Stanislawow) oblast. Grigory (Hershl) Polyanker's *Uchitel z Medzibozha* (The Teacher from Medzibozh [which happens to be the Besht's town]) writes about the heroic role of a Jewish teacher in the resistance. His "Fate of an Artist" describes the experience of a Jewish painter with the Red Army through the war and the camps, which makes him paint and exhibit a series of Holocaust paintings.

Holocaust stories are to be found among the translated works of Riva Rubina, *V"etsia nit* (The Thread Unwinds) (Moscow, 1982).

Many items in Yiddish on the Holocaust, and on other subjects as well, have no Russian or other translation. Neither Der Nister's collection *Vidervuks* (Growing Again) (Moscow, 1969) nor Itsik Kipnis's *Tsum Lebn* (To Life) (Moscow, 1969) was translated, and I have seen only excerpts translated from Perets Markish's *Der Trot fun Doyres*, or *Postup pokolenii* (The March of Generations) *(Literaturnaia Rossiia, 1963, no. 34).*

The Holocaust in Yiddish Poetry

Several poetry collections which appeared in Russian translation include poems on the Holocaust, for instance, Iosif Bukhbinder's *Tebe, moi drug* (To You, My Friend) (Moscow, 1980), David Bromberg, *Niti godov* (The Thread of Years) (Moscow, 1982), and Aron Vergelis, *Volshebstvo* (Magic) (Moscow, 1985). A comparison of two poetry collections, one in Yiddish, *Horizontn* (Moscow, 1965), and the other of Russian translations, *Sovetskaia evreiskaia poeziia* (Soviet Yiddish Poetry) (Moscow, 1985) may offer some clues to the inclination to publicize Jewish works on the Holocaust.

An important reservation must be made: this is not a comparison of like with like. The Russian collection appeared twenty years later than the Yiddish volume. Though the number of poets represented in both is similar (48 and 50), in the Yiddish collection still figure several poets who left the USSR and until recently were treated as non-persons. There are about 400 poems in the Russian collection and close to 500 in the Yiddish. In the latter there are thirty-six items on the Holocaust or with strong references to it by twenty-one poets; several poets are represented by several poems on the subject: Moyshe Tayf—six, Dora Khaykina and Yankl Shternberg—four each, David Bromberg—three. Nineteen of the poems were written between 1950 and 1965, that is, over a period of fifteen years, with some distance from the direct experiences of the war. In the Russian collection fifteen poets have poems on a Holocaust subject or with clear references to the Shoah, and there are six poems by six poets written after 1950, so within a time span of thirty-five years. In these poems the image of the ditches that became the mass graves of Jews keeps returning, and so does the issue of memory. Memory seems to be, in my understanding, the subject matter of a poem by Aron Vergelis, "Anne Frank" (1980). On a faraway nameless island some unearthly creatures build a wailing wall to Anne Frank and to the one-third of the nation who perished in the war. No human footsteps can be seen there; maybe the sea waves wash them away, and maybe the wall exists only in the elusive twilight of a dream. Nevertheless, the poet is sure that the shadows of the murdered and Anne herself come there.

It is obvious that Yiddish literature, translated or not translated, had to comply with certain demands, shun certain themes, and beware of any shadow of nationalism or Zionism. In the introduction to *Sovetskaia evreiskaia poeziia,* Valentin Kataev wrote: "Soviet Jewish poetry is the child of October and all her blood links are with October. It is oriented towards the future. . . . Patriotism and militancy have never been lacking." In the introduction to Dobin's *Rasskazy* it is said that Dobin is full of life-confirming pathos and, without avoiding the special Jewish calamities, sees the Jewish fate as inextricably linked with the general fate of other Soviet nationalities. Ties of friendship, brotherhood, and solidarity bind all of them together, particularly in the war against the Nazis. In her review of Misha Lev's *Trial After the Sentence* Josephine Woll rightly points out that the author played down the role of the Ukrainian guards and emphasized those among the Poles living around Sobibor who behaved humanely toward escapees from the death camp rather than those who were actively hostile. One might also look askance at certain novels and short stories about Jewish resistance and gentile assistance where Communists are given sole credit. Although we may not meet an accurate proportion of anti-Semites and collaborators in these works, we do meet them. In the novels I read, excluding those that are clearly anti-Zionist, one rarely meets Jewish collaborators; Jews with weaknesses in their character, moral weaknesses, yes, but outright collaborators, exceptionally. The traitor in Falikman's *Fire and Ashes* is a Karaite; in Shulmeyster's *Tsena svobody* (Shulmeyster is not a Yiddish writer), a collaborator is a former member of Ha-shomer Ha-tsair, but this organization itself is described sympathetically. There is a predilection to present Jewish active resisters, but individuals representing "the silent majority" are also there. There is, however, very little about "the silent majority" among the general population. But this may be a general weakness of Soviet *belles lettres.*

The Holocaust in Theater

It seems that the Holocaust was not a subject reflected in the Soviet theater, despite the popularity of the war theme. Aleksandr Borshchagovskii's play *The Ladies' Tailor* was printed in a Yiddish translation by Note Lurie in *Sovietish haimland* (1982, no. 9) under the title *Di nakht erev Babi Yar* and appeared in the original Russian in the monthly *Teatr* (a review of the play appeared in *Soviet Jewish Affairs,* vol. 12, no. 2, pp. 67–72). The play has been put on by the Moscow Jewish Dramatic Ensemble (a review appeared in *Sovietish haimland,* 1981, no. 7). We have no information about the play being staged in any Russian or other Soviet theater.

About twenty years earlier an Italian ensemble visited Moscow and among the plays presented was *The Diary of Anne Frank* by Francis Goodrich and Albert Hackett *(Sovetskaia kultura,* 27 April 1963). While other plays had five performances each, *The Diary of Anne Frank* had only two *(Jews in Eastern Europe,* September 1963). The restrictions on that play were not exclusively the result of the current political exigencies (the Yevtushenko "Babi Yar" controversy was still relatively fresh), for the play had been criticized much earlier, in 1959 *(Sovetskaia kultura,* 3 December 1959), on the ground that it was not founded on the principle of political struggle against fascism but was instead concerned with the idea of nonresistance to the enemy. Nevertheless, the play was put on in the Griboedov Theater in Tbilisi in 1964 *(Zaria Vostoka,* 15 March 1964).

A play about Korczak and his children by Vadim Korostylev was performed at the Moscow Children's Theater with music by M. Vaynberg, but there was no indication that the characters in the play were Jewish.

The Czech novel by Jan Otcenasek, *Romeo, Juliette, and Darkness,* a story of a wartime love between a Czech student and a Jewish girl, was made into an opera by K. Molchanov and presented in the Leningrad Small Opera Theater in 1963 *(Muzikalnaia zhizn,* 1963, no. 22). In 1964 a translation of the book was issued by "Molodaia gvardiia" in 100,000 copies.

The above enumeration is unlikely to be complete. But it conveys the impression that the Holocaust events were rather outside the interest of the Soviet theater. There were Holocaust-related vignettes in some plays; for instance, Vadim Sobko's drama *A Kiev Notebook* (published in *Raduga,* 1964, no. 8) includes the German radio announcement that on 29 September 1941 Jews had to assemble with their belongings.

The Holocaust in Film

The Holocaust was also extremely rarely reflected in the Soviet film. This is attested in an article by Shimon Chertok on Jewish themes in the Soviet cinema *(Soviet Jewish Affairs,* vol. 16, no. 3), a subject about which the author has had inside knowledge, and in information that appeared in the Soviet press in the glasnost years about films that were banned and films that did not get past the planning stage. The overall picture is that the subject of the Holocaust and Jewish subjects in general were avoided. In 1945 Mark Donskoi presented a tremendous scene of the Babi Yar massacre in the film *The Unconquered,* based on a wartime novel by Boris Gorbatov. (The inclusion of Jewish characters and their fate in this novel had already drawn attention during the war.) Later films on the theme of the war portray the Holocaust as a sign of the times and avoid emphasizing it. A 1962 film, *Footsteps in the Night,* by the Lithuanian film director Romualdas Vabalas, tells the story of the escape from the Kaunas IX Fort on Christmas Eve, 1943, but while in reality all the escapees were Jewish, in the film only one of them is a Jew.

A 1962 film by Roman Karmen, *The People's Trial,* included several Holocaust scenes *(Gudok,* 1 September 1962). But in 1964, when work started on a 1946 Holocaust story by Valentin Kataev, the script had to be rewritten twenty-one times. The film, *Otche nash* (Our Father), was directed by Boris Ermolaev. It is not clear from the account in *Sovetskaia kultura* (29 June 1989) whether the film was shown at that time or was one of the films taken off the shelves.

In 1963 a screenplay of *God Be With Us* by V. Zakliavicius and Grigory Kanovich, with the ghetto as one of its main themes, was not permitted to be filmed at the Lithuanian Film Studio. In 1965 another effort to make a film reflecting the heroism of Lithuanian Jews during the war, with a scenario by Itskhok Meras and Mikhail Kalik, was unsuccessful.

In 1964 Lev Ginzburg told about a film scenario by him based on the 1963 trial of war criminals in Krasnodar *(Iskusstvo kino,* 1964, no. 7). We do not know what happened to this project.

In 1967 Aleksandr Askoldov's film *The Commissar* was banned. This is a Civil War story which in 1967 was deemed unacceptable because it not only portrayed sympathetically a completely non-revolutionary Jewish family but also included a forward flash showing the family, wearing Stars of David, being marched to their death. The film was finally screened in 1988 all over the USSR and abroad. Whether the analogy made in the film between the White pogroms and the Holocaust will be appreciated in the new Russian dispensation is rather doubtful.

In 1977 Larissa Shepitko's film *The Ascent* was shown. It is based on Bykov's *Sotnikov,* mentioned above, and it includes the scene about the imprisoned Jewish girl who refuses to tell who gave her shelter.

In 1981 a documentary film, *Babi Yar,* was made. The tendency was to show the massacre in the context of the outrages of fascism, reaction, imperialism, and Zionism. The film was shown on television on the forty-fifth anniversary of the massacre, but with a different tendency in the narrative. The narrator was Vitaly Korotich.

In 1987 there appeared a report about a film by Elem Klimov, *Go and See,* about Nazi rule in Belorussia. The screenplay is by Klimov and the leading Belorussian writer, Ales Adamovich, who has to his credit several works on the subject.

In assessing this list of films that were made or were intended to be made, one has to take into account the paucity of foreign films on Holocaust themes shown in the USSR. Nevertheless, some were shown, mainly Polish and East German productions. In 1988 Lanzmann's *Shoah* was shown to a select audience, and in 1989 Soviet television presented Miller's *This Happened in Vichy.*

Final Observations

How the period of the Great Fatherland War and the Holocaust will fare after the revolutionary changes in 1991 it is much too early to say. One interesting and entirely understandable phenomenon should be mentioned which seems to influence to some degree the perception of Nazi atrocities, namely the preoccupation with the Soviet past and with the murders and terror under Stalin and other Soviet leaders. The following Soviet reaction to *Shoah* was reported in the Polish weekly *Tygodnik Mazowsze* (no. 245): "We should do such a film on the Armenian genocide, on our own history under Stalin." Even more pointed was a reviewer's reaction to a recently published book of Holocaust recollections, *Pisma mojej pamiaci,* in Belorussian by Anna Krasnoperko. In *Literaturnaia gazeta* (10 January 1990) Olga Ipatova from Minsk drew a parallel between the commemoration of the Holocaust and the martyrology of her own and other Soviet peoples under Stalin and pointed to the prohibition against honoring the dead of Kuropaty during the Dziady of 1989.

All this opens an interesting question: how did the Soviet attitude toward the memory of the Holocaust relate to official attitudes toward other tragedies such as the Armenian genocide or the enormous human loss in the blockade of Leningrad. The Soviets permitted a limited commemoration of the Armenian genocide in Armenia but rejected any idea of all-Union functions. They permitted the publication of Franz Werfel's *The Forty Days of Musa Dag* in Armenian but refused to publish a Russian translation. With regard to the siege of Leningrad, only very recently was a film on the suffering and mass death of the civilian population released; previously the military side of the story was the center of attention. The treatment of the Holocaust in the USSR may have been influenced by special reasons, including the regime's assimilationist policy toward Jews as well as anti-Semitic attitudes. But the cases of the Armenian genocide and the Leningrad blockade seem to point to more general attitudes present in Soviet communism as possible roots of the treatment of the Holocaust as well.

A Monument Over Babi Yar?

WILLIAM KOREY

"No monument stands over Babi Yar." This was the opening line of Yevgeny Yevtushenko's famous poem of September 1961, the then rebellious poet's powerful indictment of the Kremlin's suppression of information about the single greatest episode of the Nazi Holocaust on Soviet soil. Yevtushenko linked the suppression to traditional Russian anti-Semitism. At this moment in history, the poet's hope for a monument may finally be consummated.

An initial effort to erect a moment in response to worldwide criticism came in 1976. Thirty-five years after the Babi Yar tragedy, and after several false starts, a monument was finally erected at the site of the ravine on the outskirts of Kiev. But the character of the monument as well as the inscription upon it emptied the episode of its martyrological significance. Along with all other facets of the Nazi genocidal program against Jews, the Kremlin chose to plunge the Jewish torment at Babi Yar down history's "memory hole."

The fifty-foot-high monument, built at a cost of $1.8 million, contains nothing that even remotely suggests the Jewish agony at Babi Yar. Instead, the bronze sculpture, with eleven entwined figures, is characteristic of dozens of other Soviet memorials which dotted Eastern Europe from the Brandenburg Gate to the Urals. The stereotyped group included the following: a young girl weeping over the slain figure of her boyfriend; a sailor shielding his mother with his body; a woman, her hands tied behind her back with barbed wire but still suckling a child; another wounded young woman about to fall into the abyss; and, finally, a Red Army soldier and a partisan. It is the last two figures in the tableau that sum up the central theme of the monument. A description by the Novosti Press Agency highlighted the typical "positive heroes" of this example of socialist realism: "Proudly raising their heads, implacable and unconquered, the imprisoned soldier and the partisan are struck by the volley of bullets. Even in their last moments, they terrify the enemy with their hatred."

In keeping with this distorted image of Babi Yar was the inscription on the plaque placed at the bottom of the monument. It read: "Here, in 1941–43, the German Fascist invaders executed over 100,000 citizens of Kiev and prisoners of war." And further to empty the memorial of meaningful reference to the Jewish carnage, the structure was placed not at the specific site of the ravine but about a mile away.

That the monument and its placement as well as the entire frieze, along with the inscription, scarcely conform with the historical evidence is apparent from a careful reading of the Nuremberg records, the proceedings of a subsequent major trial in Darmstadt, West Germany, in 1967, and a host of documentary and literary sources. Distortion and falsification abounded in the Soviet monument.

What then happened at Babi Yar? The Babi Yar story began on 19 September 1941, when a fifty-man advance party of Sonderkommando 4A of Einsatzgruppe C entered the city of Kiev. Two days later, the chief of the Sonderkommando, Colonel Paul Blobel, arrived, and on 25 September the rest of the 150-member unit marched in.

Final preparations were made for the decisive action "carried out exclusively against Jews with their entire families," as a top secret Einsatzgruppe report revealed. On 28 September, some 2,000 notices were posted throughout the city calling upon "all Jews of the city of Kiev and its environs" to appear at 8 o'clock the following morning at an intersection near the city's cemetery. Failure to appear would result in their execution. The notices were accompanied by a word-of-mouth rumor, a deliberate falsehood spread by the Kommandos, that the Jews were to be evacuated and resettled elsewhere. Since the designated intersection site bordered on a railway station, the rumor seemed to have a plausible foundation. A secret official report spoke of the "extremely clever organization" utilized to overcome "the difficulties resulting from such a large-scale action."

The Jews who gathered in the streets of Kiev on 29 September were mostly mothers and children, the elderly, and the sick. The young men had left the city with the retreating Red Army. The late Ilya Ehrenburg described, in a moving section of his memoirs, how "a procession of the doomed marched along endless Lvovskaya Street—the mothers carrying their babies, the paralyzed pulled along on hand carts." The unexpected size of the crowd made for a slow procession through the principal streets. It was not until late morning or early afternoon that most of the victims reached the cemetery. At that point, the street was blocked with a barrier of barbed wire and antitank obstructions. A passage had been left through the middle, guarded on both sides by Kommandos assisted by Ukrainian *polizei*. The victims were ordered to remove their clothing.

An eyewitness, Sergei Ivanovich Lutzenko, the warden of Lukianovka Cemetery, related, in an official Soviet account, the grim finale of the march:

> They were ordered to deposit on the ground in a neat pile all the be-longings they brought with them and then, in tight columns of one hundred each, were marched to the adjoining Babi Yar.... I could see well how at the ravine's edge the columns were stopped, how everyone was stripped naked, their clothes piled in orderly bundles.

Before the shooting began, the Jews were required to run a gauntlet of rubber truncheons or big sticks as they entered the long passage. The Ukrainian *polizei* were especially brutal with those who dallied. As described by the Soviet novelist Anatoly Kuznetsov, they were "kicked, beaten with brass knuckles and clubs, . . . with [a] drunken viciousness and in a strange sadistic frenzy."

Colonel Blobel testified, in 1951, that his unit had been divided into squads of thirty men each; a squad would shoot for an hour and then be replaced by a second squad. The shooting continued until night, when the Germans retired to their quarters, herding the remaining Jews into empty garages. Early in the morning, the massacre was resumed. That evening, an eyewitness reported, "the ravine was dynamited so as to cover with earth both the dead and those still alive." An official Einsatzgruppe comment would express pride in the total operation: "The transaction was carried out without friction. No incidents oc-curred."

At the end of the thirty-six hours, the precise calculations of the Germans showed 33,771 dead. But the Einsatzgruppe continued to hunt down Jews in hiding to feed their unsatiated machinegunners at the ravine. As related in a letter by a Babi Yar survivor, Dina Pro-nicheva: "After a massacre of the Jews, the Germans combed apartments and houses. If they found children of a Jewish mother they killed them, even when, as in our case, the father was Russian."

During the subsequent two years of German occupation, the death roll of Babi Yar victims continued to mount with executions of others —Soviet prisoners of war, partisans, and communist activists. Still, the uniquely Jewish feature of the extermination procedure remained. Characteristic was the selection process by which Soviet prisoners of war were chosen for execution at Babi Yar. An Einsatzgruppe directive specified that "the racial origin has to be taken into consideration." Thus, a November 1941 report of executions noted, "the larger part were again Jews, and a considerable part of these were again Jewish prisoners of war who had been handed over by the Wehrmacht."

For the Einsatzgruppe killers, Babi Yar represented an apotheosis of their anti-Jewish objective. In March 1942, Colonel Blobel was driving in the vicinity with Gestapo agent Albert Hartel when the latter noticed that the surface was agitated by pressures from below—the spring thaw having released gases from decaying corpses. Blobel proudly explained: "Here are my Jews buried."

Soviet authorities from the very beginning attempted to blur this aspect of its character. The official government report on the massacre, published some six months after Kiev's liberation, spoke of Nazi crimes at Babi Yar against Soviet citizens generally rather than against the Jewish community specifically.

Apparently, the local authorities were anxious to remove all traces of Babi Yar, for they initially planned to build a modern market on the site. Ehrenburg, at the time, asked the Ukrainian premier, Nikita Khrushchev, to intervene and was promptly advised by the premier "not to interfere in matters that do not concern you."

The Soviet anti-Semitic campaign which burst forth in late 1948 required that Babi Yar be erased from historical memory. A poem by the Ukrainian-Jewish writer Savva Golovanivsky was singled out for attack in March 1949 because he had dared to suggest that Ukrainians and Russians "had turned their backs on an old Jew, Abraham, whom in 1941 the Germans had marched through the streets of Kiev to be shot." The poet was charged with "nationalist slander" and "defamation of the Soviet nation."

Another Ukrainian-Jewish poet, Leonid Pervomaisky, was also denounced for "repeating Golovanivsky's defamation of the Soviet people." The theme of Babi Yar was no longer countenanced in literature, and scheduled plans for a memorial at the site were quietly shelved. These plans included a design by the prominent architect A.V. Vlasov that would have shaped the monument in the form of a "strict, simple" prism.

The later "thaw" was an opportune time for sensitive Soviet intellectuals brooding over the double tragedy of Babi Yar—the Holocaust there and then suppression of any reference to it—to voice concern. The distinguished Soviet writer Viktor Nekrasov, upon learning that the Architectural Office of the Kiev Town Council planned to flood Babi Yar, fill it, and "turn the site into a park, to build a stadium there," wrote a long letter to *Literaturnaia gazeta* which appeared on 10 October 1959:

> Is this possible? Who could have thought of such a thing? To fill a. . . deep ravine and on the site of such a colossal tragedy to make merry and play football? No! This must not be allowed!

Nekrasov noted that other sites of Nazi atrocities had been turned into memorials, and "lest people ever forget what happened," he boldly demanded similar "tributes of respect" for the Kiev citizens who had been shot in Babi Yar.

A much larger community of opinion extending far beyond Soviet borders was to be stirred by Yevgeny Yevtushenko's poem in September 1961, almost twenty years to the day after the Babi Yar tragedy. In an autobiographical sketch published later in the Parisian daily *L'Express,* Yevtushenko explained how he had come to write his courageous and moving "Babi Yar." He had waited for a long time, he said, to publish a poem on anti-Semitism, but an appropriate form had not presented itself until after he had visited Babi Yar in the early fall of 1961 to see the place and sense the Holocaust. Upon his return to Moscow, he wrote the poem in "only a few hours." In it, he identified himself with "each man they shot here. . . every child they shot here," and in his profound mourning, he was transformed into "one vast and soundless howl."

The storm of criticism that followed the poem's appearance was not unexpected. Five days after "Babi Yar" was published, *Literaturnaia zhizn',* the journal of the Writers' Union of the Russian Soviet Federated Socialist Republic, carried a response in the form of a poem by another Soviet writer, Aleksei Markov, which questioned

Yevtushenko's patriotism. "What sort of real Russian are you?" asked Markov. By referring to Jewish martyrdom at Babi Yar and to Russian anti-Semitism, Yevtushenko had attempted to defile (with a "pygmy's spittle") "Russian crew-cut lads" who fell in battle against the Nazis.

A less crudely violent, if more trenchant, attack appeared in the same journal three days later. Written by a well-known Soviet critic, Dmitri Starikov, the article challenged the view that Babi Yar represented the martyrdom of Jewry. The "destinies of persons who died there cry out" against the notion that Babi Yar was "one of history's examples of anti-Semitism."

The attacks did not, however, undermine the popularity of the poem, especially among Soviet youths. The highest Party authorities became concerned. Khrushchev was later to reveal that the "Party Central Committee has been receiving letters expressing anxiety that in some works the position of Jews in our country has been depicted in a distorted way." He referred specifically to the Babi Yar poem.

At a Moscow meeting of several hundred intellectuals called by the Party leadership on 17 December 1962, the poem became a key issue. When Yevtushenko recited a part of it to the audience, Khrushchev interjected, "Comrade Yevtushenko, this poem has no place here." It was time for the "appropriate" discipline to be applied and for the customary public denunciations to be made.

A Kremlin conference of writers and artists held on 7–8 March 1963, and covered in detail in the public press, provided the setting for the disciplinary action. Khrushchev singled out Yevtushenko's "Babi Yar":

> Events are depicted in the poem as if only the Jewish population fell victim to the Fascist crime, while at the hands of the Hitlerite butchers there perished not a few Russians, Ukrainians, and Soviet people of other nationalities.

The pressures exerted upon Yevtushenko had the desired result. It was first made apparent, ironically, in the musical field. By December 1962, one of the USSR's most prestigious cultural figures, Dmitri Shostakovich, had completed his Thirteenth Symphony, a musical and choral setting of five poems by Yevtushenko, including "Babi Yar." The work received its first performance in Moscow on 18 December 1962, and was accorded a tumultuous reception. But no review appeared in the major press organs.

The official reaction to the Shostakovich symphony was hardly surprising. Just the day before its public debut, at a specially called meeting held in Moscow of top Communist Party leaders and leading Soviet intellectuals, the Party's then principal ideologist, Leonid Ilyichev, criticized Shostakovich for choosing an undesirable theme for his symphony and therewith failing to serve the true interests of the people. Public performances ceased.

To meet the powerful Party thrusts, Yevtushenko made two additions to the text. At one point, a line was added: "Here, together with Russians and Ukrainians, lie Jews." A second insertion read: "I am proud of the Russia which stood in the path of the bandits." Yevtushenko vehemently denied in a Paris interview, in February 1963, that he had capitulated to Party pressures. The fact is, of course, that the additions do violence to the spirit and intent of the poem, which had treated Babi Yar as a distinctive Jewish episode of martyrdom. After Shostakovich incorporated the revisions in the symphony, performances were renewed and *Pravda*, on 10 February 1963, observed that it was now a truly "Russian" work.

The toll had been taken. Discussion about Babi Yar disappeared from the public arena, not to reemerge until the summer of 1966, when the Kremlin, for a short period, relaxed its pressure upon the literary community. In August 1966, *Iunost*, a liberal literary monthly, initiated a three-part serialization of a powerful documentary novel, *Babi Yar*, by Anatoly Kuznetsov. With painstaking detail, graphically presented in a compelling format, the novelist catalogued the overpowering events of Babi Yar. It was the first time since the war that the Soviet public would learn the full dimensions of the Nazi massacre.

Kuznetsov did not hesitate to define the initial Nazi objective as being aimed exclusively against Jews. One of his characters, the grandfather, bursts into the household on 28 September 1941 to report the German plans: "Here's news! Not a Jew will be left in Kiev by tomorrow."

If a few non-Jews were killed during those two days, it was because they had appeared accidentally in the line of march or at the ravine. The author's candor further required him to take the difficult step of showing that some Ukrainians had welcomed the conquering Nazis, that others had actually collaborated in the mass killings, and that many had passively accepted German rule, striving in every way possible to survive.

Following his defection from the USSR in July 1969, Kuznetsov revealed in the London *Daily Telegraph* that his novel had stirred up a hornet's nest: "There was an unpublicized row over my book. They suddenly decided that it ought not to have been published. At *Iunost'* they told me that it was practically an accident that it had ever appeared at all and that a month later its publication would have been out of the question. In any case, they forbade the reprinting of it."

When Kuznetsov's work was published, a considerable amount of his original draft had been edited out. The excised portions, significantly, provided much anecdotal material concerning the widespread anti-Semitism among Ukrainians.

Public reaction to the appearance of the Kuznetsov volume was slow in coming. On 22 November the journal that had first printed the Yevtushenko poem, *Literaturnaia gazeta,* carried a powerful endorsement of the book by the liberal literary and film critic, Aleksandr Borshchagovsky. Its "destiny," he wrote, "is beyond doubt."

Terming the book "a marvel of art," Borshchagovsky went on to say that "Soviet literature has gained a passionate and talented work." He gave emphasis to the overwhelming fact of Jewish martyrdom: "The first act of the [Babi Yar] tragedy [was] when the Jewish population of Kiev was murdered, wiped out and cast into the ravine in the course of a few days." Shortly afterward, another strongly favorable review appeared in the liberal *Novyi mir.* The critic, Ariadna Gromova, stated that the Babi Yar story is "vitally necessary both here and abroad."

The open discussion of Kuznetsov's *Babi Yar* was accompanied by related developments which suggested that strong pressures from the liberal intelligentsia for a memorial to the victims of Babi Yar were having some impact on the political authorities. The earlier outcries of Nekrasov and Yevtushenko seemed, in 1966, to have found the appropriate milieu for fulfillment.

The first hint that consideration was being given to a Babi Yar memorial came in April 1965, when the President of the France–USSR Association, André Blumel, was told by the Mayor of Kiev about such plans. And, indeed, early in 1966, Novosti, the Soviet press agency, announced that the Ukrainian Architects Club in Kiev had placed on exhibit over 200 projects and some thirty detailed plans for a memorial at Babi Yar.

After the exhibition, the entries would be judged by a special panel consisting of representatives from the Academy of Sciences and other cultural institutions. Significantly, the inscriptions on the submitted projects avoided reference to Babi Yar as a symbol of Jewish martyrdom.

Those who might be disappointed with the projected character of the memorial could still take heart from the fact that at least the idea for a memorial was alive. Further verification came on 29 April 1966 when the London *Daily Telegraph* correspondent in the Soviet Union, John Miller, cabled his newspaper that he was "emphatically" assured by Ukrainian writers that "Babi Yar would have its monument in time for next year's fiftieth anniversary of the Revolution." Final assurances about the memorial came on 9 September 1966, when Peter Tempest, the correspondent in Russia of the British Communist daily, *Morning Star,* cabled from Kiev that "the memorial at Babi Yar to 200,000 people, mostly Jews, massacred here during the war will definitely be erected next year."

So heady was the atmosphere that on 29 September 1966, the twenty-fifth anniversary of Babi Yar, many Kiev citizens spontaneously assembled at the site in what has been described as "a very impressive scene." Dina Pronicheva, Viktor Nekrasov, and the Ukrainian liberal writer Ivan Dzyuba addressed the audience.

Dzyuba's remarks, preserved in the *Chornovil Papers,* are remarkable for their courage. He demanded from the authorities that they "let the Jews know Jewish history, the Jewish culture, and the Yiddish language and be proud of them." The character of the event prompted some cameramen from the Kiev newsfilm studio to rush down to film it. According to Kuznetsov, this act resulted in "a great row in the studio," followed by the dismissal of the director and the confiscation of the film by the secret police.

Although the authorities were sufficiently alarmed to place at the site, a few days later, a granite plaque on which was written the commitment that a monument would be erected there to the victims of fascism, the actual plans for building it were shelved. The celebrations of the fiftieth anniversary of the Revolution produced no memorial at Babi Yar.

Instead, the superpatriots struck back. It was hardly unexpected that the principal criticism of the Kuznetsov book would appear in a journal of the military—always the repository of correct national pride. The rhetorical title of the review in *Sovetskii voin* (August 1967)—"To a Full Extent?"—set its tone. The reviewer, Aleksei Yegorov, asserted quite simply and dogmatically that Kuznetsov's portrait of Babi Yar was a distortion. Equally false, Yegorov argued, were the reviews by Borshchagovsky and Gromova.

What Yegorov found particularly distasteful was the Kuznetsov description of those Russians and Ukrainians who had been "fascist lackeys and obeyed their criminal orders." References to Russian and Cossack collaborators, Ukrainian pro-Nazi policemen, Soviet black marketeers who pandered to the Germans, ordinary citizens who cooperated with occupation authorities (some by turning over their Jewish wives or informing on other Jews) were, from Yegorov's viewpoint, nothing short of "offensive" and hardly appropriate for a "historical work."

Not much better was Kuznetsov's ethnic characterization of the martyred. In a sarcastic introductory remark, Yegorov reminded his audience that Kuznetsov is "not the first artist who chose the tragedy of Babi Yar as a topic"; Yevtushenko had "touched upon it and, as is known, twisted historical facts." The same type of "twisting" was to be found in the Kuznetsov book, the critic contended. The novelist, he insisted, was confused about who the martyred had been. Kuznetsov should have said:

> In Babi Yar there lie buried many Russians, Ukrainians, and other people. Here were shot the sailors of the Dnieper flotilla, the railway workers of the Kiev region, workers and employees of Kiev, Red Army soldiers and commanders who were taken prisoner.

Not Jews.

A decade had elapsed since the Kremlin spoke of plans to build a monument at Babi Yar. On 2 July 1976, the Babi Yar memorial was finally unveiled. Why at this late date? International reaction to the Helsinki pact, signed by Leonid Brezhnev, may have had something to do with the question. A barrage of criticism had been directed at the USSR for not implementing the Helsinki pact's provisions, especially those demanding respect for the rights of minorities.

The failure to build a monument at Babi Yar had come to symbolize throughout the world, and within the USSR, the repression of both Jewish culture and Jewish consciousness, of which the Holocaust is an essential ingredient. The pursuit of detente by the Kremlin, in the post-Helsinki atmosphere, required the building of the long-promised memorial at Babi Yar, if only as a gesture of good faith. But the memorial deliberately violated the historical facts. It is Yegorov's perverted perception of what happened at Babi Yar that is incorporated in the monument.

Jewish activists who dared to say publicly that Babi Yar was symbolic of the Holocaust faced jail sentences. In 1969 a young Jewish radio engineer in Kiev, Boris Kochubiyevsky, was placed on trial, in part for declaring at a Babi Yar memorial service: "Here lies part of the Jewish people." The activist was convicted of the "crime" of "slander" for this and similar statements and sentenced to three years in a labor camp. Organizing prayer services like the Kaddish at the site was risky without official approval. But when Kiev Jewish activists applied in 1978 for permission to hold a Kaddish service at the ravine site, they never received the courtesy of a reply.

Soviet elementary and high school textbooks avoided mentioning Babi Yar as the site of a Jewish massacre even as it failed to deal altogether with the Holocaust. The Holocaust had simply been engulfed in almost total silence. At the historic first All-Union Congress of Jewish Organizations held in Moscow in December 1989, the several hundred delegates moved a resolution that bitterly complained: "There are no historical studies and publications in the USSR devoted to the genocide of Soviet Jews; in the school books, the tragedy of the Jewish people is not mentioned."

An exception occurred in October 1980. The Moscow Jewish Drama Ensemble was allowed to perform at a tiny theater a play about Babi Yar entitled *The Ladies' Tailor,* by Aleksandr Borshchagovsky, the critic who had defended Yevtushenko when he was subjected to a fierce onslaught in the Soviet literary community. But the play was permitted only a one-week run. At approximately the same time, a Kiev Jewish film producer, Aleksandr Shlayen, was preparing a documentary for television on the Babi Yar trauma. He was forced to drop his final plans in December 1980 when he became seriously ill. Others took over the editing process. As later described by Shlayen, the documentary was "murdered" by editor "assassins." When shown on television in 1981, the 70-minute Babi Yar film had been virtually emptied of meaningful martyrological content. Jews were mentioned but once, while Zionists were equated with Nazis.

On the occasion of the fortieth anniversary of Babi Yar in September 1981, the official Soviet reaction to any kind of Jewish ceremony at the site was negative. There was to be no assemblage and no memorial service. Moscow Jews who were planning to make the journey to Kiev were threatened with arrest. Five activists were arrested by the KGB. Only four persons succeeded in breaking through the police barriers. They were finally permitted to lay a wreath; nothing more.

A significant change came in 1987. With glasnost in full swing and Mikhail Gorbachev calling for filling in the "blank spots" of history, the authorities permitted in September a commemorative event concerning the Babi Yar massacre. It was held not in Kiev but just outside Moscow at the Jewish section of a local cemetery. Several quite disparate Jewish groups, with obvious government encouragement, were allowed as sponsors of the event. Yosef Begun, the prominent refusenik and Jewish cultural advocate, eloquently addressed himself to the absence of any reference to Jews in the Babi Yar memorial. A non-refusenik but strong critic of anti-Jewish bigotry, Yuri Sokol, called upon Soviet society to face up to anti-Semitism.

The third to speak was Samuil Zivs, the deputy chairman of the notorious and officially sponsored Anti-Zionist Committee. His theme was that the Jews who had died at Babi Yar were defending their Soviet homeland. His corollary theme was that the "refuseniks" were "Zionist-Fascists" who considered Israel as their motherland. The crowd reacted with vehement booing. Attended by several hundred Jews, along with a sprinkling of KGB and militia officers as well as Pamyat members, the ceremony—according to outside observers—had a moving and impressive character. An old refusenik, Shimon Yuntofsky, read the prayer to the dead. Candles were lit and the crowd sang "Heveinu Shalom Aleichem."

In September 1988, the Moscow authorities again gave approval for a commemorative event at the same cemetery. Some 500 were in attendance as three refuseniks of the unofficial Soviet-Israel Friendship Society, one non-refusenik (Sokol) of the same Society, and two Supreme Soviet deputies—Lev Shapiro and Viktor Pushkarev—shared the platform. A leading refusenik, Yulian Khassin, declared Babi Yar to be the beginning of the deliberate genocide of Soviet Jews by the Nazis, and he stressed that it was necessary to erect a specifically Jewish memorial at the site. Later, he wrote to the liberal journal *Ogonek,* whose editor was Ukrainian, asking for its support for this initiative.

The leading Soviet refusenik at the time, Yuli Kosharovsky, was the principal speaker. On the one hand, he urged Soviet Jews to commemorate the tragedy by steeping themselves in Jewish history and culture, along with the Hebrew language. On the other hand, he warned of the growing danger to Soviet Jews posed by Pamyat and its sister organizations. This warning was also reiterated by the other refusenik speakers and by Sokol.

Strikingly, for the first time Soviet television gave the ceremony some coverage, noting specifically its Jewish character. And Moscow Radio reported on the meeting, commenting that "problems facing Soviet Jews today were raised." In the meantime, four prominent refusenik-wives who were members of "Jewish Women Against Refusal" (JEWAR) went to Kiev to participate in a memorial service. They laid a wreath at the memorial site. On the wreath was the following dedication: "For the Holocaust generation from the generation of revival."

As significant as the modest internal development was a major gesture taken by the American Secretary of State, George P. Shultz. In April 1988, while on official visits to Moscow and Tbilisi, he arranged for a short stopover in Kiev so that he might visit Babi Yar. He told reporters accompanying him that the stopover was deliberate, for Babi Yar was "among the first places where we saw the Holocaust, the slaughter of Jews." He continued with a ringing comment: "We have to say to ourselves, always, 'Never again.' "

With 1991 marking the fiftieth anniversary of Babi Yar, a milestone appears to have been reached. For the first time, the secular authorities in Ukraine are according the Holocaust at Babi Yar lengthy and solemn recognition. Ceremonies will run from 29 September to 6 October, with the final day devoted specifically to memorial services at which representatives of Soviet and world Jewry will be in attendance (6 October was selected because Succoth falls on 29 September). The Ukrainian Government has finally spoken out: "For far too long the truth about Babi Yar has been hushed up and distorted." Acknowledged now is the fact that the ravine is "a symbol of Jewish martyrdom." Heading the organizing committee for a week of commemorating the tragedy is the Ukrainian Deputy Prime Minister, Serhiy Komissarenko. His associate is Aleksandr Shlayen, the Jewish producer of the "murdered" film on Babi Yar.

Komissarenko promised: "we will lay a cornerstone that will serve as a base for a new monument which will tell the true story of Babi Yar." It is to be erected on the very 1941 massacre site, not a distance away. He stressed that "we certainly must not forget the over 40,000 Jewish children. . . who have not been respectfully memorialized."

The twenty-ninth of September has been declared by the city of

Kiev an official "Day of Memory and Sorrow." The city will fly its flags at half-staff with public prayers to be held by all religious organizations. The week of ceremonies will include an academic conference to be chaired by Yad Vashem and which is to lead to student exchanges with Israel, the United States, and other countries. Ukrainian television and radio will carry a series of programs dedicated to the tragedy which will include a special Kiev–Jerusalem hook-up.

President George Bush, following in the footsteps of George Shultz, laid a wreath at Babi Yar while on a visit to Ukraine. The gesture was remarkably significant. No other head of state had visited the killing fields of Babi Yar. His speech caught the spirit of Yevtushenko's poem even as it offered up a commitment of the civilized world to the martyred dead: "We vow this sort of murder will never happen again. We vow never to let the forces of bigotry and hatred assert themselves without opposition."

Part 2

Soviet Policies
During the Holocaust

Escape and Evacuation of Soviet Jews at the Time of the Nazi Invasion

Policies and Realities

MORDECHAI ALTSHULER

For Soviet Jews, escape and evacuation marked the watershed between a chance to live and almost certain death. Most of the Jews who were able to flee or be evacuated to the rear had as reasonable a chance of staying alive as the rest of the population. Those who remained in the Nazi-occupied territories, by contrast, were marked for death; only a handful of them avoided annihilation by finding non-Jewish protectors or joining partisan units. Nevertheless, this subject has been given scanty attention in the vast Holocaust literature published outside the Soviet Union. Soviet and Western historiographies of the war refer only incidentally to the escape and evacuation. The few studies on this subject have confined themselves to the difficulties and success of the transfer of factories from the German-occupied areas. Accounts of the reactivation of factories in the rear, and their contribution to the war effort, have attracted special attention. The civilians who fled or were evacuated from the Nazi-occupied areas are mentioned mainly in this context of factory relocation, and here, too, the matter is treated as marginal. Hence it should not astonish us to find diverse estimates of the number of civilians evacuated from the areas overrun by the Nazis, ranging from 10 to 20 million. These estimates are largely the results of educated guesswork, with no basis in systematic research.[1]

Most of the sources available to us fail to distinguish between evacuation and escape. For ideological reasons, most Soviet publications preferred to speak of evacuation *(evakuatsiia)*. This term evokes the notion of a planned and organized operation, even when what actually happened was a panic-stricken and spontaneous escape. Very rarely do Soviet sources mention that "In addition to planned evacuation. . . there was an unplanned migration of population from areas at risk [of Nazi occupation]."[2] The term "evacuation" may have been used not only for ideological reasons but for lack of any objective possibility of differentiating between evacuation and escape, since refugees who fled for their lives, first by covering hundreds of kilometers on foot and later by boarding evacuee trains, were considered evacuees and were treated as such. Even Soviet émigrés who describe the panicky flight generally refer to it as an evacuation. Neither can this paper differentiate unequivocally between the two phenomena, although it will attempt to allude to both.

Evacuation Policy

Whenever one speaks of "evacuation policy," one should distinguish between the inclusive policy of the central institutions and that invoked in the field. With regard to the possibility of escaping the Nazis' tentacles, the policy that mattered was the latter. Hence the question to ask is whether the Soviets had any comprehensive policy for evacuating civilians from the territories threatened by the Nazi war machine.

One of the first orders issued by the Presidium of the Executive Committee on 22 June strictly forbade any entry or exit from areas declared to be under martial law *(voennoe polozhenie)*.[3] Any individual attempting to flee his or her place of residence could be considered a panic-monger, who, according to the orders in effect at the time, was subject to trial before a military tribunal. This kind of martial law was declared in all the territories annexed by the Soviet Union since the beginning of the war (Latvia, Lithuania, Estonia, eastern Poland, Bessarabia, and Northern Bukovina), in all of Belorussia, and in large sections of Ukraine—territories where the vast majority of Soviet Jews dwelled.

Two days later, however, the central authorities took note of the damage that might be caused if property and skilled manpower, essential for the war effort, were captured by the Germans. Consequently, an eight-member Supreme Evacuation Council was appointed on 24 June.

Its chairman was Lazar Kaganovich (1893–1991), a confidante of Stalin's; his appointment attests to the importance ascribed to the committee. Kaganovich's deputy was Nikolai Shvernik (1888–1970), chairman of the All-Union Council of Trade Unions. The council members were recruited from various government ministries. Although the tasks assigned to them seem to have been rather vague, the members understood that it was their duty to plan the evacuation of industrial plants and assets so that they could be exploited for the war effort. As they probed the subject, they realized that there were no contingency plans for the eventuality of such an evacuation. Hence they tried to learn from the experience of World War I, during which industrial plants and their workers were evacuated to the rear. The council staff were sent to public libraries in search of written material on the subject, but were unable to turn up anything.[4] In view of this description of the work of the Supreme Evacuation Council, it is hard to speak of any evacuation policy during the first days of the war, as the Wehrmacht drove into the Soviet Union at a rate of dozens of kilometers a day.

On 27 June the highest state and party institutions made an initial decision "to evacuate and relocate quotas of persons and assets of value,"[5] with priority for "factories that produce military wares along with metallurgical and chemical industries."[6] After this decision in principle was made and its implementational instructions attached, several days seem to have passed until it was applied in the field. This delay was of great significance as the German juggernaut drove on. On 29 June the Central Committee of the Communist Party and the Soviet government addressed all the governing institutions, stressing that "Trains should be evacuated [during the withdrawal]. . . . The enemy should not be left with even a kilogram of grain or a liter of fuel. . . . It is imperative to destroy any valuable property that cannot be taken, including noble metals, grain, and fuel."[7] On 3 July 1941, in Stalin's first speech after the German invasion—a speech that had a massive impact on the population—the Soviet ruler urged that:

Wherever Red Army formations are forced to withdraw, all the rolling stock should be removed. The enemy must not be left with a single engine or car, nor with a single pound of bread or bottle of kerosene. Members of kolkhozes should remove the animals [and] deliver their seed stocks to state institutions for evacuation. . . . All irremovable property of any value—grain, fuel, non-ferrous metals—should be destroyed.[8]

Although the government announcement and Stalin's speech do speak of evacuation, the objects to be evacuated were property; no mention was made of the civilian population. However, notwithstanding the order of 22 June forbidding the abandonment of places of residence, from the very first days of the war there were refugees who took to the roads and availed themselves of the few means of transportation that still functioned. This being the case, the Supreme Evacuation Council drew up regulations for the establishment of "evacuation stations" that would help refugees arrange transportation and food. These regulations were approved by the Politburo on 5 July. Pursuant to the regulations, a discussion was held about arrangements for people to be evacuated along with the equipment of workplaces.[9] In the first ten days of July, when most of the Soviet-annexed territories, most of eastern Belorussia, and parts of eastern Ukraine had already been occupied by the Germans, a more-or-less general policy for the evacuation of factories and their workers had coalesced, and the means of discharging this task were taking shape. On 16 July the Supreme Evacuation Council was reconstituted with these goals in mind. Shvernik was named chairman, and deputy prime ministers Alexei Kosygin and M. Pervukhin were appointed as his deputies. Each member of the council was placed in charge of the evacuation of a particular industry, and a high-ranking official in each ministry was given personal responsibility for implementing the evacuation.[10] Decisions concerning the evacuation of factories were taken in accordance with the rapid changes on the front; the Evacuation Council interacted closely with the National Defense Committee, established on 30 June, which had been granted exceedingly broad governing powers. In setting the date for the evacuation of factories and their workers, the council was caught between the hammer of dwindling time and the anvil of production imperatives. The National Defense Committee ordered the Evacuation Council "to produce until the very last moment and to begin dismantling [factories] only when a representative of the National Defense Committee or the ministry," with which the factory was affiliated, gave an order to this effect.[11] As a rule, the dismantling of factories, at least during the early weeks of the war, began only when the enemy approached. Hence it is no surprise to discover that the evacuation even of essential factories with their workers and families, especially during the first few weeks of the war, was generally haphazard and implemented under bombardment. The Soviet Yiddish writer Leizer

Katsovich described the chaos that prevailed during the evacuation of a factory in eastern Belorussia:

> The workers' families, preoccupied with their bundles, trundled along-side trucks meant for the transport of people *(tepliushki)*. Women with children draped in summer blankets ran from wagon to wagon, search-ing with worried eyes for their relatives. . . . People hoisted to their shoulders the few belongings that they had managed to take out of their houses and hauled them hastily to the train. After they had managed to lay their bundles in one of the cars, they sighed with relief and seated themselves helplessly, resting their weary heads on one of the bun-dles.[12]

In fact, the factory-evacuation policy, which was similarly chaotic, coalesced—more or less—only in mid-July. Notably, however, the evacuation of workers' relatives was marked with considerable le-niency; employees of the evacuated factories were allowed to bring not only spouses and children but also parents, siblings, and even more distant kin; others were allowed to escape and not join the evacuation of the plant in which they had been employed.[13] Hence the individual's willingness to be evacuated with his factory was a matter of import-ance, even in cases where the evacuation was carried out in accordance with orders from above, and *a fortiori* when residents fled or joined evacuations by their own initiative.

The evacuation of civilians not directly connected with factories, too, was discussed in early July 1941. On 5 July the government adopted a resolution "on measures for the evacuation of the population in wartime." The resolution differentiated between areas in which mili-tary action was taking place and those adjacent to the front or in danger of being overrun by the enemy. The authority to evacuate civilians from areas of the first type was given to the military commanders in the field; evacuation from areas of the second type was subject to approval of the Supreme Evacuation Council.[14] Since the location of the front was exceedingly fluid, the evacuation of civilians from vast territories was theoretically and, *a fortiori*, practically entrusted to the local military commander and depended largely on his attitude and assessment.

A commander's decision to evacuate the civilian population of a given area involved a large set of considerations and evaluations, one of the most important of which was the extent to which this action would undermine local defense efforts (digging trenches, erecting anti-tank barricades, and so on). Indeed, local military commanders forbade evacuation in quite a few instances because they needed workers to erect fortifications. Commanders also had to ask themselves how seri-ously the evacuation might sow panic among the civilians, undermine the motivation of combat units, and impede the transport needs of fighting or retreating units. All these considerations were, of course, informed by the local commanders' expectations of the probability and date of the occupation of the locality by the Germans. Information available to commanders was often false or, at least, incomplete and imprecise. Hence it is not surprising that the occupation of many towns took not only the civilian population but also the military commanders by surprise. In view of the scarcity of information and the numerous and diverse factors that had to be weighed in taking a decision to evacuate civilians, different attitudes toward evacuation and escape were taken in different sectors and in different towns.

Thus the Supreme Evacuation Council dealt chiefly with the evacu-ation of factories and civilians from areas adjacent to the front and from localities at risk of occupation, including Leningrad and Moscow. Since the Germans did not succeed in occupying the latter cities, the evacuation of their civilian populations does not fall within the pur-view of this article. The major importance of the Supreme Evacuation Council for the evacuees—with factories or otherwise—was the assis-tance it provided for refugees in their places of resettlement. In terms of its organization of such evacuations themselves, the council was less of a factor.

On 26 September the Supreme Evacuation Council established a Population Evacuation Administration, the major duty of which was to meet the needs of civilians who had left their places of residence irrespective of any connection with a factory. The administration oper-ated for only four months; it was disbanded on 31 January 1942, when the momentum of the flight had largely dissipated.[15]

It may therefore be said that, during the first six weeks of the German–Soviet war, the Supreme Evacuation Council was equipped with nothing more than general guidelines for the evacuation of vital industries and their workers; there was no real policy for the evacua-tion of civilians in general. The actual evacuation of factories and, *a fortiori*, of civilians not connected with factories, depended on the judgment of civilian and military local authorities who operated in a milieu of multiple contradictions and lack of clear information. In the absence of a comprehensive, clear-cut evacuation policy, the scale of flight depended largely on people's subjective willingness to leave their homes and on the objective conditions that permitted them to follow through on such a decision. The decision to flee was, at least to a certain extent, a direct result of information possessed by civilians, especially Jews, as to the Nazis' attitude toward them.

How Information on the Germans' Attitude Toward the Jews Affected the Decision to Flee

Historiography of the past few decades has largely based itself on a perspective articulated by Solomon Schwarz in his 1951 study:

> Throughout the period preceding the Soviet Union's entry into the war, readers of the Soviet press were kept in ignorance of the Nazi anti-Jewish policies; the government's neutrality blinded Soviet Jews to the mortal danger threatening them. When, on June 22, 1941, the Wehrmacht suddenly invaded the Soviet Union, the Jewish population was largely unaware of the persecution and extermination that awaited them; many of those who might have fled remained where they were and perished.[16]

Schwarz regards the press as the Soviet Jews' sole source of information, totally ignoring other media. But even if the Jews had had access to all information available at that time, they could not have known of the danger of extermination, because the Reich kept the orders governing this action, which were evidently issued between March and May of 1941, as one of its darkest secrets; the annihilation of the Jews began only after the Nazi invasion of the Soviet Union. It may therefore be said that the Soviet Jews were inadequately informed as to discrimination against and persecution of Jews in Germany and the countries it had occupied.

In the Soviet Union, more than in free countries, information is acquired from two sources: official channels—the press, radio, films—that disseminate an abundance of information, and an unofficial system of word-of-mouth dissemination. The influence of the latter is no less, and some say even greater, than that of the former. Whenever one speaks about available information, both systems should be considered.

Until the middle of September 1939, Soviet Jews had access to information from the official Soviet press and publications, and, for all intents and purposes, from them alone. Until May 1939, these channels published a steady stream of reports on attacks on Jews in Germany, Austria, Danzig, and Czechoslovakia. Following Kristallnacht, the stream of information in the Soviet press on the persecution of Jews increased. Between 11 November 1938 and the end of January 1939, *Pravda* published thirty-nine reports, articles, and columns on attacks on Jews in territories under German rule. *Izvestiia* printed twenty-eight reports and articles on the subject during the same period. The Yiddish press covered the subject with special intensity; in this period of time, the Yiddish daily *Der Shtern* printed approximately a hundred reports, articles, and columns on Nazi attacks on Jews. Many of the articles provided detailed accounts of the beating of Jews, their incarceration in concentration camps, torching of synagogues, looting of property, and so on. Even though some of the information was buried in the inside pages of the Russian-language papers, many Jews presumably gained considerable insight from these sources on the fate of their brethren under Nazi rule. Two Soviet films, *Professor Mamlok* and *The Family Oppenheim*—produced in 1938, shown in many cinemas and factories, and lauded by the Soviet media[17]—did much to disseminate information on the persecution of Jews in Germany. Indeed, several witnesses interviewed by the author noted that they had learned about the extreme anti-Jewish discrimination in Germany—the yellow patch, dismissal from workplaces, and so on—from these films.[18] The screening of the films, like the media coverage, came to an end when the Ribbentrop–Molotov Pact was signed on 23 August 1939. Precisely then, however, the flow of unofficial information gathered strength.

From the day of the German invasion of Poland (1 September 1939) until the 17th of the month, when Soviet forces began to occupy eastern Poland, hundreds of thousands of Jewish refugees congregated in the districts that were to be occupied by the Soviet Union. This flow continued with virtually no restrictions until 22 October 1939, at the very earliest. Many of the refugees had personally experienced German brutality in the first few days of the occupation. Even after the two occupation powers had sealed their new border, several months passed before unauthorized crossing became altogether impossible.

Smugglers on both sides of the border were active in spiriting Jews from Nazi-occupied Poland into the Russian zone, where many of the refugees, with relatives on the German side, continued to use such smugglers to bring them letters and accounts of developments in the German-occupied area.[19] Moreover, postal connections between the Soviet Union and German-occupied Poland were fairly regular during the months that the Nazi–Soviet pact held firm. Although the letters were laconically phrased, they conveyed much about the situation of Jews in occupied Poland. Hence it is reasonable to assume that the refugees in eastern Poland—the area annexed to the Soviet Union—knew that on 26 November 1939, the Nazi authorities in the General-gouvernement—that is, most of Nazi-occupied Poland, had conscripted Jewish civilians for forced labor, and that the first ghetto on occupied Polish soil had been established at the end of that month (that of Piotrkow, which had been annexed to the Reich). Nor could they have been unaware of the decree of January 1940, which quarantined Jews in the Generalgouvernement to their places of residence and proscribed their use of the railways. All of this was in addition to the daily incidents of plunder and murder, which were undoubtedly corroborated by refugees who crossed the border. It is hard to believe that this relatively large quantity of information, flowing through diverse channels (individuals, letters, attestations), remained hidden from very broad segments of the Jewish public.

Some of the refugees migrated to the Soviet-annexed Baltic countries. Between October and December 1939, some 2,500 Jews from the Suwalki area were expelled to Lithuania after having experienced German brutality first-hand.[20] Information on German cruelty toward Jews, albeit not on the policy of genocide that in fact did not yet exist, was therefore available to large segments of the Jewish communities in all of the annexed territories.[21] Did the Jews in these territories keep this information to themselves, or did they disseminate it among the Jewish communities in territories that had been part of the Soviet Union before 17 September 1939?

All civilians in the Soviet-annexed territories, including two million Jews, were deemed to be Soviet citizens. The sole exceptions were the refugees from German-occupied Poland, who did not desire this citizenship and hence were exiled to the far reaches of the Soviet Union. However, the Soviet authorities, regarding their new citizens with suspicion and mistrust, kept the old Soviet border in place. To cross into the interior of the country, that is, to the areas under Soviet rule before 1939, the new Soviet citizens had to obtain special permits—for a job offer, travel on official business, membership in an official delegation, and so forth. Between November 1939, and February 1940, however, the Soviet authorities propagandized vigorously among the refugees in an effort to recruit them for volunteer labor in various localities in the Soviet Union proper. Consequently, thousands of Jewish refugees in the annexed territories did make their way into the Soviet hinterland. Some of them subsequently returned to the annexed territories, but quite a few who reached Kiev, Minsk, and other cities remained there at least until the Nazi invasion. As many testimonies show, the information provided by these refugees was an important source for Jews in various localities of the Soviet Union.[22] Thus, for example, a witness from the town of Lechitsy reported:

> Until the [Soviet–German] war, rumors [about the Germans' treatment of the Jews] circulated among us. . . . Refugees from Poland reached us in 1939. They rented rooms in our house and worked in a bakery. They had fled from the Germans and told us everything. . . but we didn't believe them.[23]

It is reasonable to assume that the refugees' accounts did not remain within the narrow circle of the people who heard them directly; they must have been passed on by word of mouth to large groups in the Jewish community.

Furthermore, Red Army formations including Jewish enlisted men and officers were serving in the annexed territories (eastern Poland and the Baltic countries). When these men went on furlough, they must have told their friends and relatives what they had heard from the refugees. Moreover, groups and individuals were sent to the annexed territories for work purposes. The Jews among them maintained regular liaison with the local Jewish communities—sometimes with the encouragement of the authorities. Hence it is quite reasonable to assume that they, too, were not oblivious to information that they had received about the Nazis' Jewish policy in the Generalgouvernement and that they passed it on to friends and acquaintances in the Soviet Union. Indeed, Hersh Smolar notes that Joel Lipschitz, chairman of the Journalists' Union in Belorussia, had learned much about these developments from a trip to liberated western Belorussia [i.e., the area annexed to the Soviet Union], during which he brought with him [to his hometown of Minsk] a yellow Star of David that a Jew from Warsaw had torn from his clothes after he had crossed the Soviet border.[24]

On 7 July 1941, in the pages of the Yiddish-language newspaper of Kiev, the Soviet Yiddish author Faivel Sito (1909–45) described his impressions of an encounter he had had with a throng of refugees in Brest in November 1939:

> Never shall I forget the hair-raising story that the Jewish refugees told me then. An old Jew who had just come from Warsaw... told me how a German had killed his wife before his eyes and had raped his 15-year-old daughter and then murdered her. The same Jew told me how Hitler's thugs forced him to clean the sidewalk on Marszalkowska Street with his tongue.[25]

It is hard to imagine that the writer did not share his harrowing experiences, which he could not publicize in the press at the time, with relatives and friends. It seems, then, that information of this sort was fairly common among Soviet Jews inside the September 1939 borders. It served as a source of inspiration for Peretz Markish's poem "To the Jewish Ghetto Dancer," which he even recited to an audience of colleagues in Moscow in April 1941.[26]

Thus we may certainly say that even during the twenty-two months of the Ribbentrop–Molotov Pact, when the Soviet media refrained from covering the Nazis' anti-Jewish atrocities, a relatively large segment of Soviet Jewry had access to a significant amount of information on the subject.

The scale of official information made available in the pre-pact period, and the unofficial information that became available afterwards, increased with the German invasion of the Soviet Union. *Professor Mamlok* returned to the cinema screens. As early as 26 June, *Pravda,* the Party's major organ, printed an article under the headline "Hitler's Murderers in Warsaw." The article stressed that while the bread ration for the population of Warsaw was 350 grams a day, the Jews were given only 750 grams per week. The author of the article, asserting that she herself had left Warsaw only a few weeks earlier, noted that

> The entire population [of Warsaw] was divided into three groups: the
> Germans, masters and possessors of all privileges—the entitled elite;
> the plundered Polish people, subjugated and dispossessed of all rights;
> and finally the Jews, who have been brought to the threshold of destitu-
> tion and annihilation. [The latter] are downtrodden in the extreme. . . .
> The atrocities of the Spanish Inquisition pale before the cruelty applied
> by [the Germans] to the Jewish population of Warsaw. They forcibly
> sterilize Jews and the German authorities forbid the provision of medi-
> cal assistance to anyone below the age of 3 or past the age of 60.[27]

On 27 June, the very next day, the same paper printed an article
entitled "Unbridled Hatred for the German Occupier," with vivid descriptions of the persecution of Jews in Warsaw: the establishment of
the ghetto, distinctive markings on clothes, and various types of brutality.[28] On 29 June the Red Army newspaper published an interview
with a group of Soviet engineers who had returned from Germany. The
interviewee stressed that

> The humiliation of Jews in Germany has almost reached its limit.
> [Jews] are no longer allowed to visit public parks and gardens. Yellow
> benches marked with a J [for Jew] are stationed next to the public parks,
> and only there are Jews allowed to sit. All the stores have signs saying
> "Jews allowed to enter after five o'clock," by which time the shelves
> are already bare. Jewish physicians are allowed to treat Jewish patients
> only. . . . A Jew is forbidden to visit public places that Germans fre-
> quent. They are not even allowed to use German restrooms. Jews are
> absolutely forbidden to enter bomb shelters. The Fascists demand,
> backing the demand with violence, that Jewish physicians inscribe on
> their plaques, in addition to their names, the word Israel, and that fe-
> male Jewish physicians add the word Sarah.[29]

Accounts of this sort, publicizing the persecution of Jews in Germany
and the occupied territories, were almost certainly published in the
local press, which we have not been able to examine thus far. Within
six weeks of the German invasion of the USSR, a Jewish source became part of the propaganda system that exposed German crimes. On
11 August 1941 a Russian-language pamphlet by A. Golubeev, entitled
"Hitlerian Murders in Poland," appeared in Yiddish translation. The
author stressed that in German-occupied Poland "Jews are being uprooted with particular cruelty—not only are they being expelled from

western Poland, they are also being murdered."[30] On 24 August 1941, before the ink on this pamphlet had dried, all Soviet radio stations broadcast an assembly of "representatives of the Jewish people," during which the speakers described the Nazis' cruelties toward the Jews.[31]

Thus, accessible information about the Germans' anti-Jewish atrocities had returned to the official Soviet media from the very first days of the German–Soviet war. The Germans, too, in their own propaganda, stressed that they were waging war principally against the Jews and Communism. In the afternoon of the very first day of the German–Soviet war, German planes overflew Bobruisk, in eastern Belorussia, scattering thousands of leaflets. The leaflets stated that the Germans were fighting the Jews and the Bolsheviks, and that Bolshevism was the handiwork of the Jews, the enemies of humankind. The goal of the war, the leaflet explained, was to destroy the Jews and Bolshevism and to bring prosperity to the Russian people.[32]

A few days before the Germans occupied Kiev (19 September 1941) the Russian author A. Anatoly (Kuznetsov) reported that German planes had dropped leaflets, of which "every one had printed on it in big letters: KILL YOUR OFFICERS YIDS AND WOPS, SLOSH 'EM IN THEIR UGLY CHOPS."[33]

The Nazis used the radio waves, too, to disseminate similar anti-Jewish propaganda throughout the war, and we may assume that the Jews, especially those near the war zone, were aware of this. This German propaganda now became part of the information delivered to the Jews by the refugees streaming eastward. In fact, we corroborated the existence of information on German anti-Jewish brutality in a survey that we conducted concerning refugees from eastern Belorussia. The survey included fifty-eight respondents from fourteen towns in which approximately 70 percent of the Jews in eastern Belorussia had lived. The findings show that 56 percent of the respondents had known of anti-Jewish discrimination and assaults (8 percent having learned of them from the media, publications, and Soviet cinema; 20 percent from Polish refugees; 28 percent did not cite their source of information). According to the results of another question in the survey, concerning relatives who had not fled, the respondents believed the main reason that only 13.6 percent of their relatives had failed to flee was "a positive assessment of the Germans" that might have been caused by a lack of information about German policy toward the Jews. Thus we may assert, with a fairly high level of certainty, that many Jews, before the German invasion of the Soviet Union and *a fortiori* afterward, were aware of the Nazis' discrimination against and persecution of Jews (although they had no information about genocide); therefore, lack of information should not be considered a very important factor in their decision to refrain from fleeing.

It is true that the information provided by the Soviet media was not very reliable. Even the refugees reported that many Jews treated their information skeptically, regarding it as mere propaganda. Hence, it seems that it was not the availability of information but skepticism regarding its reliability that was one of the important factors in causing many Jews to decide to remain in their places of residence and not to abandon their property.[34] A young Soviet immigrant to Israel told the author that his grandfather, who had resided in Homel on the eve of the war, said that he had not intended to leave the city and abandon his cows, which were his only possessions; only after being persuaded by a Belorussian official did he agree to be evacuated to the interior.[35] Many other accounts confirm that the attachment to belongings was a significant factor in the decision to stay put.

Members of the older generation, who remembered German rule during World War I, were especially inclined to disbelieve reports about the Nazis' policy toward the Jews. They regarded the Germans as a nation of cultured, polite, order-loving people; it was hard to reconcile these traits with the allegations of German atrocities against Jews. In the prevailing milieu of perplexity and powerlessness, these individuals' opinions were often decisive. Thus, for example, a woman refugee from Minsk fled seventy or eighty kilometers east with her family (including an elderly grandfather and aunt) before beginning to weigh the advantages of turning back or continuing to flee. At this critical juncture, one of the people nearby said, "The Germans aren't so dangerous; we remember them from 1918, when they were pretty good." This statement sufficed to tip the balance in favor of going home, to Minsk, which the Germans occupied several days later.[36] Indeed, memories of the Germans' deportment in 1918 were frequently the deciding factor in the decision to stay.[37]

Moreover, Jews whose property had been confiscated by the Soviets and their relatives arrested, exiled, or even executed, were less inclined to trust the information provided by the Soviet media; they believed their situation could only improve under German rule.

Flight, especially during the first weeks of the war, was extremely difficult in view of the physical effort it entailed, whether this meant walking tens or hundreds of kilometers or exploiting the few available means of transportation. Such an effort exceeded the capabilities of the elderly, the ill, and those with other constraints. Hence it is not surprising that many young people were willing to flee but forwent this option because it meant abandoning elderly parents or ill or weak siblings. Under these circumstances, the close family relations for which the Jews were legendary became a trap that prevented the escape of no few young people.

Thus the decision to flee was influenced by a complex web of motives, of which available information on the German treatment of Jews was only one factor, and perhaps not the most important. Furthermore, the fateful decision had to be taken in great haste: the war had just broken out, contradictory rumors chased one another, and, most importantly, there was no official or Jewish institution that might issue clear instructions. An individual's decision to flee also depended, of course, on the objective conditions under which he or she might fulfill the decision, such as distance from railroads, availability of transportation, and the attitude of the military and civilian authorities toward escape or evacuation. Unsurprisingly, then, a highly important factor in the dimensions of escape and evacuation was the time that elapsed between the Germans' invasion of the Soviet Union and their occupation of a particular locality.

Flight and Evacuation as a Function of the Date of German Occupation

The possibilities of escape were conditioned by the unique circumstances of every community, which, even in a single town, sometimes changed with the passage of mere hours or days. In general, although further detail is warranted, escape and evacuation may be divided into two main areas, differentiated by the dates of their occupation by the Germans. (A special case, not discussed here, is the evacuation of the Caucasus, to which many factories and evacuees had been relocated at the initial stage of the war, and from which the refugees themselves were subsequently evacuated.)

1. The first area was that occupied during the first six weeks of the war, that is, by early August 1941. This area included the annexed

territories with the exception of part of Estonia, most of eastern Belorussia, and the western part of Ukraine within its 1939 borders.

2. The second area was that occupied by the German forces in the last five months of 1941 and early 1942. It included most of the Ukraine, the Crimea, and broad swathes of the RSFSR.

The First Area

22 June 1941 fell on a Sunday, and most people were looking forward to another day of leisure. At 4:00 A.M., however, thousands of German aircraft bombed airfields, railway junctions, and cities in the Soviet Union. At dawn the Wehrmacht mounted a lightning offensive along the border. At 4:30 A.M. the Politburo and the Red Army senior command assembled for an urgent discussion. Stalin, a prisoner of his assumption that the Germans would not attack immediately, and plagued by his suspicions of provocation by the capitalist countries, did not appreciate the gravity of the situation and ordered his staff to establish immediate contact with the German embassy in Moscow in order to solicit its response. During these hours, Marshal Timoshenko, the defense commissar, telephoned the front-line commanders and instructed them not to engage the Germans without an explicit order to this effect. Viacheslav Molotov, Soviet foreign minister at the time, appeared at the Politburo meeting and announced that Germany had declared war on the Soviet Union. Only then were orders given to activate the "red package," that is, the plan for defending the country's borders. By this time, however, the front-line formations were already retreating in panic, thwarting any possibility of orderly implementation.[38] Word that the war had begun was forwarded hastily to party institutions in the western republics (Belorussia, Ukraine, Lithuania, Latvia, and Estonia). In the capitals of these republics, the highest party echelons gathered in the morning and discussed the new division of responsibilities in wartime. The debates focused on defense arrangements, insofar as such were required, and administration of the economy in accordance with the new needs.[39] Even as the Wehrmacht was driving into Soviet territory and the Luftwaffe was sowing destruction in Soviet population centers, most citizens still did not know that war had broken out. Only at noon did Molotov announce, over loudspeakers installed on street corners and in private residences, that the German invasion had taken place. The announcement was followed by

mass assemblies in public squares, halls, and factories, at which party and state functionaries urged the population to organize for the defense of the Motherland and to pledge their vigor and strength to increased production. The orators tried to instill faith and hope that the Red Army would quickly deal the enemy a crushing blow. This was more than an attempted "whitewash" on the part of propagandists and government and military officials who, in view of the breakdown of communications, did not know what was happening at the front. At 9:00 P.M. on the first day of the war, military headquarters ordered the ground forces to counterattack at once and carry the combat into enemy territory, at a time when the front-line formations were already crumbling and the Wehrmacht had advanced scores of kilometers inside Soviet territory.

Many inhabitants, who may have regarded war with Germany as imminent, were nevertheless surprised by its onset and regarded it, at least initially, as a repeat of World War I. Thus everyone's first priority was to stockpile food. "Long queues developed at shop entrances," remembered a witness who had been in the town of Uzda. When the war broke out, "People rushed to the shops in order to lay hands on anything. . . . Everyone was looking for a way to avoid famine."[40] People were not reliably informed on developments in their immediate vicinity. Announcements on Soviet radio were laconic and largely confined to reports on the enemy's grave casualties. Local authorities, too, operated under conditions of absent or contradictory information. Some local authorities seemed to believe it proper to encourage escape from the bombed and burning cities; others assumed that this would only magnify the panic and disorder. According to one witness, the local radio station in Minsk proclaimed that "The city center is extremely dangerous; everyone should flee to the forests." Another witness, describing the situation in Rafalovka, writes that "The Soviet authorities asked the entire population, especially the Jews, to leave their homes and retreat to the east."[41] On the whole, such behavior was exceptional. Most members of the Soviet establishment were concerned for themselves and their families above all, and they strived to calm the populace and prevent panic-stricken flight.

With the German invasion, all men born between 1905 and 1918 (i.e., between the ages of 23 and 36) were mobilized; those aged 19–22, who were already in active service, were not discharged. The mobilization—which, of course, was implemented in a disorderly fashion in many locations occupied during the first days of the war—left many families without young men who could have taken the fateful decision to flee. Many families had only women with children, who were hardly capable of fleeing on foot or making use of the few transportation possibilities still available. Indeed, many Jewish families stayed behind and fell into Nazi hands simply because they had no way of fleeing with their young children. The Russian author Vladimir Popov (born 1907) communicates something of this situation in his novel *Stal' i shlak,* and numerous testimonies corroborate his account.[42]

On the first day of the war, the inhabitants were told to report to their workplaces and not to foment panic.[43] The decrees warned that anyone leaving his place of work would be considered a deserter and would be tried accordingly; when order finally collapsed, it was, on the whole, too late to flee. During the few days when there was still a reasonable possibility of fleeing, a large number of local authorities took measures to calm and deceive the populace, while they themselves made feverish preparations to run away and evacuate their offices. When Jews asked the authorities to issue them with evacuation permits, they were frequently told: "Have you really no confidence in the might of the Red Army? You're sowing panic."

In this sense, the following testimony of a Jewish woman from the town of Khmelnik, in the Vinnetsa district, is typical:

Evacuees from the western Ukraine already began to reach [the area] in early July 1941. There was great fear in the city. The residents ran to the raispolkom [the executive committee of the district soviet], and everyone discussed evacuation [with his friends] at work. This was the end of the matter. We weren't released from our jobs and no trains were made available. Among the [Jewish] residents, the question of evacuation became more acute from day to day and from hour to hour, but no one was allowed to leave work. Leaving work was punishable under martial law. When they went to the chairman of the raispolkom to speak with him about evacuation, he would say, "You've got nothing to fear; you're not Party members." Suddenly the report spread. . . that the city of Lvov had been recaptured [by the Red Army] and that 40,000 [Germans] had been taken prisoner. The implication was that there was no need to evacuate. So almost all the Jews stayed put.[44]

However, beyond the ruling circles' differing attitudes toward escape and evacuation, the factor that frequently tipped the scales was the very feasibility of these actions, especially with regard to transportation. Flight and evacuation took place on trains, motor vehicles, carts, and on foot. The train was the most suitable and conventional way to transport large numbers of people, but the Germans targeted railroad junctions and main stations for heavy aerial bombardment. The movement of trains was seriously disrupted; in the area occupied during the first six weeks of the war, it came to a virtual standstill. Most cars were owned by state institutions, party organs, and factories. Some of them were mobilized—more accurately, confiscated—by the army and the authorities, who used them to escape along with their families. Even the fortunate few civilians who had access to motor vehicles were not always able to make effective use of them because the roads were clogged with refugees and fleeing soldiers. To maximize the chaos on the roads, the Germans infiltrated groups of their own, sometimes in Red Army uniform.[45] Not only motor vehicles but also horse-drawn carts were "requisitioned" by the army and the authorities, and the few civilians who retained such modes of transportation moved slowly and were frequently overtaken by the Germans. Thus the possibility of escape was naturally confined, in the main, to young people. Quite a few of them faced an exceedingly cruel dilemma: to effect their own escape, they would have to abandon their parents and other elderly people who were unable or unwilling to leave their houses and flee to the unknown. Quite a few young Jews who had decided to flee ultimately chose to stay with their parents and relatives, unwilling to leave them to their fate.

There were also cases—though not many, to the best of our knowledge—in which the non-Jewish population obstructed Jews who sought to flee. One witness reports that she had managed to acquire horses and a cart for the purpose of escape, whereupon "The chairman of the kolkhoz came and took the horses, saying, 'Go find your Stalin on foot.' "[46]

The Germans' plan for the invasion of the Soviet Union was meant to induce the collapse of the military and governmental system in the shortest time possible. Thus the Wehrmacht penetrated quickly, isolating the Soviet forces and ignoring small pockets of resistance. Not only did this situation catch the armed forces off balance; it also maximized civilian chaos. As a direct consequence of this form of advance, many refugees were forced to retrace their steps after having found their path east blocked by the invaders. A witness from the city of

Mogilev-Podol'sk, in the Vinnitsa district, occupied on 19 July 1941, recalls precisely this situation:

> In the first days of the war [the Jews] believed that the enemy would never cross the Dniestr River, but when Stalin spoke on the radio [on 3 July], the city burst into panic, especially because the local radio announced that the last train of evacuees would be departing soon. Everyone took whatever they could of their movable possessions and headed for the train station. [Finding that] the refugee train had already pulled out, everyone began to walk. We trudged all night and finally in the morning, aching and exhausted, we reached Sharigorod. We decided to rest there for a day and then keep going, but the Germans overtook us.[47]

These refugees had no choice but to retrace their steps, and most of them were eventually murdered. Many refugees who fled their homes were soon forced to turn around because the Wehrmacht had outpaced them.[48]

These obstacles and problems that faced those confronting the decision to flee—a decision that had to be taken in the first few weeks of the war, at great haste and in an atmosphere of uncertainty and conflicting rumors—dictated the actual result: very few ran for their lives. Moreover, even the few Jews in the annexed territories who took to the roads encountered an unexpected obstacle: the old Soviet border. The restrictions on entry by residents of the annexed territories to the USSR proper remained in force on most fronts. Access was confined largely to Soviet functionaries and their families, who had entered these districts from the Soviet Union. Citizens of the annexed territories, mainly Jews, were delayed at the border for several days, and the consequences of the delay were fateful. Some border guards ordered the refugees to retrace their steps, threatening to shoot anyone found loitering near the border. Some of the refugees complied; they fell into the clutches of the Nazis. Officers at some border crossings understood that the old orders should be set aside in wartime; they allowed the refugees to cross. At other border points, however, the refugees were obstructed until the border guards themselves fled. This obstacle further diminished the Jews' prospects of fleeing the annexed regions. Here it should be noted that the refugees were treated humanely in some cases, and that NKVD officials in certain towns distributed certificates that made it relatively easy to cross the old border. But these cases were exceptional, and they were initiated by local functionaries rather than being ordered by higher authorities.[49]

During the first few weeks of the war, the proportion of Jewish civilians who fled the areas under threat of Nazi occupation was indeed quite low. Of approximately 2,000,000 Jews who lived in the Soviet-annexed territories on the eve of the Nazi invasion, only about 8 percent, some 140,000–180,000 people, managed to flee. However, the refugee rate was not the same in all districts. In the small towns along the old Soviet border, which were occupied at later dates, the rate of escape was higher than in places that the Wehrmacht entered on the first or second day of the war. The importance of time as a decisive factor in the Jews' flight was particularly salient in Estonia, which was not completely occupied until August; almost 50 percent of its small Jewish population escaped.[50] Of roughly 185,000 Jews in eastern Belorussia, which was occupied by the end of July, 38 percent managed to escape. Here, too, the difference between districts by date of occupation was particularly conspicuous. In the part of Belorussia occupied by the end of June, which was home to almost half the Jews of the Belorussian Republic within its borders of 17 August 1939, only 11 percent of the Jews managed to escape, whereas the share of Jewish escapees from the area overrun in the second half of July was nearly half. A similar picture is portrayed in eastern Ukraine, that is, the section of Ukraine within the 1939 borders. In the areas overrun by the Nazis by the end of July, approximately one-third of the Jewish population managed to escape.[51]

It is worth noting here that "escapee" is not coterminous with "survivor." Escapees who got caught up on the roads amidst disintegrating army formations were easy prey for German pilots who strafed the congested byways. Trains, too, were bombed persistently. In all, the number of casualties cannot be estimated but was certainly large.

The Second Area

More than 30 percent of the Jews whose towns were occupied dwelled in the areas that the Germans entered in or after August, 1941. It was in August, too, that the results of the battle of Smolensk, the first spanner in the wheels of the Blitzkrieg, began to be felt in the evacuation zone. After the German advance was braked at Smolensk, Hitler decided to mass his forces for the conquest of Ukraine and Crimea, areas rich in farmlands and raw materials with which Nazi Germany might fight a protracted war.

The slower German rate of advance toward Moscow, coupled with second thoughts in the German high command about the wisdom of concentrating the thrust in one area, also permitted the evacuation system to organize itself to some extent. In the areas occupied during this period, the "lead time" for evacuation was somewhat longer. Here many factories, along with their workers and distant relatives, were evacuated. Moreover, growing numbers of refugees who had fled the Nazi-occupied towns, including some who had crossed the front lines after having experienced the new regime first-hand, reached cities in these areas. The Jews of Kiev were massacred at Babi Yar on 29–30 September 1941, and the atrocity was covered extensively by the Soviet media. Not only did these factors combine to whet the Jews' desire to flee; the objective conditions—means of transportation and official encouragement to use them—improved as well. Secret German reports increasingly included accounts of the escape of Jews. A report by the Einsatzgruppen on 4 September is a case in point:

> Jewish intellectuals residing in the large cities continued to flee en masse, successfully, from the eastward advancing German armies; it may be stated with certainty that the Jews, who once tended to return to their homes after fleeing to the forests, no longer return so quickly or do not return at all. . . . This proves that the Jews are aware of the activities of the SIPO, which makes it impossible to keep up the same pace of liquidation [of Jews] as heretofore.[52]

In this passage, which contains a measure of self-justification before superiors for the small number of Jews being murdered, the emphasis on the nature of the Jewish refugees—chiefly intellectuals and residents of the larger cities—deserves attention.

Einsatzgruppe C, which was active on the Zhitomir–Kiev–Poltava–Kharkiv axis, delivered the following report on 11 September:

> There is an advantage to the rumors that the Germans are killing all the Jews; this evidently explains why the Einsatzkommandos are finding fewer and fewer Jews now. One can see in every location that 70–90 percent of the Jews have fled, unlike the previous situation, when only influential Jews had run away.[53]

The reports of 12 September and 9 October repeat this information. Although one must treat these reports cautiously, they do support the hypothesis that early August marked a major watershed in the proportions of Jews evacuated from the territories facing German occupation. One reason for this was better organization of the evacuation effort; another was the Jews' greater willingness to leave their homes. This finding is corroborated by statistical estimates, according to which nearly 70 percent of the Jews in central Ukraine were evacuated to the interior of the Soviet Union.[54] A similar or even slightly higher percentage of Jewish evacuees was found in the German-occupied sectors of the RSFSR. Several districts occupied by the Germans at a relatively late date were nevertheless noted for lower evacuation rates because of special conditions. Thus, for example, only 60 percent of the Jews in the Crimea, which was fully occupied only in mid-November, managed to flee.

As a rule, then, we may state that the later an area was occupied by the Germans, the higher the proportion of Jews who fled or were evacuated. Furthermore, the percentage of Jews who managed to flee or be evacuated was higher in the major cities than in smaller towns and villages. Transportation, especially rail transportation, was more available in the large cities than in the towns and villages, which in some cases were tens of kilometers from the nearest railroad station. Moreover, Jews somehow connected with the Soviet establishment were more likely to escape. Priority in evacuation was given to the Soviet apparatchik, cultural and scientific organizations, and large factories. Jews evacuated in these contexts could, as stated, bring their families with them, and the notion of "family" sometimes included distant relatives. However, the rank-and-file Jew, who had no relatives employed in high-priority institutions or workplaces, had to invoke various schemes and stratagems to find a slot among the evacuees. The young, too, were more likely than their older counterparts to flee or be evacuated successfully. There were two reasons for this: the younger people had integrated themselves into the Soviet establishment with greater success, and they displayed greater audacity in assuming the risks of escape and evacuation.

Was There a Policy Favoring Rescue of Jews?

Summing up, the question to ask is whether there was a policy favoring the rescue of Jews.

Even as the war still raged, rumors circulated in the Soviet Union that the Soviet authorities were engaging in the rescue and evacuation to the rear of Jews residing in the territories about to be occupied by the Germans. The Jewish Anti-Fascist Committee, which was interested in fostering sympathy for the Soviet Union, especially in the United States, repeatedly stressed that hundreds of thousands of Jews had been evacuated from the districts about to fall into Nazi hands and were thus spared the bitter fate of genocide. Soviet publications propagated this message in the postwar period until recent years.[55]

Even Jewish public opinion outside the Soviet Union—including circles with no affiliation with the left—tended in the 1940s to accept the notion that it had been Soviet policy to evacuate Jews from areas about to be overrun by the Nazis. Jews all over the world were impressed by the fact that hundreds of thousands of Jews in vast areas of the Soviet Union had been rescued from murder by means of escape and evacuation, as opposed to the small numbers of survivors in other European countries.

In the 1950s, as the Cold War gathered momentum, Western Jewish opinion tended to emphasize the Soviet Union's complicity in the annihilation of the Jews, citing the period of the Ribbentrop–Molotov Pact and the failure of the Soviet press to print information about Nazi atrocities against Jews.[56] The propagation of these views, however, was meant above all to serve transient political goals. Only recently have we witnessed the beginning of serious and even-handed research that may answer the question, at least in part.

During the first months of the German invasion of the Soviet Union, one cannot point at any deliberate and central policy of evacuation, let alone evacuation of the Jews. The attitude toward evacuation and even toward escape was largely shaped by the authorities in each locality. Thus it is correct to speak not of one evacuation policy but of many. The local authorities' considerations originated largely in their assessments of war needs; they drew no distinction, to the best of our knowledge, between Jews and non-Jews. At that stage, in any case, civilians' movement toward the rear is to be construed as escape rather than organized and orderly evacuation.

In the second stage, starting in August 1941, the major conduit for the transfer of factories and people to the rear was organized evacuation, directed to some extent from on high. Again, we have no knowledge of any intentional policy directives that gave the Jews special priority. In certain towns, however, as the result of local initiative, the authorities—military commanders, party officials, soviet bureaucrats —encouraged the Jews to leave, stressing that they faced greater danger than the others.

Thus, while it is difficult to speak of an intentional policy to rescue the Jews, the proportion of Jews among the refugees and evacuees was higher than their proportion in the population at large or even the population of a particular town. Thus, for example, a Jew visiting Kiev on 8–10 July 1941, had the impression that "Most of the passengers [fleeing on the ship Felix Dzerzhinsky] were Jews, including a large number of women, children, and old people, refugees from the cities and towns of the Ukraine."[57]

There were four major reasons for the high proportion of Jews among the refugees and evacuees: (1) most of the escapees and evacuees, as noted, came from the larger cities, where the Jews were over-represented vis-à-vis the general population; (2) the percentage of Jews associated with evacuated agencies, bureaucracies, and factories far exceeded their share of the general population, and these evacuees took with them their immediate families and more distant relatives; (3) the Jews were more mobile than the population at large and more willing to relocate; and most important of all, (4) the Jews knew that their fate under Nazi rule would be worse than that of the rest of the population, even though they did not imagine, initially, that their lot would be genocide. Hence it is not astonishing that Jews were more amenable than others to assuming the risks of escape and evacuation. The fact that the Jews were heavily represented among the refugees and evacuees created the impression that they had been given preference as a matter of policy. Although this was not the case, the Soviet authorities in some towns did encourage the Jews, in particular, to flee.

By virtue of escape and evacuation, hundreds of thousands of Jews remained alive in the Soviet Union and survived the Holocaust. This, however, does not suggest that there was an intentional policy of saving them; nor does it attest to any preference given to the Jews during the period of escape and evacuation.

Notes

1. For a more extensive treatment of this issue, see M. Altshuler, "Evacuation and Flight of Jews from Eastern Belorussia, June–August 1941," *Yahadut zemanenu,* 1986, vol. 3, pp. 121–23 (Hebrew).

2. Sh. Munchaev, "Druzhba narodov SSSR—vazhneishee uslovie v reshenii problemy evakuatsii v gody Velikoi otechestvennoi voiny," *Vestnik Moskovskogo universiteta: Istoriia,* 1972, no. 6, p. 56.

3. Kommunisticheskaia partiia v Velikoi otechestvennoi voine, *Dokumenty i materialy* (Moscow, 1970), p. 38.

4. P. Pogrebnoi, "O deiatel'nosti soveta po evakuatsii," in *Eshelony idut na Vostok* (Moscow, 1966), p. 201. N. Dubrovin, "Eshelon za eshelonom," in ibid., p. 208–9.

5. *Istoriia Velikoi otechestvennoi voiny Sovetskogo Soiuza* (Moscow, 1962), vol. 2, pp. 56, 143.

6. M. Pervukhin, "Pereobrazovanie promyshlennosti," *Sovetskii tyl v Velikoi otechestvennoi voine* (Moscow, 1974), vol. 2, p. 13.

7. *Resheniia partii i pravitel'stva po khoziaistvennym voprosam* (Moscow, 1968), vol. 3, p. 39.

8. I. Stalin, *Sochineniia* (1967), vol. 2 (xv), p. 8.

9. Pervukhin, p. 13; *Istoriia VOV,* vol. 2, p. 547; I. Belonosov, "Evakuatsiia naseleniia iz prifrontovoi polosy v 1941–1942 gg.," in *Eshelony idut na Vostok,* p. 16.

10. Pervukhin, p. 14; Pogrebnoi, pp. 201–2.

11. *Istoriia VOV,* vol. 2, p. 143. Concerning the impact of this factor in the timing of the evacuation of the Gomsel'mash factory in Homel, see P. Kalinin, *Partizanskaia respublika* (Minsk, 1968), p. 26.

12. L. Katsovich, *Fun heim tsu heim* (Moscow, 1946), p. 3 (Yiddish).

13. Ibid., pp. 15–16.

14. *Istoriia VOV,* vol. 2, p. 547; Belonosov, p. 16.

15. *Velikaia otechestvennaia voina, 1941–1945* (Moscow, 1985), pp. 801–3.

16. S. M. Schwarz, *The Jews in the Soviet Union* (Syracuse: Syracuse University Press, [1951]), p. 310. The author took the same attitude in his subsequent books. See S. Schwarz, *Antisemitizm v Sovetskom Soiuze* (New York, 1952), pp. 125–26; *Evrei v Sovetskom Soiuze s nachala Vtoroi mirovoi voiny* (New York, 1966), pp. 45–47. Other historians followed his example. See S.W. Baron, The Russian Jew under Tsars and Soviets, New York, 1976, pp. 249–50; Sh. Ettinger, *Modern Anti-Semitism* (Tel Aviv, 1978), p. 244 (Hebrew).

17. *Sovetskie khudozhestvennye fil'my—Annotirovanny katalog* (Moscow, 1962,) vol. 2, pp. 171–74.

18. Oral History Division, The Institute of Contemporary Jewry, The Hebrew University of Jerusalem, Interview no. 7(58), p. 12.

19. Y. Litvak, *Polish-Jewish Refugees in the USSR, 1939–1946* (Tel Aviv, 1988), pp. 21–70 (Hebrew).

20. S. Neshamit, "The Deportation of the Jews of Suvalki and the Surrounding District in October–November 1939 and Rescue Activities on Their Behalf," in *Studies on the Holocaust Period* (Tel Aviv, 1981), vol. 2, pp. 202–16 (Hebrew).

21. D. Levin, *They Fought Back: Lithuanian Jewry's Armed Resistance to the Nazis, 1941–1945* (Jerusalem, 1974), pp. 23–25 (Hebrew); D. Levin, *The Jews in the Soviet-Annexed Territories, 1939–1941* (Tel Aviv, 1989), pp. 191–213 (Hebrew).

22. One of the witnesses reported that "Refugees from Poland began to reach Minsk in 1939. They told us about the Germans' atrocities. Some of the Jews didn't believe it, because they still remembered the German occupation of Minsk

in 1918, which was relatively comfortable, and thought it preferable to the oppressive Soviet rule." *Minsk Memorial Anthology* (Jerusalem, 1985), vol. 2, p. 398 (Hebrew). Another witness notes that "The refugees from Poland told us about how the Germans abused the Jews" (ibid., p. 411).

23. The witness was born in 1928; the transcript of the interview is kept at Yad Vashem, no. 033C/963.

24. H. Smolar, *Fun minsker geto* (Moscow, 1946), p. 4. The author omitted this episode from the Hebrew version of his book, even though he has much to say about Lipschitz. See: H. Smolar, *Soviet Jews Behind Ghetto Fences* (Tel Aviv, 1984), pp. 29–32 (Hebrew).

25. *Der shtern*, 7 July 1941.

26. Kh. Shmeruk, "Polish Jewry in Yiddish Literature of the Soviet Union," in *Studies on the Holocaust Period* (Hakibbutz Hameuchad Publishing House, 1969), vol. 1, p. 137 (Hebrew).

27. I. Barzitskaia, "Gitlerovskie raizboiniki v Varshave," *Pravda,* 26 June 1941.

28. T. Krushevski, "Nenavist' k germanskim okkupantam bezgranichna," *Pravda,* 27 June 1941.

29. Fashistskaia Germania—tiurma narodov, *Krasnaia zvezda,* 29 June 1941.

30. The quotation is cited from Y.A. Gilboa, *The Black Years of Soviet Jewry* (Tel Aviv, 1972), p. 28 (Hebrew).

31. *Pravda,* 25 August 1951; Sh. Redlich, *Propaganda and Nationalism in Wartime Russia: The Jewish Antifascist Committee in the USSR, 1941–1948,* 1982, pp. 39–43.

32. A. Rozin, *Main veg aheim* (Jerusalem, 1981), p. 277.

33. A. Anatoli (Kuznetsov), *Babi Yar,* tr. David Floyd (New York, 1970), p. 140.

34. Yad Vashem, Testimony no. 03/2750, pp. 5–6.

35. Oral testimony given the author by Eli Weinerman. Another witness, who happened to have been in the town of Berezin on 26 June, several days before the German occupation, notes that "Jews did believe it desirable to flee, but they thought it a shame to leave their belongings behind." Yad Vashem, Testimony no. 033/263, p. 2.

36. Oral History Division, The Institute of Contemporary Jewry, The Hebrew University of Jerusalem, Interview no. 20(58), p. 10.

37. In the village of Shchedrin (where approximately 2,000 Jews resided), for example, "The kolkhoz people harnessed their horses and were willing to head east, but one. . . of them addressed them and said: 'Jews, where do you intend to go, abandoning everything? You have nothing to fear. Don't you remember 1918, when the Germans occupied the area and even came into our town, and they treated the civilian population politely? Unharness the horses! . . . " (M. Kiakhovitskii, "Hundert yor ekzistents fun a yiddish shtetl," *Sovietish haimland,* 1982, no. 1, p. 38). These remarks triggered a spirited argument, during which crucial hours were wasted. Ultimately most of the village's Jews indeed stayed put and were murdered. A Jew from Poland, reaching the town of Proskurov on 3 July 1941, while fleeing eastward, related the following: "I went into the home of some Jews, where several Jewish refugees were staying too. . . . An elderly Jew, who boasted that he had known the Germans as far back as World War I, tried to persuade me that they were a cultured people who should not be feared. I told him

about the massacres perpetrated by the Germans in occupied Poland, but I had the impression that he wasn't convinced by my arguments" (L. Fisher, *A frizier in lager* [Tel Aviv, 1975], pp. 36–37). Similar testimonies appear in *Bobruisk Memorial Book* (Tel Aviv, 1967), p. 770 (Hebrew). See also Yad Vashem, Testimony no. 033C/963, concerning a Jewish doctor in the town of Smoliany, Vitebsk district, who convinced the public not to flee. See Ehrenburg archives, Yad Vashem, Document no. 40/3.

38.   G. Zhukov, *Vospominania i razmyshlenia* (Moscow, 1990), vol. 2, pp. 7–10; I. Boldin, *Stranitsy zhizni* (Moscow, 1961).

39.   *Istoriia Minska* (Minsk, 1957), p. 409; *Ocherki istorii Kommunisticheskoi partii Ukrainy* (Kiev, 1964), pp. 501–4.

40.   Yad Vashem, Testimony 03/3282, p. 1. See also Oral History Division, The Institute of Contemporary Jewry, The Hebrew University of Jerusalem, Interview No. 24(58), p. 22; I. Grinshtein, *Ud mkikar haiovel* (Tel Aviv, 1968), p. 10; *Pinkas Slutsk uvnoteha* (Tel Aviv, 1962), p. 376; Rozin, p. 276.

41.   Oral History Division, The Institute of Contemporary Jewry, The Hebrew University of Jerusalem, Interview no. 17(58), pp. 92–93; A. Shvartsblat, "Bevitsot Uveiaarot Polesia," *Yalkut moreshet*, 1989, no. 46, p. 133.

42.   V. Popov, "Stal' i shlak," *Znamia*, 1949, no. 2, pp. 25–29.

43.   Yad Vashem, Testimony 03/3952, p. 2.

44.   Letter to the Jewish-Russian author Ilya Ehrenburg, Yad Vashem Archives, P–21/3/3, p. 3.

45.   A. Rubin, *Magafaim humot, magafaim adumot* (Tel Aviv, 1977), p. 12.

46.   Yad Vashem, Testimony 03/3954.

47.   *Birobidzhaner shtern*, 22 July 1988.

48.   Concerning those who turned back, consult the Ehrenburg archives at Yad Vashem for testimony in Yiddish about the town of Chmelnik. Kantor describes the atmosphere and commotion that prevailed among the refugees as they retraced their steps; see P. Kantor, "Tate-mame," *Sovietish haimland*, 1989, p. 5, p. 21.

49.   See the sources cited in notes 19 and 21 *supra*.

50.   See the sources cited in notes 19 and 21 *supra* and D. Levin (ed.), *Pinkas hakehilot—Latvia veEstonia* (Jerusalem, 1988), pp. 307–12; Sh. Specktor, *The Holocaust of Volhynian Jews, 1941–1944* (Jerusalem, 1986), pp. 44–52 (Hebrew).

51.   See Altshuler, op. cit. note 1 *supra*, and Sh. Specktor, "The Fate of the Jews of the Soviet Ukraine (within the 1939 Borders) during the Nazi Invasion— Numbers and Estimates," *Shvut*, 1987, no. 12, pp. 55–66 (Hebrew).

52.   "Der Chef der Sipo und SD," *Ereignissmeldung der UdSSR*, no. 73, p. 18.

53.   Ibid., no. 80, pp. 9–10.

54.   See Specktor, op. cit. note 51 *supra*.

55.   D. Rozenberg, "Sovetn-farband hot geratevet tsen mol mer yidn vi ale andere lender tsuzamen genumen," *Morgen fraihait*, 3 July 1943; B. Goldberg, "Vi men hot evakuirt yidn beisn krig in sovet rusland," *Der tog*, 21 February 1947; M. Kaganovich, *Der yidisher onteil in der partizaner bavegung in soviet rusland* (Rome, 1948), pp. 187–88.

56.   See the publications cited in note 16 *supra* and M. Mirski, "Soviet Evacuation in World War II," *Jewish Currents*, 1980, July–August, pp. 15–18; and J. Litvak, "The Rescue of Jewish Victims of the Nazis by the Soviet Authorities during the Holocaust," *Behinot*, 1970, no. 2–3, pp. 47–80.

57.   Fisher, p. 39.

A Soviet View of Palestine on the Eve of the Holocaust

RAFAEL MEDOFF

The sudden spate of contacts between the Soviet government and leaders of the world Zionist movement during World War II is commonly attributed to the Kremlin's desire to attract international Jewish support for the Soviet war effort against Nazi Germany. Historians have therefore dated the beginning of the relationship between Moscow and the Diaspora Zionist leadership to the period subsequent to the 22 June 1941 invasion of Russia by Germany.[1]

In fact, however, the first significant meeting between a Zionist leader and a representative of the Soviet government actually took place in January 1941, five months before the Nazi invasion of the USSR. From the timing of the meeting alone, it is clear that the traditional interpretation of Soviet motives for agreeing to such contacts must be revised. More significant is the content of that conversation, which indicates a level of Soviet interest in the Palestine problem that exceeds prevailing assumptions and may have been stimulated by the Polish Jewish refugee crisis of 1939–40.

The immediate context of the meeting was an attempt by the London-based Zionist leadership to interest the Soviets in a commercial transaction by which "the Russian Government should purchase oranges in Palestine and pay with furs in New York," as Chaim Weizmann framed it.[2] The oranges-for-furs proposal was the basis of Weizmann's 30 January 1941 appointment with Ivan Maisky, the Soviet ambassador to London, at the Soviet Embassy. As it turned out, the exchange proposal occupied only a small portion of the conversation between Weizmann and Maisky.

The content of their discussion is known because Weizmann paraphrased it in some detail at a subsequent meeting of the Jewish Agency
Executive in London; Maisky unfortunately chose to omit all mention
of Weizmann, Palestine, and Zionism from his memoirs.[3]

The oranges-for-furs idea seemed to appeal to Maisky, Weizmann
reported: "M. Maisky said that he was no businessman, but the proposition sounded reasonable to him, and he would communicate it to his
Government and put in a good word for it."[4]

That subject having been disposed of pending a formal Soviet
response, the bulk of the conversation was then devoted—evidently at
Maisky's initiative—to the situation in Palestine. Maisky asked
Weizmann "how the war was affecting Palestine," and Weizmann provided "some idea of what the economic situation there was."

The Zionist leader and the Soviet ambassador then turned to "political questions." Weizmann characterized Arab–Jewish relations in Palestine as being "frozen," noting that there was "some semblance of
cooperation between the two peoples." The signs to which Weizmann
was referring included the fact that Arab rioting had come to an end
(following the promulgation of the British White Paper of 15 May
1939); and the large numbers of Arabs and Jews who had recently
volunteered for a joint Arab–Jewish infantry regiment of the British
Army—so many, in fact, that a second company was formed.[5]

Maisky expressed keen interest in the question of what would become of Palestine after the war. He prefaced his remarks about the
future of Palestine by pointing out "that a great Jewish problem would
face them after the war." The Soviets were, of course, intimately familiar with the Jewish problem that already existed. In the wake of the
German invasion of Poland, some 350,000 Polish Jews took refuge in
the Soviet-occupied region of eastern Poland.

The Soviets were not necessarily pleased by this development; there
were many instances in which the Soviet authorities turned away Jews
who were seeking haven in the area under their jurisdiction.[6] In the
summer of 1940, Moscow undertook its own unusual solution to the
Polish-Jewish refugee problem by offering the refugees a choice between repatriation to German-occupied Poland and Soviet citizenship.
When the majority chose repatriation, the Soviets interpreted their selection as evidence of disloyalty and punished them by exiling them to
the interior part of the Soviet Union. Hence the period between the
German–Soviet invasion of Poland and the German invasion of the

Soviet Union was a time when the Soviet authorities were confronted by a virtual flood of Jewish refugees and grappled with possible solutions. Considering the facts on the ground, the "great Jewish problem" to which Ambassador Maisky referred in his January 1941 talk with Weizmann was probably on the minds of many Soviet officials at that time.

The likelihood that the Polish-Jewish refugee crisis stimulated some Soviet officials to mull various possible solutions to the problem may help explain the otherwise inexplicable views which Maisky expressed to Weizmann. After referring to that "great Jewish problem," Maisky asked the Zionist leader "whether it was Dr. Weizmann's opinion that the only solution lay in Palestine." When Weizmann replied in the affirmative, "M. Maisky said that there would have to be an exchange of populations," that is, an exchange involving the removal of Arabs from Palestine to facilitate the establishment of a Jewish homeland.

The Soviets had not previously expressed support for the aims of Zionism. On the contrary, Moscow's pronouncements on the subject throughout the two previous decades had been consistently hostile toward Zionism. Although Weizmann's paraphrased account of the conversation does not say so explicitly, one would expect that he was at least somewhat surprised to hear a senior representative of the Soviet regime not only speaking in terms of the creation of a Jewish homeland, but advocating methods toward that end which were typically proposed only by the most militant elements in the Zionist movement.

Weizmann responded to Maisky's suggestion by estimating "that if half a million Arabs could be transferred, two million Jews could be put in their place." He added: "That, of course, would be a first installment; what might happen afterwards was a matter for history." This was not the first time that Weizmann had privately expressed cautious approval for the Arab "transfer" notion. As Yehoshua Porath has shown, Weizmann energetically pursued the Middle East peace plan concocted by Harry St. John Philby, according to which funds raised by the Zionists and the Allied powers would be used for the development of Saudi Arabia in exchange for Saudi absorption of a large number of Palestinian Arab farmers.[7] What distinguished Weizmann's interest in the Philby plan from Ambassador Maisky's idea was the question of Arab consent. The Philby scheme was based on the assumption that Zionist officials and Arab leaders would agree that the plan was mutually beneficial, and the Palestinian Arabs would consent to emigrate because of the financial incentives. Maisky, by contrast, was less sensitive to the Arabs' wishes. When Maisky said to Weizmann "that they in Russia had also to deal with exchanges of population"—possibly a reference to the harsh deportations of about 10 million Ukrainian peasants[8] during 1929–33—Weizmann "explained that they were unable to deal with [the Arabs] as, for instance, the Russian authorities would deal with a backward element in their population in the USSR. Nor would they desire to do so."

That said, Weizmann turned to some of the technicalities of effecting such a population transfer. "[T]he distances they had to deal with in Palestine," Weizmann pointed out, "would be smaller" than those involved in Soviet population movements, since the Zionists "would be transferring the Arabs only into Iraq or Transjordan." When Maisky wondered if there might be a problem "in transferring a hill-country population to the plains," Weizmann pointed out that it might be possible to ease the transition by beginning "with the Arabs from the Jordan Valley"; in any event, the Zionist leader continued, "conditions in Transjordan were not so very different from those of the Palestine hill-country."

Weizmann then turned the conversation to the subject of Palestine's Jewish communal settlements, a subject of natural interest to the Soviet ambassador, and one which Weizmann no doubt hoped would arouse Soviet sympathy for the Zionist endeavor. As they shook hands and parted, Maisky remarked "that he had learnt a great deal about Palestine and the Jewish problem."

Did Maisky's statements to Weizmann reflect only his own unorthodox ideas on Palestine, or do they suggest a certain fluidity of thinking among some Soviet officials on how to deal with "the great Jewish problem" that they had seen first-hand in Poland and expected to face again at war's end?

If recent changes permit greater access by Western researchers to the internal correspondence of Soviet embassies abroad during the war years, an answer to that riddle may yet be found. In the meantime, the chronology of the relationship between Moscow and Jerusalem must be moved back by almost half a year, and the list of reasons for the initiation of those contacts must be reexamined.

Notes

1. For examples of this tendency among historians, see Jacob Hen-Tov, "Contacts Between Soviet Ambassador Maisky and Zionist Leaders During World War

II," *Soviet Jewish Affairs* 8 (1978), 46–47; Yaacov Ro'i, "Soviet-Israeli Relations, 1947–1954," in Michael Confino and Shimon Shamir, eds. *The USSR and the Middle East* (Jerusalem: Israel Universities Press, 1973), 123; Shimon Redlich, "Relations and Contacts between the USSR, Soviet Jews and the Yishuv in Palestine" (Hebrew), in *Annual of Bar-Ilan University Studies in Judaica and the Humanities* 24–25 (1989), 157; and Alden H. Voth, *Moscow Abandons Israel for the Arabs: Ten Crucial Years in the Middle East* (Lanham, MD: University Press of America, 1980), 42.

2. "Short Minutes of Meeting Held on Thursday, 30 January 1941, at 77, Great Russell Street, London, N.C.1" (hereafter referred to as Short Minutes), p. 1, Weizmann Archives (hereafter referred to as WA), Weizmann Institute, Rehovot, Israel. Unless otherwise stated, all quotations attributed to Weizmann and Maisky in this essay are from this document.

3. Ivan Maisky, *Memoirs of a Soviet Ambassador: The War, 1939–1943* (New York: Charles Scribner's Sons, 1968).

4. Subsequent correspondence between Weizmann and Maisky on the subject suggests that Weizmann was overly optimistic in his assessment of Maisky's view of the proposal. "[A]s I anticipated during our conversation, I am afraid this plan is of no interest to the Soviet Government in that as a rule the USSR does not import any kind of fruit from abroad," Maisky wrote on 10 February. See Maisky to Weitzman [sic], 10 February 1941, WA.

5. "Palestinian Force Arrives in France," *New York Times*, 29 February 1940, 6; "More Jews and Arabs to Enlist," *New York Times*, 9 November 1940, 3.

6. Dov Levin, "The Attitude of the Soviet Union to the Rescue of Jews," *Rescue Attempts During the Holocaust* (Jerusalem: Yad Vashem, 1977), 228–29.

7. Yehoshua Porath, "Weizmann, Churchill and the 'Philby Plan,' 1937–1943," *Studies in Zionism* 5 (1984), 239–72.

8. For the various estimates, see Robert Conquest, *The Harvest of Sorrow: Soviet Collectivization and the Terror-Famine* (New York: Oxford University Press, 1986), 126–27.

Soviet Jewry in the Thinking of the Yishuv Leadership, 1939–1943

Some Preliminary Observations

DAVID ENGEL

The Jews of the Soviet Union are not the subject of what is to follow, but rather may provide a part of the answer to a question about another group of people altogether. That question concerns the behavior of the leaders of the Palestinian Yishuv in response to the news that the Jews of Nazi-occupied Europe were being subjected not merely to an extended and cruel pogrom but to a systematic program aimed at taking the life of each and every one of them. As any number of studies have already established, that news began to filter out of the killing zone as early as mid-1942, although until November of that year it was met with considerable skepticism and public efforts at denial.[1] As denial became increasingly more difficult, however, the Yishuv leadership felt pressure to become involved actively in efforts to rescue Europe's Jews from their mortal danger. The extent to which it did so is, of course, a matter of considerable controversy, both academic and public, and a full consideration of the problem is beyond the scope of what can be attempted here.[2] It does appear, though, that there were considerations that tempered the willingness of the Yishuv's leaders to explore certain rescue possibilities—an inference suggested by, among other items, the following story.

On 16 November 1942 a group of sixty-nine Jewish citizens of Palestine who had been trapped in Nazi-occupied Europe since September 1939 was brought to the British holding camp at Atlit, near Haifa, having been exchanged for a similar contingent of Axis nationals detained in Allied countries. During the next several days the exchangees were interviewed by members of the Jewish Agency Executive in Jerusalem, who inquired about conditions for Jews under Nazi rule. Their eyewitness testimony appears to have convinced those who heard it that there could no longer be any room for doubt: all of European Jewry had been placed under a sentence of death, and that sentence was already well on its way to being carried out *in toto*.[3] In response the Agency Executive and the General Council of Palestinian Jews *(Va'ad Le'umi)* proclaimed three days of "sounding the alarm, protest, and outcry," culminating, on 2 December, in a twelve-hour work stoppage in all nonvital enterprises.[4]

Beyond this public outpouring of grief, however, the leaders of the Yishuv, ideologically committed to a view of themselves as the vanguard leadership of world Jewry as a whole, began to explore practical possibilities of rescuing whatever Jews might still be saved. This exploration led, at a very early stage, to the London-based Polish government-in-exile. Because Poland had been set by the Germans as the primary arena in which the murder of Jews from all over Europe was to be carried out, it appeared logical to assume that Polish cooperation could be an important determinant of the success of any rescue effort. And, quite felicitously, it turned out that at the very moment when the testimony of the sixty-nine exchangees had raised the concern of the Yishuv leadership for the fate of European Jewry to a new level of intensity, a senior official of the Polish government—Stanislaw Kot, a former interior minister and ambassador to the Soviet Union and a close political confidant of Prime Minister Wladyslaw Sikorski—was visiting Palestine, ostensibly for a three-month period of rest and relaxation but actually for reasons of internal Polish politics.[5] Thus a series of meetings was arranged between Kot and various officials and leaders of the Yishuv to discuss, among other things, how the Polish government might contribute to the rescue enterprise.[6]

At these meetings, which continued from late November 1942 through the end of January 1943, Jewish representatives, including David Ben-Gurion, chairman of the Jewish Agency Executive, presented a series of demands for action by the Polish government. Among the demands were calls for a broadcast instruction to the population of the occupied homeland to come to the aid of threatened Jews, for a decision that any Polish citizen involved in the killing or persecution of Jews would be held accountable for his crime, for the dispatch

of "confidential agents" from Palestine to occupied Poland for the
purpose of "mak[ing] contact with the Government delegates and
send[ing] exact news about the situation of Jews in Poland through the
channels available to the Polish Government," for Polish government
support for the establishment of a Jewish army to fight alongside other
Allied forces, and for the establishment of a special cabinet-level Ministry of Jewish Affairs.[7] Kot responded to these entreaties with what
was essentially his own demand for political *quid pro quo:* the Jews,
he claimed, could be of value to the government-in-exile in its efforts
to make certain that Poland's eastern territories, which had been annexed by the Soviet Union in 1939, would be returned to Polish sovereignty following the conclusion of hostilities.[8] As he explained to
Yitzhak Grünbaum, the doyen of Polish Zionists who now headed the
Jewish Agency's recently established Rescue Committee *(Va'ad
HaHatsalah),* he had hoped to find "a person or a Jewish body with
whom a general agreement could be reached, [an agreement] that
would represent the Jewish people as the ally of the Polish government."[9] In the same conversation he also indicated that "the time has
already come to prepare the peace now," stressing that "in this field the
Jews possess the ability to help the Poles"—a thinly veiled hint that
Jews might use their purported influence among opinion-making circles in the West to win hearts and minds, especially within the British
and U.S. governments, for Poland's territorial postulates.[10] Grünbaum
evidently understood Kot's intention, and he was ready with a response:

> With regard to western Poland there will be no disagreements; the main
> issue is Poland's eastern areas. This matter concerns Russia especially,
> and that complicates things considerably.... With regard to Bolshe-
> vism the Jews' attitude will depend upon the regime; if the regime will
> be as it was before the war, then certainly they will oppose any annexa-
> tion [of the eastern Polish territories] to Russia.... But it is possible
> that things will change, and in that case our attitude will change as well.
> The Jews must deal extremely cautiously in their relations with Rus-
> sia.[11]

In other words, the official of the Jewish Agency Executive formally charged with the development and conduct of plans to rescue as
many Jews from Nazi-occupied Europe as possible explicitly refused

to strike a bargain with a leading official of the Polish government, a step without which there was virtually no possibility of involving that government in any significant rescue action. It appears, moreover, that his response to Kot had been considered beforehand by other members of the Executive and that in offering it he believed that he was acting in the name of that body; in any event no objection was raised to his response by any of the other twelve members present, including Ben-Gurion and the members of the Executive's Committee on Polish Jewry (which consisted, in addition to Grünbaum, of Eliyahu Dobkin, Emil Schmorak, and Moshe Shapiro).[12] The Polish spokesman had made it clear that in their relations with the Polish government the Jews possessed at least a modicum of leverage that was painfully absent in their dealings with the principal Western allies, and yet at a most critical juncture the use of that leverage was abjured. The question is, of course, what was the thinking that stood behind this response?

Several factors in this thinking have been identified elsewhere,[13] including the possibility that the response was in part a reflection of a legacy of distrust of Polish politicians among Jewish leaders—a distrust engendered by disappointment with previous political agreements that had aimed at securing the future of Polish Jewry—and in part an indication of a perception of the Yishuv leadership that the Soviet Union was likely to assume a position of decisive importance in determining the future of Palestine (in particular the future of the Zionist enterprise in that country) once the war was over. There does not appear to be any reason to doubt that these two considerations were present in the mind of Grünbaum and other Jewish leaders as they spoke with the Polish diplomat; in fact, there is direct documentary evidence that the highest echelons of the Zionist movement gave careful consideration, both before and even as the meetings with Kot were being arranged, to the proposition that winning the sympathy of the Soviet Union for the Zionist cause should be regarded as one of the movement's primary aims.[14] But from a careful reading of the exact words that Grünbaum employed in refusing Kot's entreaty it appears that yet another thought may have entered into the Jewish spokesman's calculations. Grünbaum explained to Kot, in effect, that the Zionist movement preferred to keep its options open vis-à-vis the USSR because it believed that following the war there was a reasonable chance that the character of the regime in Moscow would change to the Zionists' benefit. Only if such a change were not forthcoming, he suggested, would the Zionists prefer that Poland control the territories in dispute; otherwise they would rather see those territories remain under Soviet rule. This explanation makes no sense if the only thing that the Zionists sought was Soviet support for their political aims in Palestine. In that case it would have been a matter of indifference to them who ruled the contested areas or what type of regime was installed in them, and their choice of sides would have been determined exclusively by considerations of political expediency. Yet Grünbaum indicated that the nature of the regime that would control those lands was of vital interest to the Zionist movement and even of decisive importance in determining its stand on the Polish–Soviet dispute. Assuming that Grünbaum was not being disingenuous—an assumption that seems plausible on both textual and contextual grounds—there appears to be reason to inquire why this was so.

In this connection there may be room to suspect that Grünbaum and many of his colleagues within the Yishuv leadership were hopeful that after the war the government of the USSR would permit large-scale migration of Soviet Jews to Palestine. It may even be, moreover, that after late 1942 they looked to those potential Soviet Jewish immigrants to assume the role that they had previously assigned to the now decimated Jewish community of Poland—namely, to provide the human vehicle for transforming Palestine into a country with a Jewish majority. If such were the case, they would have preferred to see the Soviet Union—a country for which many of them, especially within the labor movement, possessed a basic sympathy despite what they regarded as the evil deeds of its government in recent years[15]—in control of the postwar destinies of as many Jews as possible; they might thus be spared the necessity of negotiating with the Polish government over the fate of large numbers of potential immigrants—a task that they found distasteful despite the Poles' professed warm support for the Zionist enterprise.[16]

What are the grounds for this suspicion? In the first place, it appears that the political thinking of the Zionist movement around the time of Kot's meetings with the Yishuv leadership proceeded from the assumption that the conclusion of the war would see millions of Jews left homeless, unable to rebuild their lives in their former countries of residence. This assumption had formed the basis for the so-called Biltmore program, adopted at a conference of American Zionists in May 1942, which had raised publicly for the first time the demand to open the gates of Palestine to unlimited Jewish immigration, under the supervision of the Jewish Agency, as a prelude toward establishing the country as "a Jewish commonwealth integrated in the structure of the new democratic world."[17] Indeed, it was argued, Palestine was capable of making a decisive contribution to solving the expected worldwide postwar refugee problem, and by making this contribution the country would acquire a large Jewish majority, justifying independence under the auspices of a Jewish government. Such thinking had been formally endorsed by the Smaller Zionist Actions Committee in Jerusalem on 10 November 1942, when the Biltmore program was adopted as the official statement of the Zionist political platform.[18] Yet but a week later it became apparent to the leaders of the Yishuv that those anticipated millions of refugees might not be alive at the conclusion of hostilities and indeed might already have perished in the Nazi abyss; and as time went on it appeared more and more that the potential pool of immigrants from the countries within the Nazi orbit would not be sufficient to tip the demographic balance in Palestine to the Jews' favor.[19] Thus it is no surprise that immediately following the arrival of the sixty-nine exchangees and the absorption of the import of their testimony leaders of the Yishuv began to turn their attention more intensively than before toward the fate of the Jews in those countries that could still provide significant manpower for the Jewish state in the making. Eliyahu Dobkin, head of the Jewish Agency's Immigration Department, for example, called at the beginning of December 1942 for the dispatch of dozens of emissaries *(shelihim)* to various countries in the Middle East, seeing in the 800,000 Jews living there a more accessible body of potential immigrants than the Jews under Nazi occupation.[20]

Not surprisingly, the same thought appears to have occurred with regard to the several millions of Jews living within the boundaries of the Soviet Union. In fact, not only before the turning point in understanding the situation of the Jews under Nazi occupation but even before the USSR's entry into the anti-German alliance, the Zionist leadership had been searching for ways to cultivate Soviet favor for their enterprise in Palestine, with the hope that such favor might result not only in support for Zionist political plans but also in expanded immigration from that country. In late 1940 Dobkin and Jewish Agency Treasurer Eliezer Kaplan had sought to develop commercial relations between the Yishuv and the USSR, based initially upon the

exchange of Russian furs for Palestinian oranges, evidently in the hope
that such relations might lead to negotiations with the Soviet government over permitting the immigration of certain categories of Jews
under Soviet jurisdiction to Palestine.[21] In April 1941 the Council of
the General Federation of Jewish Workers in Palestine (Histadrut) discussed the vital need for the Zionist labor movement to make inroads
among Soviet Jewry in order to develop new sources of manpower for
the Yishuv. The importance of such inroads was explained, among
others, by Yisrael Idelsohn, a central figure in the HaKibbuts
HaMe'uhad movement:

> To reach that Jewish community [in the USSR] is an extremely import-
> ant question for us. After all, a third of world Jewry is located there.
> Everything that can be done to reach those Jews must be done, [includ-
> ing] negotiating with the authorities, even if it is 100 percent certain
> that such negotiations will not succeed. We must try again and again, if
> only we shall be permitted [to negotiate]; but we must negotiate, for this
> is the way in which we shall reach Russian Jewry and make it part of
> our enterprise.[22]

If Idelsohn does not appear to have been terribly sanguine over the
prospects for success of the efforts he proposed, those involved in the
negotiations on the economic front seemed more hopeful. Joseph
Linton of the Jewish Agency office in London noted with satisfaction
in a letter to Moshe Shertok, head of the Agency's Political Department in Jerusalem, that even if nothing were to come directly of the
furs-for-oranges proposal, the idea had at least brought about the rees-
tablishment of high-level contacts between the Soviet government and
the Zionist leadership. The plan, he observed, had served as a pretext
for a meeting between Chaim Weizmann, president of the World Zionist Organization, and the Soviet ambassador in London, Ivan Maisky,
the first meeting at such a level to have taken place in many years. The
Soviet diplomat, according to Linton, had given the Zionist president
"a very friendly reception," a fact that evidently led him to conclude
that "the Russian Embassy contact . . . may prove useful in obtaining
facilities for our refugees to leave Russia when we can give them
immigration certificates."[23]

This hope that the Soviet government might be made to see the
merit of the Zionist cause in Palestine grew markedly following the

USSR's entry into the war in June 1941. Almost immediately Zionist bodies and organizations began to contemplate with satisfaction the prospect of renewed contact with the Jews of the Soviet Union.[24] On 17 July, for example, the Histadrut Executive debated a proposal of one of the Left Poalei-Zion factions calling for the raising of a volunteer brigade from the Yishuv to fight on the Soviet front. Among the reasons advanced in support of this idea was the prospect that "by bringing their faithful assistance to the defenders of the Soviet Union, volunteer units of Palestinian workers would be carrying the message of Jewish labor Palestine to the masses of Jews now fighting shoulder to shoulder with all other Soviet nationalities . . . for the national and social liberation of all enslaved and oppressed peoples."[25] Although the proposal was ultimately rejected, virtually all who participated in the debate expressed the view that the time was ripe for spreading the Zionist message in the Soviet Union; disagreement was only regarding the proper vehicle for doing so.[26] Such thinking also undoubtedly underlay the August 1941 decision of the Jewish Agency Executive to activate a Committee for Dealing with Matters [Relating to] Russian Jewry (Va'adah leTippul beInyanei Yahadut Rusiyah), whose mandate included, among other things, "exerting pressure to permit the exit of Jewish refugees from the Soviet Union" and "a special demand to free veteran and new Zionist prisoners . . . and to permit them to emigrate."[27]

Zionist spokesmen who attempted to probe the Soviet government for signs of a change in its historic attitude toward their movement, however, soon found the situation to be a bit more complicated than they might at first have imagined. Emanuel Neumann of the American Emergency Committee for Zionist Affairs and Maurice Perlzweig of the American Jewish Congress, who met with USSR Ambassador Konstantin Oumansky in Washington on 17 July 1941, noted that although the Soviet diplomat had agreed that "the recent developments which have ranged Soviet Russia on the side of the democracies seemed to offer an opportunity for establishing better working relations between representatives of Jewish organizations and the Soviet Government," he had pointedly refused to enter into a discussion of his government's attitude toward Zionism in general and had insisted that the condition of Jews in the Soviet Union was altogether satisfactory.[28] Nevertheless, the two representatives observed that Oumansky had expressed a willingness to talk further about two specific matters: permitting the emigration of those Jews from Western Poland who had fled to the USSR in 1939 and establishing relief facilities for Jews who "did not fit in with the social and economic system."[29] A similar probe by Selig Brodetsky and Berl Locker of the Jewish Agency Executive in London with the first secretary of the Soviet Embassy in the British capital yielded similar results, with the additional hint that veteran Russian Zionists who had been imprisoned by the Soviet regime for their Zionist activity might now be released and allowed to emigrate.[30] In short, it appeared that while the Soviets were not yet ready to consider the prospect that the bulk of their own Jewish citizens might be candidates for migration to the Zionist state in the making, they were prepared, perhaps, to mitigate what had seemed to be their previous total opposition to anything smacking of Zionism with regard to a number of clearly defined and—from their perspective—peripheral groups of people.

From the Zionist point of view, however, the groups under discussion as possible exceptions to previous Soviet practice were not peripheral at all. In particular, the body of Jewish refugees from the former Polish territories that had been captured and annexed by the Soviet Union in 1939—a body that numbered some 400,000,[31] although reports reaching Palestine often gave a much higher figure[32]— comprised, in the eyes of the Yishuv leadership, a formidable reservoir of potential immigrants, and securing their evacuation and eventual *aliyah* quickly became one of the Jewish Agency's central concerns.[33] Those responsible for achieving this goal appear to have realized that their best chance for success lay in appealing to the good will of the Soviet regime—good will that might more likely be obtained through expressions of support for the Soviet war effort than, among other things, by public statements favoring the Polish side in the Polish–Soviet conflict, as Kot had demanded as the price for Polish action on the Jews' rescue demands. Indeed, when Shertok later approached Soviet Ambassador Maisky in London with a formal proposal to approve the exit of "a certain limited number of Jews from Poland, who are now in the USSR, to reinforce the Palestine Jewish war effort," he took pains to emphasize that "there is among the Jews of Palestine a deep and widespread sympathy and admiration for the Soviet Union in its heroic struggle" and that "the Jews of Palestine are keenly conscious of the fact that, in their humble capacity, they are making a contribution to the common war effort in which the Soviet Union plays such a major part."[34] In contrast, when (inaccurate) word reached Jerusalem that Ignacy Schwarzbart, a Zionist representative on the Polish National Council in London, had publicly declared his support for Poland's foreign policy and had criticized the Soviet government's treatment of Polish Jewish refugees in their country, Shertok was advised that such a statement could have dangerous consequences, both for Jews living in the disputed border regions and for the Zionist movement.[35]

In any event, the Yishuv leadership was also faced with the question of whether the apparent chinks in the Soviets' formidable anti-Zionist defenses, as it were, revealed by their willingness to discuss the possible emigration of Jewish refugees from Poland and others, were likely to be quickly repaired, or whether they might rather eventually be widened to the point where masses of Soviet Jews might escape through them. Thus during the months following the USSR's entry into the war they attempted to gauge the Soviets' long-range intentions toward the Zionist enterprise. In this regard the opinions of Yishuv leaders who met with Soviet officials varied. Eliyahu Epstein, the Russian-born director of the Middle East section of the Jewish Agency Political Department, who held talks with the Soviet legate in Ankara in November 1941, took a pessimistic position; in a lengthy memorandum to his superior, Shertok, he indicated that "all reports that have reached me from reliable sources prove that there has been no change at all in the *internal* policies of the USSR, whatever the foreign policy stance of the Soviet government might be."[36] Epstein thus advised that "it would be a mistake to assume that we stand today before greater possibilities for Zionist activity in the USSR than we did in the past," seeing in the minimal flexibility that some Soviet officials had indicated with regard to questions concerning the refugees from Poland and Zionist political prisoners the full extent of likely Soviet concessions to the Zionist cause. Others, however, including Dobkin and Grünbaum, while acknowledging that "there is no possibility today of obtaining exit visas from Russia for Soviet citizens" and that the results of the first round of contacts with Soviet officials had been less than hoped for, not only saw no reason to cease looking for a way to approach the Soviet government on the matter of immigration, but called, at a meeting of the Committee on Russian Jewry in February 1942, for "continued negotiations with the Soviet authorities in all possible directions."[37]

Whichever evaluation was more justified by the actual state of Soviet intentions, though, the Jewish Agency and other branches of the Zionist movement continued during the second half of 1941 and throughout 1942 to seek Soviet acquiescence to their demands for refugees from Poland to be permitted to leave the country for Palestine, for Zionist prisoners to be released, for a relief mission from the Yishuv to be allowed into Soviet territory, and for the teaching of Hebrew to be permitted.[38] They also endeavored to exploit every possible occasion to impress Soviet representatives with the seriousness of the Zionist enterprise and the fundamental affinity between its values and the ideals for which the USSR purportedly stood.[39] By pursuing this course they evidently hoped to try gradually to enlarge the small openings that the Soviet government had given them so that eventually the masses of Soviet Jews might be exposed to Zionist influence. That strategy was reflected, among other places, in a letter from Arieh Tartakower of the World Jewish Congress to Binyamin West of the Committee on Russian Jewry in April 1942. Tartakower, who, largely at the behest of the Jewish Agency, had been conducting discussions with Soviet diplomats in the United States, including the new Soviet ambassador, Maxim Litvinov, about Zionist matters, indicated that so far he had been able to make significant headway only with regard to matters concerning refugees from Poland, for it was "clear to all of us that the time has not yet come to raise the matter . . . of Zionist activities in Russia proper."[40] Nevertheless, he stated that at his last meeting he had attempted to persuade Litvinov that "not only refugees from Poland but also refugees in Russia from other countries" be permitted to enjoy a benefit that had been promised the former group. He pointed out that it would be a difficult matter to induce the Soviets to acquiesce to this request and that he felt that he had to proceed cautiously. Still, though, as he told West, he "understood that [the Yishuv leadership] was interested . . . in political activity and in assistance for the Jews of Russia who are not from the occupied areas." In these matters, he explained, he still faced a stone wall, but he implied that gradually, by obtaining piecemeal concessions, that wall might be breached.

More direct in this regard was Yitzhak Ben-Zvi, chairman of the General Council. In a diary entry from late August 1942, made following his talks with two representatives of the Soviet legation in Ankara who had been visiting in Palestine—talks at which he had especially stressed the Yishuv's manpower needs—he stated that for the present he was prepared to confine his discussions with Soviet authorities to matters relating to Jewish refugees from Poland and other countries. However, he wrote, "we shall have a chance to discuss the immigration of Russian citizens to Palestine once the war is over."[41]

In the meantime, moreover, the Yishuv leadership appears to have embarked upon more direct means of forging a link between Palestine and the Jews of the Soviet Union. In March 1942 the General Council issued a formal proclamation praising the active role taken by Soviet Jewry in the fight against Hitler. This proclamation embodied what seems to have been the Yishuv's fundamental thought regarding that Jewish community:

> To be sure, the Jews of Soviet Russia . . . have been cut off from us for many years, but during all those years the Jews of Palestine have not ceased to look toward that far but near community. . . . And during all those years the hope has accompanied us that the barrier that separates us from the Soviet Jewish tribe will fall and that brothers who have been cut off and divided from one another will reestablish their relationship, working together for a common future in Zion. And even though that barrier has not yet fallen, we believe with a perfect faith that the day is not far when the ongoing process of the ingathering of exiles in Palestine will be connected once again with the Jews of Soviet Russia in an atmosphere of mutual trust and understanding.[42]

In order to reestablish that connection, the Immigration Department of the Jewish Agency sought in the same month to recruit ten to twelve emissaries from the various Zionist youth movements in Palestine to infiltrate into Soviet Central Asia via Iran and to organize the immigration of Jews from that area. Initially, of course, the emissaries were to work mainly with refugees from Poland, but it was hoped no doubt that eventually they would be able to expand the range of their contacts to Russian-speaking Jews as well.[43]

The physical link between the Yishuv and Soviet Jewry via this route was made possible by the evacuation of the Polish exile army, commanded by General Wladyslaw Anders, from the Soviet Union to Iran (and subsequently to Palestine)—a process that began in April 1942 and reached its climax the following August.[44] Moreover, the circumstances of this evacuation created a situation in which the Soviet authorities appeared relatively pliable and responsive to Jewish desires regarding immigration to Palestine. The fact that only a small number of Jews had been included in the evacuation transports was attributed by the Yishuv leadership—largely on the basis of a field investigation undertaken on behalf of the Jewish Agency by a refugee attorney named Eliyahu Rudnicki, a report of which reached Jerusalem in September 1942[45]—to discrimination by Polish officials, whereas the Soviets were perceived as willing to allow virtually all Jewish refugees from Poland to leave.[46] In this situation the Yishuv leadership had an opportunity to compare the attitudes displayed by the Polish and Soviet governments toward their postulates, and the comparison strongly favored the Soviet side. If, as Rudnicki had indicated explicitly in the introduction to his report, the investigation that he had conducted was to serve as a basis for "orienting [the Jewish Agency's] relations both with the Polish government and with the Soviets,"[47] the stance of the Yishuv with regard to the Polish–Soviet dispute was clear.

Rudnicki's report also highlighted another aspect of the Yishuv's view of the situation of Jews under Soviet rule. Rudnicki had indicated that "the condition of the Jewish refugees in Russia is horrible. At least 30 percent have died of hunger, typhus, dysentery, and other illnesses. . . . They have only one hope—that we will save them"[48] In such circumstances the leaders of Palestinian Jewry might well have viewed the extrication of these refugees from the Soviet Union as an act of rescue equal in importance to any action that might be taken on behalf of Jews in Nazi-occupied Europe—and perhaps even as one more advisably undertaken, for it seemingly enjoyed a greater prospect of success.[49] What is more, they appear to have been convinced that the difficult conditions of the refugees from Poland were shared by many Soviet Jews proper.[50] Hence it does not appear altogether surprising that even the baleful news brought by the sixty-nine exchangees did not bring about a change in the Yishuv leadership's thinking along the lines hoped for, among others, by Stanislaw Kot: the Soviet government seemed to hold the key to the rescue of many more Jews than did the Polish; and what is more, those Jews were the ones most likely to provide the basis for turning Palestine into a Jewish commonwealth after the war.

Such appears to have been the thinking embodied in a memorandum prepared by Yitshak Rabinowicz, himself a former Zionist political prisoner in the USSR and now a member of the Committee on Russian Jewry, for Shertok on 20 November 1942, four days following the arrival of the exchangees at Atlit.[51] Rabinowicz indicated that following the war "Soviet Russia. . . will have decisive influence over the question of the Jews concentrated in. . . the areas of Russian rule or occupation." "Many signs," he declared, "point to a definite movement in the direction of understanding for us [Zionists]." Thus, he concluded, "through a sensible, careful, and systematic policy we shall be able to build a bridge between us and Russian Jewry and to tear down the wall that has been built up on both sides during the last twenty years." To his mind that policy required that the Jewish Agency place itself firmly on the Soviet side in the Polish–Soviet dispute. In return for such a stance, he suggested, the Agency would be in a strong position to demand and to receive official recognition by the Soviet government as the sole body responsible for the welfare of all Jewish refugees in the USSR. This step, in turn, would give the Agency a strong foothold within the Soviet Union, a foothold that could presumably be expanded eventually to encompass Soviet Jewry proper as well.

Unfortunately, although the documentary record permits a fairly easy reconstruction of the gestation of such ideas, the documentary traces of their practical application are much fainter. It is not clear, for example, what Shertok did with Rabinowicz's memorandum—whether it became the basis for broader discussions among the Yishuv leadership and in particular whether Grünbaum might have had it specifically in mind when he formulated his response to Kot's entreaties. Perhaps more wide-ranging archival research than has been attempted here will reveal documents that speak directly to this problem. In the meantime, though, it appears quite plausible that Grünbaum's response to Kot reflected, at least in part, an opinion adumbrated within the leadership of the Yishuv at the time, that the future of Soviet Jewry was to be of greater consequence for the success or failure of the Zionist enterprise in Palestine than was the future of the Jews under Nazi occupation. For this statement about the thinking of the Yishuv leadership there is also as yet no direct documentary confirmation; hence the argument cannot be regarded at present as anything more than a suspicion. Nonetheless, the suspicion does not appear to be without foundation; the possibility that it might be true merits further careful investigation.

Notes

Special thanks are due Hagar Fynne for her assistance in assembling the documentary materials for this paper.

1. Dina Porat, *Hanhagah beMilkud: HaYishuv Nochah haSho'ah, 1942–1945* (Tel Aviv, 1986), pp. 44–67. See also Sh. B. Beit-Tsvi, *HaTsiyont haPost-Ugandit beMashber haSho'ah: Mehkar al Gormei Mishgeha shel haTenu'ah haTsiyonit baShanim 1938–1945* (Tel Aviv, 1977), pp. 42–105; Walter Laqueur, *The Terrible Secret: Suppression of the Truth about Hitler's "Final Solution"* (Boston, 1980), pp. 157–95.

2. In particular, it must be emphasized that nothing of what follows should be construed as an attempt to confront the question of whether the Yishuv's response to the Holocaust, or any part of that response, was sufficient or insufficient, proper or improper, well or invidiously motivated, or deserving of any other evaluation. In order for it to be properly understood this article must be read exclusively as a discussion of a proposition of fact, viz., that in late 1942–early 1943 certain expectations about the future of the Jews in the Soviet Union were among the various considerations that influenced the stance taken by the Yishuv leadership toward a representative of the Polish government-in-exile in discussions on the rescue of Jews from German-occupied Poland. As the article makes clear, the evidence examined to date does not permit an unambiguous affirmation of this proposition, but it does offer strong reason to suspect that it may indeed be true. The question of whether this consideration *ought to* have influenced the Yishuv leadership's stance, at all or in any particular direction, is not addressed here.

3. For the testimony of one of the leaders of the group, see Reprezentacja Żydostwa Polskiego, *Sprawozdanie z dzialalności w latach 1940–1945* (Tel Aviv, 1945), pp. 46–51. On the impact of this testimony upon the Yishuv leadership, see Porat, *Hanhagah beMilkud*, pp. 59–67.

4. For a description of the events of these three days, see Porat, *Hanhagah beMilkud*, pp. 76–87. See also Monty Noam Penkower, *The Jews Were Expendable: Free World Diplomacy and the Holocaust* (Urbana and Chicago, 1983), p. 83.

5. It appears that he was attempting to quell an incipient revolt against Sikorski by high-ranking officers in the Polish exile army then stationed in Palestine. See, *inter alia*, [Jan Drohojowski], *Jana Drohojowskiego wspomnienia dyplomatyczne* (Kraków, 1969), pp. 214–20; "Rozmowa z Min. Prof. Kotem," January 1943, Central Zionist Archives (henceforth CZA)—J25/2.

6. For the texts of the minutes of some of these meetings, see David Engel, "The Polish Government-in-Exile and the Holocaust: Stanislaw Kot's Confrontation with Palestinian Jewry, November 1942-January 1943," *POLIN*, 2 (1987): 273–309.

7. Ibid., pp. 274–76, 289–90, 293–98, 307.

8. Ibid., p. 285.

9. "Pirteikol miYeshivat Hanhalat haSochnut haYehudit leErets Yisra'el," 24 January 1943, CZA—Minute Books, Jewish Agency Executive.

10. In an earlier conversation with a delegation from the Representation of Polish Jewry *(Reprezentacja Żydostwa Polskiego)*, Kot had been much more direct: "The Jews need to stop complaining and get to work. Where is the Jews' public declaration that Lwów and Wilno ought to be returned to Poland? Why have the Jews done nothing in this matter? Either the Jews express solidarity with Polish actions, or they [should] step aside, and then they will not be able to bring

accusations against the Polish government." "Reprezentacja Żydów Polskich," 5 December 1942, Hoover Institution Archives (henceforth HIA)—Polish Government, Box 700, File "Mniejszości Żydzi." On the development of the idea that Jews possessed significant influence over the formation of Western public opinion, see David Engel, *In the Shadow of Auschwitz: The Polish Government-in-Exile and the Jews, 1939–1942* (Chapel Hill, 1987), esp. pp. 69–85; also idem, "HaSichsuch haPolani-haSovieti keGorem beHityahasutah shel Memshelet Polin haGolah laSho'ah," *Shvut*, 12 (1987):26–28.

11. See above, note 9.

12. To be sure, Schmorak, a former Polish Sejm deputy from Lwów, criticized Grünbaum for demanding the establishment of a Ministry of Jewish Affairs, on the grounds that this demand had not been approved either by the Executive's Committee on Polish Jewry or by the independent Representation of Polish Jewry *(Reprezentacja Zydostwa Polskiego)*. Grünbaum replied that he "had not made any proposals; ideas had been expressed about a Jewish Ministry or Jewish Department in the prime minister's office, but that was all with regard to such matters. Regarding the remaining matters," he added, "these have been discussed here more than once, and agreement has been reached on them." He indicated moreover that he "was convinced that he had not been speaking solely on his own authority." Neither Schmorak nor anyone else present contradicted him. This fact suggests that his response to Kot was in line with the general thinking of the Executive as a whole. Ibid.

13. Engel, *In the Shadow of Auschwitz*, pp. 210–11.

14. See, for example, Ben-Gurion to Histadrut Executive, 4 January 1942, with attached memorandum to Maisky, 13 October 1941, CZA—S25/486: "Soviet Russia will be among the few leading major Powers which will determine the fate of the world when peace comes. . . . The attitude of Soviet Russia to the Jewish problem outside [of the Soviet Union] is a matter of the greatest concern, both from the Jewish and the Labour point of view." See also Yitshak Rabinowicz, member of the Jewish Agency's Committee on Soviet Jewry, to Moshe Shertok, head of the Jewish Agency's Political Department, 20 November 1942, CZA—S25/5182.

15. For a discussion of the general attitudes of the Yishuv leadership toward the Soviet Union, see, *inter alia*, Anita Shapira, *Berl* (Tel Aviv, 1980), pp. 610ff.

16. See Engel, *In the Shadow of Auschwitz*, pp. 41–42, 48–49. Of course, at the time the Soviet occupation of all of Eastern Europe and the change in the Polish regime was not anticipated.

17. See Ben Halpern, *The Idea of the Jewish State*, 2nd ed. (Cambridge, 1961), pp. 39–40; Yehuda Bauer, *From Diplomacy to Resistance: A History of Jewish Palestine 1939–1945* (Philadelphia, 1970), pp. 234–42.

18. Bauer, *From Diplomacy to Resistance*, pp. 242–43, 250.

19. In 1942 the number of Arabs in Palestine exceeded the number of Jews by about 500,000; *Universal Jewish Encyclopedia* (New York, 1942), 8:364. In August 1943 an official of the Political Department of the Jewish Agency (probably Eliyahu Epstein) indicated to the Soviet legate to Turkey that he "hoped that a million or a million and a half of the Jews of Central and Eastern Europe would remain" after the war; "Bikkur baTsirut haRusit beAnkara," 26 August 1943, CZA—S25/486. In December 1943 Menahem Bader, delegate of the General

Federation of Jewish Workers in Palestine (Histadrut), reported that there were probably no more than 200,000 Jews, and at most 260,000, left alive in Poland; "Protokol miYeshivat haVa'ad haPo'el," 29 December 1943, Histadrut Archives (henceforth AH)—Minute Books, Executive. Earlier the president of the World Zionist Organization, Chaim Weizmann, had estimated that one-third of the post-war Jewish population of the countries of Central and Eastern Europe would be candidates for resettlement in Palestine; Weizmann to Anthony de Rothschild, 22 January 1942, in *The Letters and Papers of Chaim Weizmann* (Jerusalem, 1968–80), Series A, 20:258. David Ben-Gurion, head of the Jewish Agency Executive, had spoken of two million new Jewish immigrants as the critical mass needed to keep Palestine from "descend[ing] from the political stage." Quoted in Bauer, *From Diplomacy to Resistance,* p. 238.

20. Porat, *Hanhagah beMilkud,* p. 485.

21. See Joseph Linton, Jewish Agency, London, to Moshe Shertok, Jewish Agency, Jerusalem, 4 February 1941, CZA—S25/5182. See also Shlomo Kless, *Gevulot, Mahteret uVerihah: Pe'ilut Tsiyonit-Halutsit biVerit-haMo'atsot uKesharim im haYishuv baArets* (Tel Aviv, 1989), p. 182.

22. "Protokol miMo'etset haHistadrut ha–43," 9 April 1941, p. 61, AH—Minute Books, Council. See also the remarks of Moshe Erem, ibid., p. 25, and Aharon Ben-Shemesh, ibid., p. 45.

23. Linton to Shertok, 4 February 1941 (see above, note 21).

24. See, for example, the memorandum by Yehoshua Gordon, "Ezra laTsava haLohem vehaOchlusiyah haMeshuhreret shel Rusiyah," 8 July 1941, CZA—S6/4738. Even the breakaway Revisionist New Zionist Organization, traditionally strongly anti-Soviet, noted "the importance for Zionism of the return of Russian Jewry to the forefront of Jewish affairs." "Minutes of the Consultation of the Presidency in New York," 11 August 1941, Jabotinsky Institute Archives—G5/1/3.

25. "Yeshivat haVa'ad haPo'el," 17 July 1941, p. 25, AH—Minute Books, Executive.

26. An exception to this tendency was Yaakov Hazan, who felt that the Soviet government would not receive any official delegation from the Yishuv. Ibid., pp. 29–31.

27. Kless, *Gevulot, Mahteret uVerihah,* pp. 122–23. It is not clear whether the phrase "Jewish refugees" referred to Polish Jews who had fled eastward in 1939 or to Soviet Jews proper fleeing the Nazi advance of 1941. Although a short while later the Yishuv leadership began devoting special attention to the former group (on which see below), it appears that in the weeks following the German invasion its concern was not so limited. For example, an internal Jewish Agency memorandum of 8 July 1941 noted that "because all of the battles are now being fought in an area populated by Jews it is unavoidable that concern should be expressed primarily for the refugees who will be forced to escape into the Russian interior." "Ezra laTsava haLohem . . . " (see above, note 24). See also Magen to American Jewish Committee, 23 October 1941, CZA—S6/1494: "In the wake of the war in Russia great masses of Jews have been uprooted from the areas of German conquest. The problem of these new refugees is exceedingly sharp. . . . A great rescue effort is called for."

28. "Minute of Conference with Ambassador Oumansky at the Russian Em-

bassy," 17 July 1941, CZA—S6/4738; "Exchange of Letters between M.L. Per-
lzweig and Lord Halifax," 23 July 1941, in Lukasz Hirszowicz, "The Soviet
Union and the Jews during World War II: British Foreign Office Documents,"
Soviet Jewish Affairs, 3 (1973): 75–78.

29. "Minute of Conference with Ambassador Oumansky" (see previous note).

30. "Pirtei-kol miYeshivat Hanhalat haSochnut," 4 August 1941, CZA—Minute Books, Jewish Agency Executive.

31. On the formation of this body and its number, see Engel, *In the Shadow of
Auschwitz*, pp. 125, 268.

32. See, for example, Rafael Szafar, Tehran, to "Dear Friends," 24 May 1942,
CZA—S6/4738, which placed the number at 900,000; Jewish Agency Executive
to Arthur Lourie, 23 June 1942, ibid., which reported receiving estimates of
550,000 Jewish refugees from Poland in Turkestan alone; "He'etek Telegramah
sheNishlah leNiu-York uleLondon beAugust 1942," ibid., which estimated as
many as 490,000 refugees.

33. Eliyahu Dobkin indicated to Aryeh Tartakower that securing the exit of
Jewish Polish citizens from the Soviet Union was "perhaps the central question
for our movement at this time." Dobkin to Tartakower, 7 October 1942, CZA—
S6/831. See also Engel, *In the Shadow of Auschwitz*, pp. 139ff.; David Engel,
Facing a Holocaust: The Polish Government-in-Exile and the Jews, 1943–1945
(Chapel Hill, 1993), chapter 2.

34. Shertok to Soviet ambassador, London, 19 January 1943, CZA—S25/847.

35. Yitshak Rabinowicz to Shertok, 12 November 1942, CZA—S25/486.

36. Epstein to Shertok, 26 January 1942, CZA—S6/4738.

37. "Protokol miYeshivat haVa'adah haRusit. . . ," 3 February 1942, CZA—
S6/4551.

38. See, for example, "Pirtei-kol miYeshivat Hanhalat haSochnut haYehudit,"
20 July 1941, CZA—Minute Books, Jewish Agency Executive; Dobkin to distribution list, 18 August 1941, CZA—S6/1494; Magen to American Jewish Committee, 23 October 1941, ibid.; Arieh Tartakower to Binyamin West, 21
December 1941, CZA—S25/5182; Y. Rabinowicz to Committee on Russian
Jewry, 27 January 1942, CZA—S46/510; West to Yizhak Ben-Zvi, 8 March
1942, CZA—S6/831.

39. Consider, for example, the extensive meetings held with officers of the
Soviet ship *Mikoyan*, which unexpectedly came to anchor in Haifa port in Decem-
ber 1941 after having seen battle in the Aegean Sea. "Sihot im Ketsinei haOniyah
haRusit 'Mikoyan,' " 10 December 1941, CZA—S6/831; "Sihot baArets im
Ketsinei haOniyah haRusit," 15 December 1941, ibid.; "Siyur Sheni baArets im
vedei haOniyah haRusit," 22 December 1941, CZA—S25/486; A. Dystrowski to
L. Herman, 28 December 1941, CZA—S25/486. See also the materials about the
Histadrut sent by David Ben-Gurion to Maisky, 13 October 1941, ibid.

40. Tartakower to West, 20 April 1942, CZA—S6/4738.

41. "MiBikkurei Tsirei haMishlahat haRusit. . . ," 31 August 1942, CZA—
S25/486. On the visit of the two Soviet representatives from Ankara, see Shimon
Redlich, *Tehiyah al Tenai: HaVa'ad haYehudi haAnti-Fashisti haSovieti—Aliyato
uShekiyato* (Tel Aviv, 1990), pp. 150–51.

42. "Gillui Da'at," n.d. [attached to West to Ben-Zvi, 8 March 1941], CZA—
S6/831.

43. See, for example, Moshe Kolodny to the leaders of HaNo'ar haTsiyoni, 8 March 1942, Masu'ah Archive—NZ/8/44. The emissaries were required to speak Russian.

44. On the evacuation, see Engel, *In the Shadow of Auschwitz*, pp. 139–47. On the exploitation of the evacuation for the development of connections between the Yishuv and Jews (mainly refugees from Poland) in the Soviet Union, see Kless, *Gevulot, Mahteret uVerihah*, pp. 160–79.

45. On Rudnicki's investigation and its findings, see Engel, *Facing a Holocaust*, pp. 49–51.

46. See Engel, "HaSichsuch haPolani-haSovieti," pp. 30–31.

47. Rudnicki to Jewish Agency, 8 September 1942, HIA—Poland. Ambasada US, Box 64, File 6.

48. Ibid.

49. See Dobkin to Tartakower, 7 October 1942, CZA—S6/831.

50. See, for example, "Hatsa'ah leEzrah leYahadut Rusiyah," 25 August 1942, CZA—S6/879.

51. Rabinowicz to Shertok, 20 November 1942, CZA—S25/5182.

Part 3

Regional Studies

The Holocaust in Transnistria

A Special Case of Genocide

DALIA OFER

Introduction

Transnistria, a political unit created by the Nazis, was a region of some 40,000 square kilometers situated between two rivers, the Dniester and the Bug, in the southern corner of the Soviet republic of Ukraine. It existed for about two and a half years, from August 1941 until March 1944, when the Red Army marched in and liberated it. The creation of Transnistria, a name given to the area by Hitler, represented the wish of the Nazis to compensate Romania for the regions of Transylvania and southern Dobrudja, which had been lost to Hungary and Bulgaria. The two regions of Bukovina and Bessarabia, which the Soviet Union invaded and annexed in June 1940, were given back to the Romanians after the Red Army had fled.[1]

The history of the Holocaust in Transnistria, as in any other place in Europe, incorporates the accounts of the perpetrators and the victims. Among the leading perpetrators in Transnistria were the Romanian army and police. Their actions were a consequence of the new political situation created when the war against the Soviets began. Romania's national anti-Semitism was radicalized by the war and by wild nationalistic aspirations. Ion Antonescu, the Romanian dictator, believed that the dream of "Greater Romania," born in the summer of 1940, could be realized through alliance with the Nazis and a direct involvement in the Barbarossa campaign. The Jewish population of Bessarabia, Bukovina, and Transnistria had no place in the "New Greater Romania." Nevertheless, the fate of Romanian Jews cannot be understood without taking into account the massive killing by the Nazi Einsatzgruppen in the first weeks of the war against the Soviets.[2] From this point of view, the history of the Jews in Transnistria demonstrates the convergence of different motivations working toward the same goal: getting rid of the Jews, and killing them. The murderers included not only the Romanians and the Nazis, but also the local Germans (Volksdeutsche) and Ukrainians who actively collaborated in the process of annihilation. They were stimulated by two major motives, Nazi racism and traditional anti-Semitism; anti-Bolshevik feeling also played a central role since the Jews were identified with the Communist regime. To these factors one should add an indifference to the loss of human life, particularly Jewish life, as a consequence of the general suffering and the large number of casualties caused by the war (the Romanian Army had lost some 70,000 soldiers during the siege and the battle over Odessa).

In Transnistria the Romanian policy of expelling Jews from certain areas and the Nazi final solution were somewhat "less successful" than in other parts of Eastern Europe: 40 percent of the deportees survived. But the manifestations of cruelty, brutality, and bestiality reported from that area stand out nonetheless. Granted, there were no gas chambers in Transnistria, nothing like the death factories of Treblinka, Sobibor, and Belzec, Auschwitz, and Maidanek. Yet intentional killing through starvation, forced labor camps where people were worked to death, mass killings by shootings, and all other elements of the Holocaust did indeed exist in Transnistria.

The description of the Jewish fate in Transnistria must take account of two phases: the fate of the local Jewish population, and the fate of the deportees, themselves the remnants of their communities, mostly of Bessarabia, Bukovina, and Dorohoi. What happened in Romania reflects the main factors and issues of the Holocaust: Jews as a group were isolated and marked for death. Ghettos, forced labor camps, and death centers were established. Unlike in other areas of Eastern Europe, in Transnistria the majority of the ghetto and camp populations consisted of deportees who were complete strangers in the area, who did not even understand the language of the local Ukrainian-speaking population. The deportees were brought to Transnistria stripped of their valuables, with no money or means of livelihood, and completely disorganized. However, the Jewish community was not completely dismembered. As it became clear that some kind of organization offered the only chance of survival, the stronger elements among the deportees started to organize their brethren into some sort of community. A few individuals who managed to smuggle in some money succeeded in setting up self-help institutions and bringing a measure of order into the ghettos and camps assigned to them. The problems of many Jewish leaders in Transnistria, who were caught between their obligations to the Romanian authorities and their brethren, resembled those of heads of Judenräte in Poland and other parts of Europe, except that in most camps and ghettos in Transnistria the people came from different places and backgrounds, and so had no real core. Their first task, as they saw it, was to establish a community, with some sense of identification and loyalty.

In light of the above, the history of the catastrophe in Transnistria can be viewed as the Holocaust in microcosm, yet there were some unique elements. As mentioned above, the Romanians, not the Germans, did most of the killing. Indeed, independent Romania was the only German ally involved directly in mass killings. (The Croatian militia was involved in mass killings of Jews and Serbs, but Croatia was really a puppet state established by the Nazis.) Although the Romanian government and army set out on the path of the final solution with great zeal, once Nazi victory no longer appeared certain, they started to hesitate and to explore options. On the whole, Romania adopted a much more independent policy, its "Jewish policy" being a case in point. The government thus resisted Nazi demands to deport the remaining Romanian Jews (of the Regat) to the killing centers in Poland.[3] In this respect, the fate of the Jews in Romania, and to a lesser extent in Transnistria, was influenced by political considerations.

These political shifts, and the existence of an established Jewish community in Romania (notwithstanding the great economic losses and humiliation it suffered), gave some leeway for rescue efforts in Transnistria. Two other factors account for the uniqueness of the Transnistrian case: the general disorder that prevailed among the Romanian officials and their lack of a systematic plan for killing the Jews, on the one hand, and the normative use of bribery among Romanian politicians and bureaucrats, on the other hand. These factors enabled the Jewish leadership to work out a strategy of aid and rescue for Transnistria. From the spring of 1942 (almost a year after the mass killing started, and not more than six months after most of the deportations were carried out), different forms of aid reached the Jews in

Transnistria. Although late in time and not enough in volume, it was an important contribution to the survival of the Jews in Transnistria. No other Jewish community under Nazi rule received such massive aid.

Life in Transnistria's ghettos and camps, its similarities and dissimilarities compared with the general history of the Holocaust, and the unique case of Transnistria, will be described below.

The Fate of the Local Jews

According to the census of 1926, the last one taken before the war, there were 2,495,000 inhabitants in Transnistria: 1,070,000 Ukrainians, 710,000 Russians, 300,000 Jews, 290,000 Romanians (Moldavians), and 125,000 Germans. In addition, there were small groups of Lithuanians, Bulgarians, Greeks, Armenians, and Gypsies. More than half of the Jews of Transnistria, about 180,000 of them, lived in Odessa, the largest town in the region, which contained approximately 600,000 inhabitants. Other towns were much smaller, numbering between 7,000 and 30,000 people each. In some of these the local Jews comprised the majority. Most of the non-Jewish Ukrainian population were farmers living in small villages.[4]

Because so very few of the local Jews escaped with their lives, the evidence and testimonies about their fate once the German Eleventh Army and the Third Romanian Army crossed the Dniester on 15 July 1941, following the hasty retreat of the Red Army, are very scarce. During his trial, Otto Ohlendorf, head of Einsatzgruppe D, which operated in the area with the help of the Romanian troops, gave some information about what took place. According to his account, the area was divided into Einsatzkommandos 10a-b, 11a-b, and 12, but in the latter's reports there is no distinction between the killings in Bessarabia and Northern Bukovina and those in Transnistria. Rather, the reports describe one continuous operation—from the first stage of killings in Soviet territories, to the annihilation carried out after the Germans crossed the Dniester, down to the last operation in the Crimea.[5] (The siege of Odessa was left to the Romanian military forces, who received some needed help from the Germans.) Einsatzgruppe D reached the Crimea in September 1941, but Einsatzkommando 12 held back for another few months. The first wave of murder took a heavy toll in Jewish life; in just six weeks, 50,000–60,000 Jews were dead.[6] A second wave of killing followed soon after.

On 30 August 1941 German and Romanian army officers convened in Tighina to sign an agreement on the governing of Transnistria. The Romanians took over the civil administration, keeping the Soviet administrative division of the region (raions). However, the Romanian lei was not introduced as the legal tender; instead, a special mark "Reichskreditkassenschein" (RKKS), was issued, which could be used only in the region. As for security, a Romanian special security force, Esalon-Operativ, which had been established for the purpose of killing when the war started, was placed in Transnistria.[7] One of its main tasks was internal security, which was to be maintained together with the local gendarmerie. The primary military control remained in Germans hands, although the Romanian Army stayed in Transnistria. The local Germans in Transnistria enjoyed special rights. They were also recruited by the Einsatzgruppen command to VOMI (Volksdeutsche Mittelstelle), an agent of the SS.[8] A Ukraine militia was also formed and collaborated with the other security forces. Although the Romanians proclaimed sovereignty over Transnistria, in spite of many German offers they never actually annexed it. For Antonescu, Transnistria was never a part of the "Great Fatherland," but rather a bargaining chip in future permanent territorial arrangements.[9] From the Jewish perspective, the cooperation between the Romanian gendarmerie, the Esalon-Operativ, Einsatzgruppe D, VOMI, and the Ukrainian militia summed up the very nature of the Holocaust in this region. The killings of the local Jews were carried out by all these organizations.

When Odessa was captured (October 1941), the second wave of mass killings started. Some 20,000 to 30,000 Jews were killed out of the 80,000 that were left in Odessa after the Soviet evacuation.[10] This was carried out on 23–24 October by the Romanian Army. It was claimed that the Jews were responsible for terrorist and sabotage acts in the city. The remaining 35,000–40,000 Jews were put in a ghetto in appalling conditions.

A third wave of killing started when the Jews of Odessa were deported to camps in the region of Brezovca. This region was heavily populated by Volksdeutsche, and within one year most of the Jews were murdered by VOMI troops. The same happened to the rest of the Jews in the southern part of Transnistria, who were deported to forced labor camps in Bogdanovka and Domanovka: they too were murdered by VOMI Einsatzkommandos (in both cases, the Romanian special forces were operating with VOMI). Out of the 210,000 local Jews of

Transnistria (taking into account that some 90,000 had evacuated Odessa and other places with the Soviets), some 80 percent were murdered during the first six months of the occupation. Their killing was a part of the final solution. They were murdered by the same methods— that is, shooting—that were used by all Einsatzgruppen in the Soviet-occupied territories. After the first major wave of brutality and murder, the Jews were marked, isolated, deprived of their property, and finally deported and killed (Order No. 23 of 11 November 1941). This followed the model developed by the Nazis in Poland. The distinct character of Transnistria was reflected in the massive role played by the Romanians and the Volksdeutsche in the killing. Unlike the other collaborating minorities, such as the Ukrainians in the rest of occupied Ukraine, or the Lithuanians, who served as auxiliary forces to the Einsatzgruppen, here the collaborators were the planners, the initiators, and also the executioners. The VOMI was practically an arm of the SS, and the Romanians contributed their army and state security units.

The assault on the unprepared Jewish population was swift and brutal. There was no escape; there was no time to prepare, or to hide. The Jewish population outside of Odessa lived in small and medium-sized towns and villages. Yet even the large Jewish population of Odessa was left completely bewildered once half its members were evacuated. Those who remained were confused, with no leaders, and completely at the mercy of the conquerors, who immediately implemented massive punitive acts (23–24 October) aimed exclusively at the Jews, who were considered to be the nucleus of the Bolshevik regime. This onslaught was reinforced by and gave legitimacy to the widespread deep anti-Semitism, and at the same time was an endorsement of the extreme nationalistic and victorious sentiments of the Romanian Army, which had lost so many soldiers in the siege of Odessa.

The ghetto at Odessa, which was in existence for no more than a few weeks and was afflicted by poverty and disease, had little opportunity for self-help and resistance. The non-Jewish population of Odessa in general experienced a milder occupation than their kinsmen under direct German occupation in the rest of Ukraine. After the first few months of occupation, the Romanian administration tried to bring life back to normal. But by that time the Jews had already been deported, and most of them were dead.[11]

The Deportations to Transnistria

According to the census of 1930, there were 206,958 Jews in Bessarabia and 107,975 in Bukovina—314,933 Jews in all. At the start of the war, on 21 June 1941, the numbers were slightly higher. In a census taken on 1 September 1941, the number of Jews in both regions was 126,434. What had happened to the other 188,499?

Some 30,000 to 40,000 Jews fled with the Soviets (some of them were caught again in Odessa). About 150,000 to 160,000 were murdered. Einsatzgruppe D was responsible for the area of Bessarabia, which included the large Jewish communities of Kishinev and Belz. However, most of killing was done by the Romanian army, the Esalon-Operativ, and the gendarmerie.[12] Those Jews who survived the massacres of the summer of 1941 were interned in four camps in Bessarabia and two others in northern Bukovina (about 64,000 people), and shortly afterward they were deported to Transnistria.

The major organized deportations to Transnistria started on 6 October 1941 and lasted until January 1942. Most of the 118,847 Jews from Bessarabia, Bukovina, and Dorohoi were transported to the northern end of Transnistria, whose major city was Moghilev. The second wave of deportation, which included the 4,650 remaining Jews from Cernauti, took place in the summer of 1942; a third one in September 1942 involved 2,238 deportees. It included Jews from the central part of Romania (the Regat), who were punished for what the authorities called political crimes. During 1943 a few hundred Jews were deported to Transnistria as a punitive measure, among them the main leader of Romanian Jews, Dr. Wilhelm Filderman, who was expelled to the ghetto of Moghilev in July 1943. The total number of Jews deported exceeded 130,000.[13] The inhuman treatment and the horrible conditions inflicted on the deportees are described in detail in diaries, memoirs, and reports. One is shocked by the depths of human cruelty, by the measures taken to humiliate thousands of innocent people, by the utter misery inflicted on the expelled Jews. The roads of Transnistria were littered with corpses left unburied or covered by snow. The deportations to Transnistria could be rightly called "Death Marches."[14]

The first wave of deportees was the group that established the patterns of life in Transnistria. In general the deportees could be divided into three groups: people who had lived under Soviet rule in Bessarabia and northern Bukovina since June 1940; those who remained under

Romanian domination in southern Bukovina; and those from Dorohoi, a region of central Romania that had been administratively annexed to Bukovina in 1938.

Those Jewish communities which were subjected to Soviet rule had already lost the main features of their community structure. Jewish social and political institutions had been abolished by the Soviets, and a number of political and spiritual leaders were deported to Siberia. Economically, the Jewish middle class had lost much of its wealth, and the community in general was in economic distress. As a consequence, these communities were already weakened when the war started. Yet, there was a crucial difference between the first and second groups, attributable to their experience during the first months of the war—mass killings, and concentration in camps and ghettos in Bessarabia and Bukovina. In July and August 1941 the Romanians started to expel more than 38,000 Jews to Transnistria, but the German Army and the Einsatzgruppe D command raised strong objections, since the deportations interfered with their operations. The Romanians were instructed to stop their unplanned deportations and the Jews were pushed back east of the Dniester. At that time Einsatzgruppe D was already busy killing the local Jews. Some 4,000 of the nearly 25,000 Jews who reached the eastern bank of the Dniester lost their lives in the forced marches back and forth from Transnistria, or were murdered by Einsatzkommando 10b, which was operating near Moghilev. The returnees were concentrated in the camps, and found there other deported Jews who had been stopped before crossing the river. These Jews were already living in appalling conditions, stripped of everything they had, and terrorized by the Romanian soldiers. Many of them lost their entire families in the killings or the marches.

Until October 1941, when the deportations began, the Jews of southern Bukovina and Dorohoi had not suffered directly from the war. They were spared the massacres and the acts of revenge by the local Romanian population. The Jews of Cernauti too were saved from the massacres and deportations.[15] Thus, these Jews were still in their homes when the order of deportation was announced. They had some time to prepare for the evacuation and could therefore manage to take with them food, clothing, money, and jewelry. Most of the people set out on the forced journey with their families, and some were even able to rent wagons and other means of transportation to make the long marches easier.

The Deportees in Transnistria: The General Framework

There is very little evidence of any planning or preparation on the part
of the Romanian authorities concerning the settlement of the deportees.
On 11 November Gheorghe Alexianu, the Romanian Governor of
Transnistria, made public Decree No. 23 concerning the organization
of Jewish life; this decree became the "constitution" of the ghettos and
camps. According to the decree, Jews were confined to those villages
and towns where local Jews or Russians had lived before. The local
gendarmerie was authorized to select the places of residence. The decree further limited their movements and stipulated that they had to
earn their living by forced labor for the benefit of the authorities (in the
Agreement of Tighina, clause 7 referred to Jewish forced labor for the
German Army). A fixed wage of one mark per day for simple workers
and two marks for professionals and specialists was to be paid by
allotment of food, which was to be supplied by the authorities.

The decree also dealt with the internal structure of the community
(called "colonie" in the text). Every community had to choose a "head"
from among the deportees to serve as its spokesman, pending the approval of the pretor of the region (usually a Romanian officer). The
"head" was personally responsible for fulfilling all the demands for
labor set by the Romanian authorities and for detailing workers for
different tasks, some of them very difficult. The workers were divided
into groups of twenty, headed by a chief who also had to be approved
by the pretor.[16]

Decree No. 23 was little more than a deception. It gave the impression that there was a clear Romanian Jewish policy for Transnistria,
and it referred to what might be considered as the "normal life" of
deported people in war conditions. But, although the decree covered
elements of regular daily life—dwelling, food supplies, work and self-
organization—in reality the physical and material condition of the deportees was completely disregarded. The expelled Jews were unable to
organize regular life. They needed hospitals and basic medical help,
food and clothing, orphanages, and so forth; instead, they were moved
aimlessly, again and again from one ghetto to another and from camp
to camp, none of which had even the minimal facilities to accommodate them. Even the "choosing" of a leader, the head of the community, was a sham.

As to a definite Jewish policy, this too was far from clear. The future of Transnistria itself was debated. If Transnistria was not to stay Romanian, the need to plan for the future was minimal. In Transnistria the Jews were one more element to be exploited in the process of expediency. In any event, the deported Jews were not to return to Romania. Thus for the Romanians, unlike the Germans, the killing of Jews was not an aim in itself; it was the outcome of certain circumstances.

When the convoys of Jews arrived in Transnistria, they found an area laid bare by the advancing troops and heavily bombarded. In the towns and villages where the ghettos were established (ghettos were usually established inside a town or village, while camps of different types were outside regular settlements),[17] many buildings were ruined and roads and rail lines were destroyed. The people arrived without any accommodation, or any means to buy food. The newcomers, in their poor conditions and frightful appearance, were a threat to the local population and raised fear and resentment. Shortages in all commodities were intensified by the notorious looting of the Romanian soldiers.

Since the towns and villages in the northern part of Transnistria were very small, the Jews were spread in small numbers. In the region of Moghilev, for example, the Jews were divided into fifty-three ghettos and one camp. Only nine ghettos had more than a thousand people; thirty-six of them contained up to 500 people. The Balta region contained twenty-one ghettos and camps, of which four contained more than 1,000 people; the others held less than 500.[18] Many of the deportees lived during the first month in pig barns, horse stalls, and cowsheds. When they finally found better dwellings, as many as fifteen to eighteen people had to share one room. In most places there were not even the simplest sanitary facilities; there were no detergents for basic disinfection, or clean water. The death toll was extremely high, in particular during the first winter, 1941–42, when 30–50 percent of the people perished in a typhus epidemic that raged throughout the ghettos and camps.[19]

The accounts of the survivors and the earliest records abound with descriptions of death and misery. Many people moved about naked; children were covered with rags or newspapers, because they had to sell their clothing for bread. Corpses lay in the fields, along the routes of the marches, or were piled high next to living people in the barns.[20] The hardships were further aggravated by the fact that the deportees were complete strangers; only very few could speak Ukrainian. Moreover, as already mentioned, most of the local Jews had already been killed by the Einsatzgruppe D, so there was no place to turn to for help. Individual helplessness was utter and complete.

It is hard to compare the situation in Transnistria to other deportations in Eastern Europe. In Poland, for example, according to Reinhardt Heydrich's order of 21 September 1939, Jews were expelled from their homes in larger numbers.[21] Yet they were directed to large Jewish communities that had some infrastructure and a social tradition to accommodate them. The situation in a city like Warsaw, where hundreds of thousands of refugees were concentrated, was awful, and when the ghetto was established it became even worse. But even under these dreadful conditions the death toll was 12–15 percent; in Transnistria, the death toll reached 30–50 percent during the first winter. The only comparable case were the deportation to Lublin of Jews from Czechoslovakia, Austria, and Germany in the fall of 1939, but this was smaller in scale and lasted for only a few months.[22]

Everyday Life in the Ghettos and Camps

The nearly two and a half years of the deportees' sojourn in Transnistria can be divided into three periods. The first, from the fall of 1941 until the spring of 1942, was the most difficult time for all the deportees, and more then a third of them perished. The second period lasted from the summer of 1942 to the spring of 1943. During this time internal organization developed and became more efficient; the deportees developed some kind of living and working capacity. Help from the Romanian Jewish community arrived more regularly, and the political interests of the Romanians started to shift. The third period, from the summer of 1943 until March 1944, when the Soviets returned, was more hopeful but very dangerous. Retreat brought German soldiers back through the region. They attacked Jews in the ghettos and camps and caused many casualties.[23] On the other hand, the plans to return orphans and other groups of people to Romania were more successful. Therefore any description of the life in the 117 ghettos and camps should take into account these periods as well as the many different situations which prevailed in the numerous ghettos and camps.

For the individual, everyday life was mainly dependent on external forces—Decrees No. 23 and 2927, and the capricious nature of the local authorities. However, internal factors were also very important in shaping the fate of the individual. These depended on the individual's personality as well as the possibility of transforming the "colonie" into a Jewish community. To achieve this transformation a sense of belonging and a strong feeling of identification with the group were needed.

The patterns and structure of the community of the deportees hardly resembled their previous communities. Their life now was completely different from the one they led before, but past experience certainly helped in their attempts to organize some community life. Having an accepted leader who enjoyed some authority or was endowed with charisma improved their situation. A leader who was able to adapt, improvise, and get aid and better conditions for the people was a critical factor in the struggle for survival.

The endeavors of Dr. Meir Teich, the head of the Suceava community, illustrate this proposition. When Dr. Teich learned from the mayor of his town about the coming deportations, he began to prepare his community for the unknown. He tried to get as much information as possible about the route and inquired how to ease the hardships of the coming days. He managed to get transportation for his people and saved them from the deadly marches. He got permission to stay for a while in Moghilev and found places to stay in. He preceded his people and reached the city of Sargorod, where their ghetto was to be organized, a few days earlier then the group, which enabled him to prepare some accommodation for them. Dr. Teich was not the only example.[24]

Naturally, people of this kind became heads of the communities, not through a vote, but as a consequence of the situation. But in many small places heads of ghettos were appointed by the prefect or mayor of the town, and there were cases when these people served their superiors rather than their own people.[25] The position of head of the community created a great number of practical and ethical problems. We already referred to the formal task of the head of the community and the committee that worked with him, namely to deliver the required number of workers for forced labor. Most people tried to avoid the work, which was very difficult and paid poorly if at all. In most cases the sites of forced labor were far from the ghetto and the workers lived in harsh conditions. Some forced labor sites were under German supervision, and many of the workers there were murdered after the assigned work was completed.

In this respect, the task of the head of the community resembled that of the Judenräte in the ghettos of Eastern Europe before the deportations to death camps. Many moral issues these Jewish leaders had to face were similar. Since the required number of workers had to be provided, regulations for enrollment and exemption from forced labor had to be established. In some ghettos very strict egalitarian regulations were set for a fair participation in this labor force. However, there were always exceptions, and implementation of the rules created a great deal of resentment among the members of the community.[26] Indeed, this issue emphasized more than others the inequality in the community, as a network of connections was an extremely important factor in defining one's position in the community. A very small number of people who had some means were able to buy themselves out of forced labor. But the majority were poor, and the little food they earned by their work was their only means of survival. People who had close ties with the head of the community or some members of the committee were often able to get easier work, in administration, or in the aid services. In Sargorod, Moghilev, and some other ghettos, the townsfolk of the head of the ghetto were usually the members of the committee and held the central positions. In many cases they were even his closest relatives or personal friends. Conflicts between different groups and complaints of abuse of position were voiced at the time and in later testimonies.[27]

The first steps in self-organization were structured according to the home communities. The help was not centralized and groups of deportees who managed to bring with them money or jewelry were better equipped to help the poor in their midst. The people that generally were in a relatively better position were from southern Bukovina and Dorohoi. They were the first to get organized and establish aid services. Dr. Teich reported that he collected 3,500,000 lei from his people by deducting 2–10 percent from each person who engaged his services to transfer money (which was illegal). This became a fund for all kinds of emergencies. Similar stories were told about the leaders in the ghetto of Moghilev, where the main figure of the ghetto was a prominent member of the community in Radautz, engineer Siegfried Jaegendorf.[28] Later the population of the ghetto was taxed by the committee.

Thus we find in Moghilev, Sargorod, Djurin, and other places, substantial differences between groups of deportees. These factors indicated a society in which the center was the group of people who could accommodate themselves to the new conditions. They had some means to influence external authorities and the initiative to carry out ideas for projects of work and aid. A network of connections placed the rest of the community accordingly, close to the center or further toward the periphery.[29] Nevertheless, those in the center were interested in helping the community for a number of reasons, for example, avoiding the spread of diseases like typhus and keeping on hand a substantial number of people to supply the demand for workers. Yet the Jewish tradition of self-help and Zedakah (charity), and a deep feeling of Jewish identity, were major motivations for the aid programs. As these efforts progressed, the services were no longer distributed in the framework of the home community, but became "universal." Still, the importance of the network of connections did not disappear. In most ghettos the committees established some kind of social help services, food kitchens (usually called canteens), medical clinics, homes for the elderly, and orphanages.[30] In some of the ghettos the committees established cooperatives—shops where certain products were sold. Actually, they were used to conceal a major source of income for the community: goods that were sent by the aid committee in Bucharest were sold to the Ukrainians, and the profits were used to support the social institutions.[31] Although the endeavors to initiate this aid started at the end of 1941, it only developed into a more orderly system in the spring and summer of 1942. A great number of the weaker people perished during that winter due to the cold, hunger, and typhus. Dr. Teich reported that in the epidemic of that winter his community lost 1,400 out of 7,000 people (this total of 7,000 included 1,800 local Jews), that is, 20 percent of the community. In other places the toll was even higher.[32]

The committees and the heads of the ghettos were controlling life from another aspect. The Romanians were not interested in the internal community life of the Jews but did impose general prohibitions on leaving the ghetto and moving around, and on having contacts with people (including family members) in other ghettos and camps. There was a ban on all communications (letters, parcels, newspapers, etc.). Nevertheless, contacts with Bucharest were maintained illegally by the committees and individual persons through the services of army personnel and businessmen, who profited well from serving as couriers. Young people in the ghettos created their own newspapers and kept up some kind of Zionist political activities, to keep alive some manifestation of the past and overcome their feelings of loneliness and despair. We have evidence of this from the ghettos of Djurin and Sargorod, and oral testimonies attest to their existence in other ghettos also.

A newspaper named *Courier* appeared in Djurin from April to September 1943. It was distributed clandestinely from house to house, and the readers were asked to destroy the last copy. Essays, poems, and descriptions of daily life were painstakingly copied by hand, and even caricatures and puzzles were included in the issues. Of the copies that were smuggled to Bucharest, six survived. Criticism of the Romanians was only hinted at in short stories and anecdotes, but the references were obvious to the readers. Songs and rhymes related to the mixture of Jews in the ghetto. Solemn lines told about the mothers who lost their children, the hunger that followed many a day and night, and the fate of those who did not have even the barest minimum for survival. However, the paper, which was written, edited, and distributed by young people, displayed some optimism and hope. Spring gave the opportunity to express longings for love; hardships were not allowed to cancel out the beauty of nature. In addition, the paper carried some serious articles on the composition of the population of the ghetto in Djurin and its social problems. It was not a real community, claimed one article, but a fictitious one. Another topic was the role of the ghetto police, who had to hand over workers to the gendarmerie. The paper expressed deep sorrow over the matter, yet with a considerable amount of understanding and even sympathy. Some of the committee members strongly objected to the whole idea of the paper. They were afraid of the consequences, if the authorities found out. The head of the community tried to stop the paper, but failed. Its means of distribution were concealed even from the committee. Unfortunately, the paper was detected by the gendarmerie; only by paying a "fat bribe" did the head of the committee manage to secure the Romanian gendarmes' silence. Thus the adventure of the paper came to an end.[33]

Another activity that seemed dangerous to the committee and its head were the Zionists' youth movements. The account of this activity came from Sargorod, where the *Noa'r Hazioni* (Zionist Youth) managed to keep their movement alive throughout the years of the ghetto. They too issued a paper, mostly for the members of the movement, and as Zionists they tried to recruit other young people to join their movement. An important part of their efforts was devoted to educating the orphans and giving these poor souls some hope. The theme was *Aliyah* (immigration) to *Erezt Israel*. In the beginning they received the support of the committee and especially of Dr. Teich. But when the youths started to criticize members of the committee, tension developed and the latter's attitude became ambivalent.[34]

The individual in the ghettos and camps was constantly on his guard: he had to be careful lest he be deported; he had to avoid, if possible, the hard conditions of forced labor, and yet he had to work in order to get food and to avoid unnecessary clashes with the authorities, both non-Jewish and Jewish. It is true that his life was regulated by many rules and hardships, but it is also true that personality and will power, as well as ability to adapt, were of the utmost importance for survival.

In the small ghettos and camps, where the aid and community support were weaker, the character of each individual counted even more. Many of the testimonies tell how people managed to save themselves, what means they used, what dangers they avoided. The need for workers in the villages during the summers of 1942 and 1943 opened up the chance to work for food under more tolerable conditions.[35]

In general, the initiative of small groups and individuals to evade regulation and try to move from the worst conditions in camps and ghettos to ones that were slightly better, increased chances of survival in Transnistria. Thanks to the fact that Romanian authorities could be bribed extensively and that from the fall of 1943 the change in the political situation reached Transnistria too, those who made it through the winter of 1943 had more chances to be saved. From the end of 1942 the Romanians were more reluctant to hand over Jews to the Germans, either for forced labor or for killing.

The Aid of the Committee in Bucharest

The description of the rescue efforts, assistance, and relief sent to Transnistria are part of the history of Romanian Jewry no less than the history of the deportees in Transnistria. The Romanian Jewish community was the only one in Europe that organized a rescue program on such a scale. It was initiated by the special Aid Committee, technically part of the Center of Romanian Jews (Centrala Evereiol din Romania), but in fact a section of an illegal Jewish coordinating council, established by the most prominent Jewish personalities in Romania, among them Filderman, Wilhelm Fisher, Beno Benvenisti of the Zionist movement, Rabbi Safran, and many others.[36] These people did their best to foil the Nazi plan to deport Romanian Jewry to the East, and also to relieve the economic deprivation of the Jewish community. The aid to the deportees in Transnistria was an integral part of the work of this council. Politically, the members of the council aimed at forcing the Romanian government to change their policy toward the deportees and return them to Romania. In these efforts they contacted Jewish international organizations (such as the World Jewish Congress, the Joint Distribution Committee, the World Zionist Organization) and the International Red Cross, offering to resettle the deportees in Palestine after their return to Romania. They also used to their advantage the growing ambivalence of the Romanian public and government about the alliance with the Nazis.[37] The legal aspect of their struggle was handled by Filderman, who pointed out the illegality of the steps taken against the Jews; Rabbi Safran and his colleagues stressed the moral aspect, in an attempt to get the support of the church, of Antonescu's wife, and Queen Helena of Romania, arguing that the inhumane actions against the Jews contradicted the Christian and Romanian tradition. Of course, the urgent necessity of providing immediate material assistance in order to reduce the death toll and the general suffering was presented as the first responsibility of all concerned.

When the first information about the massacres and pogroms reached Bucharest, appeals to help the Jews afflicted by the atrocities of the war, were addressed to Ion Antonescu. Unfortunately, his first positive answer was given only in December 1941, when the large wave of deportations was coming to an end. It took three more months for Alexianu, the leader of Transnistria, to agree to the aid program. The real intentions of the government were then reflected in the bureaucratic obstacles they put up when the program began. Large sums of money sent via the Romanian Central Bank (at the extremely low rate of exchange of 60 lei per 1 RKKS) did not reach their destination. The same happened with money sent illegally, via couriers who received 10–15 percent of the amount they transported. It was risky to use such channels to pass money, since both senders and receivers were at the mercy of the couriers. Handling the aid in this way encouraged corruption, not only on the part of the Romanians, but also among Jewish leaders. Many complaints were voiced that heads and members of committees abused their privileges and used the money for their own ends. It is difficult to know how much money actually reached the Jewish communities.[38]

A substantial change in the aid program occurred during 1943, after the first delegation of Romanian Jews, headed by Fred Saraga, visited Transnistria in December 1942. The official aim of the delegation was to explore ways to improve the distribution of aid and its use. The delegates wanted to establish direct contacts with the deportees and their leaders, and to find out at first hand what their needs were and the best ways to fulfill them.[39] The work of the delegation was very important. It helped to improve the distribution of aid by the Romanian authorities and by the Jewish heads of communities. The amounts of money and goods sent to Transnistria increased, and the direct contacts between the delegates and the deportees raised the hopes and spirits of many; they felt they were not completely deserted.

During the years aid transferred by the committee to Transnistria amounted to half a billion lei in money and goods (this corresponds to some U.S. $700,000 at the rate of exchange in 1943).[40] By any account, this was a substantial effort on the part of Romanian Jewry.

From the summer of 1943 the plans to return certain groups of deportees from Transnistria started to materialize. The difficulties of organizing the reevacuation were immense. The lack of precise information about many of the deportees, the advancing Soviet forces, and the reluctance of the Nazis posed many dangers. Yet the plan was implemented. Some 1,000 orphans were among the evacuees, some of whom would join the illegal voyages to Palestine that were conducted by the delegation of the Yishuv.[41] The case of Transnistrian deportees was also unique in this respect. They were evacuated when the Nazis were still in power and while in other areas of their domination the killing was continuing with full force.

Conclusion

The case of Transnistria illustrates the influence of the "Final solution" on traditional anti-Semitism as reflected in Romanian policy whereby removing the Jews became a central part of a radical nationalistic strategy. The activities of the Einsatzgruppen in the Soviet-occupied territories prompted and legitimated this policy, which Romanian leaders defined in terms of national interest and justified by reference to the Jews' response to the Soviet takeover in the summer of 1940.

The relatively high number of survivors in Transnistria as compared to German-occupied territories demonstrates that, notwithstanding harsh conditions, brutality, and inhuman behavior, the lack of a systematic plan of extermination permitted the survival of about 40 percent of the Jews.

Self-help and aid programs were another important factor. Jewish self-organization in Transnistria eased the life of the deportees and contributed considerably to their chances of survival. At the same time, however, it revealed the social tensions in the community and the vulnerability of the individual who lacked a connection to the central leadership or the means to bribe the authorities. Similar situations occurred within many Jewish communities throughout occupied Europe. In Transnistria, as in other Jewish communities, Zionist youth movements were a major factor in mobilizing educational activities, but they were dependent on the cooperation of the community leadership in taking care of thousands of orphans in children's homes. Finally, by introducing emigration to Palestine as a feasible proposition, they provided encouragement and hope (indeed, orphans from Transnistria left for Palestine in the spring and summer of 1944).

Notes

I would like to thank my research assistant, Mr. Raphael Julius, for his help.

1. Romania lost Bessarabia and Bukovina to the Soviets on 28 June 1940. Northern Transylvania was lost to Hungary on 30 August 1940, and on 12 September of the same year southern Dorudja was taken by the Bulgarians. All this was according to an agreement between Germany and its allies. Martin Broszat, "Das Dritte Reich und die Rumänische Judenpolitik," *Gutachten des Instituts für Zeitgeschichte* (Munich: Institut für Zeitgeschichte, 1958), pp. 102–83.

2. Raul Hilberg, *The Destruction of European Jews* (Chicago: Quadrangle Books, 1967), pp. 199–201, 492–93 (hereafter: Hilberg 1967).

3. Jean Ancel, "Plans for the Destruction of the Romanian Jews and their Discontinuation in the Light of Documentary Evidence (July–October 1942)," *Yad Vashem Studies,* vol. 16 (Jerusalem, 1984), pp. 381–420.

4. Alexander Dallin, *Odessa, 1941–1944: A Case Study of Soviet Territory Under Foreign Rule* (Los Angeles: The RAND Corporation, 1957), pp. 45–109 (hereafter: Dallin 1957).

5. Theodore Lavi, ed., *Pinkas Kehilot Romania* (Hebrew) (Book of Romanian Community) (Jerusalem: Yad Vashem, 1970), pp. 368–69 (hereafter: *Pinkas* 1970).

6. It is very difficult to arrive at a credible number of Jews murdered by the Einsatzgruppe D, which had only some 400 people and did not have enough time to accomplish its task and make Transnistria *Judenrein*. The estimate is that some 50,000 to 70,000 Jews were murdered during this time, the majority by the

Einsatzgruppen and the rest by Romanians and local people, among them the Volksdeutsche. In December 1941 a report of Einsatzgruppe D summed up the number of victims as 54,696. See ibid.; also, Samuel Ben Zion, *Yeladim Yehudim Bitransnistria Bitkufat Hashoah* (Hebrew) (Jewish Children in Transnistria During the Holocaust) (Jerusalem: Yad Vashem and Haifa University, 1990), p. 63 (hereafter: Ben Zion 1990).

7. Jean Ancel, "The Romanian Way of Solving the Jewish Problem in Bessarabia and Bukovina June–July 1941," *Yad Vashem Studies*, vol. 19 (Jerusalem, 1988), pp. 187–232 (hereafter: Ancel, *Studies* 19, 1988). Ancel sees this force as a Romanian version of the Einsatzgruppen.

8. VOMI (Reference Office for Racial Germans) was created in 1936 by Rudolf Hess on order of Hitler. It was responsible for coordinating all the party and state work concerning Germans abroad. It became part of the SS a year later. After the war started, VOMI's importance and power grew in all fields of racial policy, and it developed into a major SS power center. Heinz Hoehne, *The Order of the Death's Head: The Story of Hitler's S.S.* (London: Secker & Warburg, 1969), pp. 276–77.

9. Dallin 1957, pp. 48–54.

10. The description of the events in Odessa and the south of Transnistria is based on *Pinkas* 1970, pp. 390–93; Dallin 1957, pp. 79–88; Julius J. Fisher, *Transnistria: the Forgotten Cemetery* (South Brunswick, London: Thomas Yoseloff Ltd., 1969), pp. 119–26.

11. Dallin 1957, pp. xi-xii, 105–9.

12. Ancel, *Studies* 19, 1988, pp. 207–15.

13. For the numbers and dates, see *Pinkas* 1970, p. 356.

14. Matatias Carp, *Transnistria le'ben, leiden un umkuft fon Bessarabise, Bukoviner, un Rumanishe yeden* (Yiddish) (Transnistria, the Life, Suffering and Death of the Jews of Bessarabia, Bukovina, and Romania) (Buenos Aires: St. Martin, 1950) (hereafter: Carp 1950). This is one example of such a description.

15. The case of the Jews of Cernauti is an example of refusal of a Romanian major to obey the killing orders. Hilberg 1967, p. 200; Ben Zion, 1990, pp. 78–79.

16. For a translation of the decree see Avigdor Shachan, *Bakfor Halohet* (Hebrew) (Burning Ice, The Ghettos of Transnistria), (Tel Aviv: Beit Lohamie Haggetaot Hakibbutz Hameuhad, 1990), Appendix, pp. 382–83 (hereafter Shachan 1990). On 7 December 1942 another decree, No. 2927, ordered directly all Jews aged 12 to 60 to participate in forced labor. Meir Teich, "The Jewish Autonomy in the Ghetto of Sergorod (Transnistria)," *Yad Vashem Studies*, vol. 2 (Jerusalem, 1958), pp. 203–33 (hereafter: Teich 1958).

17. *Pinkas* 1970, pp. 359–60.

18. Shachan 1990, Appendix, pp. 377–80.

19. Carp 1950, pp. 212–306; Shachan 1990, pp. 150–65.

20. A great number of reports were sent to Jewish organizations through Geneva and Istanbul and the International Red Cross. The Filderman Archive in Yad Vashem Archive (YSA) holds many records on Transnistria. So do the Jaegendorf collection in YSA and the Carp collection in Bessarabia House in Tel-Aviv, a division of YSA. More than 150 oral testimonies were collected in YSA.

21. Hilberg 1967, pp. 127–28.

22. The plan to expel Jews to Lublin was part of a broad plan to concentrate and isolate the Jewish population in a reservation in the Nisko–Lublin area of Poland. The Nazi rationale of the plan was that, if isolated, the Jews, being parasites, would deteriorate physically, which would bring about "natural" liquidation. Two groups of deportees were sent from Vienna in 1939, one on 20 October (912 people) and a second on 26 October (672 people). A transport of deportees from Czechoslovakia was sent on 18 October (1,000 people). The deportations ceased at the end of October, as a result of organizational problems encountered by the German side.

23. *Pinkas* 1970 pp. 440–41, the case of Smerinca; pp. 443–51, the case of Tulcin.

24. Teich 1958.

25. *Pinkas* 1970, pp. 442–44; the case of Hrinovca, p. 441, the case of Adolf Herschman in Smerinca.

26. Teich 1958; Shraga Yesuhrun, *Hahitargenut haa'zmit shel yehudie Bukovina begeto Moghilev* (Hebrew) (Self-Organization of the Jews of Bukovina in the ghetto of Moghilev), master's dissertation, University of Haifa 1979 (hereafter: Yeshurun 1979).

27. Fred Saraga, 31 January 1943, "Offizieller Bericht der Jüdischen Commission die in Transnistria war" (The Official Report of the Committee That Visited Transnistria), YSA, M20/104 (hereafter: Saraga report).

28. Yeshurun 1979, p. 38.

29. For a detailed account of the ghettos and camps, see *Pinkas* 1970, pp. 389–519. Other important sources are the Izkor books (Memorial Books) of the communities.

30. Yeshurun 1979, pp. 38–61, 79–85.

31. The testimony of Mr. Moshe Katz of Djurin and a detailed description of all the institutions and activities of the committee, in Jean Ancel, ed., *Documents Concerning the Fate of Romanian Jewry During the Holocaust*, published in the 1980s by the Beate Klarsfeld Foundation (New York) in twelve volumes, pp. 527–34; (hereafter: Ancel *Documents); Memoirs of Siegfried Jaegendorf*, YVA P9/3, unpublished; Teich 1958, pp. 216–18, 226–27.

32. Teich 1958, pp. 215–18.

33. Dora Litani, "Iton Mahatarti Be Transnistria" (Hebrew) ("An Underground Newspaper in Transnistria"), *Yediot Yad Vashem* 31 (31 December 1963), pp. 40–43; Leor Kunshtatd, "Parashat haiav shel iton mahatarti bemahaneh haricuz Djurin" (Hebrew) ("The Story of an Underground Newspaper in the Concentration Camp in Djurin"), *Hadoar* (weekly of the Histadrut in the USA), New York (April 1975), no. 2, pp. 313–14.

34. Moshe Sherff, "Ken Sargorod" (Hebrew) ("The Youth Movement in Sargorod"), *Masuah* 4 (April 1976), pp. 212–14; Izhak Arzti (Herzig), "Zichronot" (Hebrew) ("Memoirs"), *Masuah* 1 (1973), pp. 126–28.

35. *Behold the Children of Our Time: Case Histories of Youth Aliyah Trainees Who Arrived in Palestine from the Deportation Camps in Transnistria in 1944* (London, 1945), pp. 1–33.

36. In December 1941, the Union of Jewish Communities, headed by W. Filderman, was dissolved by the government and a version of a Jewish Judenräte

was established, headed by a Jewish convert, Nandor Ghingold. This was the notorious *Centrala* hated and distrusted by the Jews. In a few committees of the *Centrala* some of the prominent Jewish leaders continued to serve, hoping to be able in this way to assist the community. One of these committees was the aid committee for Transnistria headed by Fred Saraga. It kept its autonomy within the framework of the *Centrala* and thus earned the appreciation and trust of the Jewish community. Saraga was a member of an illegal council of a Romanian rescue committee. Theodore Lavi, *Yahadut Rumania Bemavak a' l Hazalatah* (Hebrew) (Romanian Jewry's Struggle for Life) (Jerusalem: Yad Vashem, 1965); Yehuda Bauer, *American Jewry and the Holocaust, The American Joint Distribution Committee 1939–1945* (Detroit: Wayne State University Press, 1981), pp. 343–49 (hereafter: Bauer, 1981).

37. Ancel 1985; National Archive (NAR) Ref. 871.4016/271 to the Secretary of State from Franklin Mott Gunter, the legation in Bucharest, 19 August 1941; ibid., Ref. 871.4016/287, F.M. Gunter to the State Department, 4 November 1941. Enclosed are translations of four letters sent to Filderman from I. Antonescu, 9, 11, 25 October and 4 November 1941 about the deportations to Ukraine (Transnistria); a translation of a letter from Antonescu to Filderman, 19 October 1941; and a translation of a decree obliging the Jews to contribute to the stockpiling of clothing for the public interest, October 1941. All these materials were handed to the American legation by Filderman. Printed in Ancel, *Documents,* Vol. III, pp. 334–58.

38. Haganah Archive 14/67 report from Romania–Transnistria, Summer 1943; Moreshet Archive D.1.743 Jancu Skarlett (member of Hashomer Hatza'ir youth movement in Romania) to Bader, June 14, 1943; YVA M20/104 (Silberschein Collection) *Augenzeugenbericht* (German) (Eyewitness Report) beginning of October 1942; ibid., M20/102, *Die Hilfsaktion für die Transnitrien Deportierten Juden* (German) (The Aid to the Jewish Deportees to Transnistria) undated, but must be in the winter of 1943.

39. Saraga report.

40. Bauer 1981, pp. 345.

41. Dalia Ofer, *Escaping the Holocaust: Illegal Immigration to the Land of Israel 1939–1944* (New York: Oxford University Press, 1990), pp. 238–66.

The Jewish Community in the Soviet-Annexed Territories on the Eve of the Holocaust

A Social Scientist's View

JAN GROSS

In this paper I will analyze a cliché, which in its most succinct form may be stated as follows: Jews welcomed the Soviet occupation of southeastern Poland in 1939 and willingly collaborated with the Communist administration set up in these territories.[1] This summary account emerged and found a receptive audience during the war years. Widely shared in the Polish society at the time, it was never subsequently challenged by historiography. It thus stands out as an example of either extraordinary self-reflective lucidity in a society under occupation or else of an uncritical dullness on the part of historians who simply incorporated what was believed at the time into their interpretations.

That Jews' compliant behavior and favored status in the Soviet zone of occupation was the reason for widespread hostility of the Polish population toward Jews during and after the war also remains a cliché of contemporary Polish historiography. Hence, we have here a suitable subject matter for students of the Holocaust, because what broad segments of the Polish society thought about the Jews during the war was a crucial factor determining the likelihood of survival of Jews hiding outside the ghettos.

The stereotype of Jewish behavior under the Soviet occupation is made up of two components. First, Jews are reported to have enthusi-

astically welcomed occupation of southeastern Poland by the Red
Army. Second, Jews are known to have developed particularly good
relationships with the Soviets, as evidenced by their collaboration in
the local administration and the apparatus of coercion. One ought to
note at the outset that in their initial welcome of the Red Army and
subsequent collaboration, Jews' behavior, if not motivation, was indis-
tinguishable from that of other "minorities" (the Ukrainian population,
for example), which should, at least, have removed the odium of special rapport with the Soviet authorities. But, more importantly, the
stereotype ought to be scrutinized in the light of available evidence,
since the historical record supports a more nuanced picture. One might
even argue that on balance the record reveals the meaning of the Jewish experience to have been opposite of what the stereotype conveys.
For not only does Jewish behavior and rapport with the Soviets change
over time, and must also be differentiated by social category, but one
could even justifiably contend that Jews suffered *more* than other ethnic groups as a result of sovietization of southeastern Poland and that
they uniquely and overtly manifested hostility toward the Soviet regime.

Before the war Jews made up around 9 percent of the total resident
population in the territories later occupied by the Red Army. They
were scattered all over the area, amounting to no more than 5.2 percent
in Wilno voivodeship and reaching the high of 12 percent in Bialystok
voivodeship. Being settled predominantly in urban areas, however,
they were a more visible minority than these numbers would suggest.
If one adds to these figures some 250,000–350,000 refugees who
flocked into this territory from western and central Poland, we end up
with 1.4–1.5 million Jews living there in 1939–41, roughly 11 percent
of the total population.[2] The number of Jews in urban centers—the
largest cities, such as Lwow, Bialystok, or Wilno, for example—is
reported to have doubled within a month or two following the outbreak
of the war.

The early period following the Red Army's entry into Poland was
full of confusion. Civil war was picking up throughout the countryside.
The eastern part of Poland was swarming with refugees, as well as
conscripts and military detachments in more or less futile pursuit of
points of mobilization, concentration, evacuation, or simply food.
Thus, while Poland was at war with Germany on the western front,
what the eastern half of Poland experienced in late September 1939

was not nearly as clear-cut and unambiguous. If one is to give a proper account of the behavior and motivation of the people living there, this fundamental lack of clarity must be taken into consideration, yet it is missing from the subsequent historiography of the period.

In 1939 the Polish government and military were neither envisioning nor prepared to fight a war with the Soviet Union. Moreover, neither in September 1939 nor at anytime thereafter was Poland officially at war with the USSR. Indeed, the Supreme Commander, when informed on 17 September about the Red Army's incursion into the Polish territory, and just before evacuating himself across the Romanian border, issued orders not to oppose the Soviets (which made no difference, since communications among the scattered Polish detachments were already broken). Local Polish authorities, to the extent that they were still in place, and officers, to the extent that they retained command over various detachments, as often as not issued orders or instructions to greet and welcome entering Soviet units.[3]

To compound the confusion, it is by no means clear that the Red Army soldiers knew the general purpose of their mission. Many passing Soviet units waved and otherwise demonstrated friendly intent. Was this merely a deception that any reasonable person ought to have seen through? If so, many did not.

All over the Ukrainian countryside groups of peasants hoisted flags in the blue and yellow Ukrainian national colors in joyful celebration of the long-awaited collapse of the Polish state.[4] Occasionally a mixed crowd with church banners greeted Red Army units singing "in the confusing elation communist songs mixed with religious hymns."[5] The colors, songs, and inscriptions that one would encounter in these scenes of welcome were a confused mixture, as were the people who lined the roads. Where do the Jews fit in this situation? My first and probably the most adequate answer to this question would be: they fit into the general confusion.

The friendly reception of the Red Army detachments entering the villages, hamlets, and towns of western Ukraine and western Belorussia is a well-established fact. The cheering groups were predominantly composed of minority youth.[6] In many instances—for example, when the Germans were evacuating an area they had conquered but which the Soviets were to occupy according to the Ribbentrop–Molotov agreement—such welcoming ceremonies were organized on explicit instructions and people were forced to attend.[7] Yet we have no clear evidence by which to judge the size of the welcoming groups. We read repeatedly that the majority of local residents were fearful and suspicious of the Red Army and, invariably, that it was youth one could see cheering in the streets. Undoubtedly not more than a small fraction of the local population showed up on these occasions; but how many energetic enthusiasts does it take to make a lasting impression on witnesses eager to see confirmation of a long-held prejudice?

But what Poles and Ukrainians report, often with biting irony, the Jews do not deny: "Jews greeted the Soviet army with joy. The young people were spending days and evenings with the soldiers." "Jews received incoming Russians enthusiastically, and they [the Russians] also trusted them [the Jews]." "The first days of the Bolsheviks' presence were very nice. People went out into the streets, kept looking over tanks, and children walked after the soldiers."[8]

What could have been the motivation of the young Jews in these crowds? Undoubtedly there were Communist sympathizers among them.[9] There were some young Zionists in the streets as well.[10] But left-wing and other secular ideologies had relatively few local adherents and were not representative of the spiritual or mental outlook predominant among the shtetl Jews. The reasons that motivated people to respond to the Soviet presence one way or another were for the most part opportunistic. They were grounded less, I believe, in preconceived ideological notions than in immediate experiences and expectations of what might have happened had the Soviets not arrived.

It took a good many days before the Red Army would show the flag in the outlying areas. But it was there that the bulk of the population of this backward half of a relatively underdeveloped European country lived at the time. Wherever ethnic strife filled the power vacuum created in the interim period, a local minority (whatever that minority happened to be in a given place) might suffer brutal persecution at the hands of its neighbors.[11] Many residents of these backwaters—including Polish military settlers or landowners, who were the most exposed—expressed relief at the first sight of the Soviet military or fled into neighboring towns where the Soviets had already established their presence.[12] In the absence of landowners, Jews provided a second best target for *jacquerie,* and as peasant crowds converged on the towns of western Ukraine and western Belorussia they had innumerable shtetls to chose from.[13] As always in the diaspora, only a central authority could protect Jews from the surrounding population.

Two further points need to be made. As justification for its invasion of Poland, the Soviet government announced that it was compelled to enter Polish territory in order to protect interests of national minorities, specifically the Ukrainians and the Belorussians. This pretense at national liberation was of course but a fig leaf deployed to cover Soviet imperial ambitions. Yet initial Soviet policies (eradication of Polish statehood and class war against the Polish *pany,* for instance) as well as a variety of steps taken to follow up on the promise of national liberation (immediate promotion of local languages into the public sphere, for example) created a general atmosphere of ethnic emancipation. People belonging to ethnic minorities—and one should be mindful that these so-called minorities were a significant majority in the Soviet-occupied territories—lost the humiliating sense of being second-class citizens. One woman recalled a *bon mot* from the period which turned around a prewar Polish nationalistic slogan: "You wanted Poland without Jews, so now you have Jews without Poland."[14]

It took some time for most Jews to recognize that they had ceased to be citizens altogether, that vis-à-vis the Soviet authority they had no rights at all. At the beginning what mattered above all was the newly introduced equality, and with it a restored sense of personal dignity. I will return to this theme of emancipation, for I think it has an interesting double-edged aspect in the experience of young Jews. For now let us simply note that for the entire Jewish community this was an emancipation not solely from the discriminatory policies of the prewar Polish administration but also from the brutalities Jewish communities were suffering at the hands of the invading Germans. This is the second point that ought to be made forcefully.

Jews had been brutalized by invading Germans in September 1939, and awareness of this harsh treatment had spread among Jews in southeastern Poland by the time of the Soviet invasion.[15] How widespread this knowledge was by the third and fourth weeks of September I cannot tell precisely. But rumors travel faster than invading armies; they precede them, and if anything, in tales of *Greuelgeschichte* they exaggerate fears, or hopes, as the case may be. Even more to the point, however, Jews had experience of German treatment in a sizable chunk of the territories eventually occupied by the Red Army because the Wehrmacht had been there first. During the following months a steady trickle of horror stories reached the Jewish community through refugee reports.

Jews, naturally, were not the only people on the move during that autumn. Hundreds of thousands, perhaps millions, had been displaced by war. But the Jewish experience was again unique in its severity, especially in the vicinity of the makeshift border separating the German and the Soviet zones of occupation. Entire Jewish communities—men, women, and children—were uprooted by the Germans and driven eastward, over the river, into the Soviet zone, where as often as not they were denied entry. They would then linger for days in a no-man's-land, abused, pillaged, raped, shot at, until they bought their way in or got through by stealth or good luck.[16]

From the very beginning of World War II, Jews were extremely vulnerable. They sensed and experienced this vulnerability and responded accordingly. They were particularly endangered by the absence of central authority and by the German presence. Soviet occupation of southeastern Poland held both in abeyance. The sense of relief that was initially detectable in the Jewish community (and I have to caution that we have no evidence to judge how widespread it was, as the older generation had vivid memories of the mayhem in these areas after the October Revolution and during the 1920 Polish–Bolshevik war) at the prospect of Soviet administration must therefore be properly contextualized: the only alternative to the Soviet occupation at the time was the establishment of German administration, not the continuation of the Polish statehood.

I do not know any systematic body of evidence[17] that would support claims of massive Jewish participation in the Soviet administration. There is, on the other hand, good evidence to indicate that Jews *were not,* as a rule, involved in the Soviet-sponsored apparatus of enforcement in the villages where the vast majority of the population lived at the time in these territories. We know scores of names of village committee members and the personnel of rural militias, and Jews are only infrequently mentioned among them.[18] We also know that the higher echelons of local Soviet administration—at the county (raion), voivodeship (oblast), or city level—were staffed by functionaries brought in from the east. I seriously doubt that the intermediate administrative apparatus was predominantly Jewish.

What about the shared memory of Jews lending a helping hand to the Soviet invader? Well, there were Jews in the Soviet administrative apparatus, in the local militia, and in the secret police. And there is no reason to think that they would have been less rude or abusive than any

other such Soviet functionary. But that they were remembered so viv-
idly and with such scorn does not tell us necessarily that Jews were
massively involved in collaboration. Rather, I think, it is a reflection of
how unseemly, how jarring, how offensive it was to see a Jew in a
position of authority. That is why this remembrance was so deeply
engraved. And it was also an easy memory to carry about these exceedingly confusing times, because it simplified matters and comfort-
ably rested on the paradigmatic association between communism and
Jews *(zydokomuna)* in Polish public opinion.[19] I conclude, therefore,
that claims concerning Jewish collaborationism draw on im-
pressionistic evidence and neglect an inherently complex and confusing reality of the Soviet occupation. When they are used rhetorically as
a *pars pro toto*, allegedly to capture the meaning of the entire Jewish
experience under the Soviet occupation, then they are simply wrong
and can be refuted by solid evidence.

In the first place, one reads in the testimonies of unsympathetic
witnesses that national minorities (Ukrainians, Jews, Belorussians)
soon learned their lesson, and but a few months into the Soviet occupation grew nostalgic for Poland. Standing alone, this would be important evidence difficult to reconcile with the image of Jewish
collaborationism. But even more significantly, this change of mood
was promptly followed by overt action in the face of two policies then
carried out by the Soviet authorities. Here we touch upon the second
misunderstanding about mutual relationships between Jews and the
Soviet authorities. Conventional narrative of those years glosses over
what in effect was Jewish resistance and Soviet repression of the Jews.

In the early spring of 1940 began a registration of the residents for
Soviet citizenship (a so-called "passportization")[20] or for transfer to
Germany (in accordance with one of the stipulations of the Soviet–
German pact). In the only well-documented manifestation of their
mass behavior under the Soviet occupation, Jews refused to take up
Soviet identity cards, and signed up in droves for repatriation into what
was by then the Generalgouvernement, a part of Poland occupied by
the Germans. "Never in my life have I seen such a determined resistance as when Soviet authorities wanted to force the Jews to accept
Soviet citizenship," recalls a witness to these events. "Their resistance
defies description."[21] We need not draw on archival material to document Jews' eagerness to get away from under the Soviet rule. Nikita
Khrushchev, who as first secretary of the Ukrainian Communist Party

toured Lwow in the company of the head of the Ukrainian NKVD, the infamous Ivan Serov, wrote in his memoirs: "There are long lines standing outside of the place where people register for permission to return to Polish territory. When I took a closer look, I was shocked to see that most of the people in line were members of the Jewish population. They were bribing the Gestapo agents to let them leave as soon as possible to return to their original homes."[22]

Whatever judgment we might be ready to pronounce with the benefit of hindsight (presumably, that this was collective insanity—an opinion some witnesses were lucid enough to articulate on the spot),[23] this was undeniably a collective manifestation of defiance, an open, public, rejection of the Soviet regime. And it was treated as such. In the arsenal of Soviet power's repressive measures, one of the most ferocious was forced deportation. This involved removal into some remote part of the Soviet interior of an entire category of the population, taking all who had been targeted—including children, the sickly, and the elderly, without exception. One of the four big deportations carried out by the Soviet authorities from southeastern Poland, the June 1940 deportation, was made up of refugees from the German-occupied part of the country. It was composed predominantly of those very Jews who had queued up for repatriation to the Generalgouvernement.

Jews were sent into forced settlement in other deportations as well. Statistics compiled in 1944 by the Polish Ministry of Foreign Affairs on the basis of 120,000 personal files from Polish Red Cross records in Teheran show that among Polish citizens who found themselves in Soviet interior (for the most part forcibly deported in 1940–41) 52 percent were ethnic Poles, 30 percent were Jewish, and 18 percent were Ukrainian and Belorussian.[24] Thus, the ratio of Jews in this group was roughly three times higher than their ratio in the total population of Soviet-occupied southeastern Poland. By that measure alone the Jews were far more heavily repressed than the Poles, whose ratio among the deportees was less than double their ratio in the total population of these territories. Whatever the imprecision and inadequacy of statistics (and those who have compiled them were the first to point out how inaccurate they must be), we may safely dismiss a view stipulating that Jews were beneficiaries of Soviet rule and enjoyed some special rapport with the Soviet authorities.

Ironically, these victims of deportations turned out to be the lucky ones. It is not the death rate (some 25–30 percent) but the survival rate

among them that is remarkable when compared with the all-out extermination of the Jewish population that managed to remain in western
Ukraine and western Belorussia. In retrospect, it would have been best
for the Jews if they all had been deported into the Soviet interior prior
to the outbreak of the Russo–German war. Had the Soviets implemented such a policy, it would not have been for love of Jews.

One final note belongs not to the history of the Holocaust but to the
tangled web of clichés on the subject matter of Polish–Jewish–Soviet
relations. Once the Polish Jews found themselves in the USSR they
could not get out. Of some 130,000 prewar Polish citizens who were
evacuated from the USSR by the Polish authorities, Jews numbered
about 8,000. They made up about 30 percent of the deportees but
about 6 percent of the evacuees.[25] So much for preferential treatment.

A third dimension of Jewish experience under the Soviet rule has
less to do with mental states, real or imputed sympathies, and police
measures, but is grounded in the tedious reality of everyday life. This
is the socioeconomic aspect of sovietization and how it affected the
Jews.

Soviet authorities instituted a new economic regime. In a series of
steps, property rights were effectively suspended. Although they
stopped short of collectivizing agriculture (the peasantry was put under
gradually more oppressive tax burden and property use restrictions),
the authorities abolished private property. Jews were the ethnic group
most affected by these measures, not because they owned so much, but
because so many Jews owned so little. In sociological terms, Jews
were an impoverished stratum of self-employed craftsmen and trades-
men. Consequently, abolition of private property touched them en
masse. They had no reserves to draw on, and were additionally burdened by claims for material assistance from vast numbers of destitute
Jewish refugees. Thus, although previously unavailable employment
opportunities in industry and administration opened up for Jews, as a
group they suffered material calamity under the Soviet regime.

Sovietization affected more than the material aspects of community
life; it also radically undermined what we would today call civil society. Indeed, community institutions folded up soon after the Soviet
authorities established themselves in southeastern Poland. Pinchuk
quotes numerous memorial books as well as Yad Vashem sources to
illustrate this process. In the words of an eyewitness from Luck: "community and social life of the local Jewish organizations stopped en-

tirely. With the entry of the Red Army nobody dared to call a meeting of an organization or institution. All community or national contacts from that day on went underground."[26] Of course, the situation varied considerably from one place to another since so much depended in the early months on the zeal of local enforcers. But over time the dissolution of all institutions supporting Jewish community life became universal.

As Soviet authorities promoted all-out secularization, synagogues and all other places of worship, irrespective of denomination, were closed up or placed under an enormous tax burden, which the already impoverished population could not sustain for long. Jewish religious life was additionally affected by a ban on official use of Hebrew. Yiddish, the language of the toiling masses, was promoted instead, but only up to a point.[27] The dissolution of the Kehillah undercut the material ability of a host of religious, educational, and social welfare organizations to function. Political parties dissolved or were banned, and their leaders and prominent members were arrested. Bundists and Zionists were hunted down with particular diligence. Again I quote Pinchuk's sources, this time a witness from Pinsk: "Systematically and mercilessly all activists were removed from among the Jewish masses. All those who might or could have expressed opposition to the reeducation of the population were eliminated.[28] In a memorandum on the "state of European Jewry at the beginning of World War II," sent from the relative, if only temporary, security of Lithuanian-administered Wilno, Moshe Sneh informed Nachum Goldman that "the spiritual elite of Polish Jewry" had found refuge in Lithuania. "To Lithuania fled those Jews who were threatened equally by Nazi and Soviet occupation, i.e., the Jewish intelligentsia of Zionist and Socialist persuasion, Zionist and Bundist leaders, authors, journalists, teachers, scientists, Hasidic and non-Hasidic rabbis, the whole Yeshivot and a large section of the Jewish plutocracy."[29] The Jewish population, like the Ukrainian, Polish, and Belorussian populations, was deprived of the institutional infrastructure underpinning its community life and systematically decapitated as a broad spectrum of Jewish elites was removed through arrest or deportation or driven to flee abroad.

My sense is that the social context of Jewish life in this territory over preceding decades had rendered the Jewish community as a whole particularly vulnerable to such deprivations. During the interwar years Jews could not count on favorable treatment by the Polish-dominated state and local administration, and they were simultaneously under hostile pressure from the majority ethnic group residing in a given area. Thus, they were alien to all powers and were therefore thrown upon themselves and on their own self-reliance. Hence, the destruction of their community institutions was all the more incapacitating.[30]

But in the experience of Jewish community a confusing paradox was associated with the process of sovietization. According to the traditional pattern of discrimination familiar to national minorities, as long as they kept to themselves they were tolerated. It was when the processes of social change led segments of minority population out of self-imposed isolation, or when they actively sought assimilation, that the dominant nationality would be provoked to show anger, contempt, and frequently violence. The opposite was true under the Soviet regime: now Jewish insularity and voluntary separation from the rest of society would not be tolerated. Jews could acquire Soviet citizenship with all the rights and entitlements that went with the honor, but they could no longer sustain their community life. Once again they could not be simultaneously Jews *and* citizens of the state that had jurisdiction over them. This reversal of the pattern of discrimination was disorienting, and scores of people grew to appreciate the nationality policy of the new regime.

There was also another experience of emancipation. Due to both its self-imposed insularity and the hostile social environment, Jewish community life was all-encompassing. Those for whom the institutions, practices, and customs of traditional Jewish life felt oppressive; those who wanted out because they could not fit, or fell out, or because they had hopes, dreams, and aspirations that could not be fulfilled within the boundaries that the community drew around itself—all these, primarily young, socially marginal, unusually open-mined, gifted, or sensitive people welcomed the change. They sensed that the new regime offered an easy way out of the Jewish community, not only through the so-called "opportunities" afforded Soviet citizens but also, and perhaps primarily, because under the impact of sovietization the social control mechanisms of the Jewish community were swiftly and utterly destroyed. It was, in other words, the prospect of emancipation *from* Jewishness as much as emancipation of the Jews that drew young people into the streets to cheer the Red Army and later to work on behalf of the Soviet occupiers.[31] That these images of emancipation were mostly in the eye of the beholder matters little, for people are motivated precisely by their own perceptions of reality.

Given the socioeconomic circumstances of the Jewish population—that refugees made up such a significant fraction of the total; that Jews were predominantly self-employed, and hence belonged to the propertied, capitalist class; that the language of Jewish religious identity and practice, Hebrew, was proscribed by the Soviets, who in the name of emancipation of the common man and secularization promoted Yiddish instead—for all these reasons, the Jewish community, though not deliberately discriminated against as an ethnic group, suffered probably the heaviest adverse impact of sovietization. I am, however, hesitant to engage in comparisons of collective sufferings, since each was undermined by different aspects of Soviet policies. Jews, for instance, were relatively unaffected by the destruction of the Polish state institutions and administrative apparatus. Here, Poles were the primary victims. Ukrainians and Belorussians would have been the main victims had forcible collectivization been implemented. But, undeniably, as individual property owners or as persons who came from a foreign country and had close relatives living abroad, Jews were singularly ill-suited for incorporation into the fold of Soviet society. Hence the sorry fate of the Jewish population, persecuted not as Jews per se but rather as members of politically and socioeconomically unacceptable social categories.

As a consequence of the Soviet rule over the area, Jewish communities were dramatically weakened on the eve of the Holocaust. The Jews were rendered more vulnerable as they were pauperized and by and large deprived of their indigenous institutions and their leaders, who had been skimmed off in accordance with the Soviet policy of removing elites. Would the fate of the Jewish community have been different had it been richer in material resources and human capital when the destructive fury of the Nazis was unleashed against it? Only the incomprehensibility of the Holocaust prevents an obvious answer to this seemingly tautological question.

Notes

1. How widespread this opinion had been we can now tell with great precision, thanks to the existence of a detailed record of all references concerning Jews ever made in the Polish underground press during World War II. This useful record was compiled by Paweł Szapiro, a researcher at the Zydowski Instytut Historyczny in Warsaw.

2. Shimon Redlich, "The Jews in the Soviet Annexed Territories 1939–1941,"

Soviet Jewish Affairs, 1971, no. 1, p. 81, quotes the figure of 2 million, but includes in it Jews from the Baltic states and Bessarabia, incorporated into the USSR in 1940. See Bernard Weinryb, "Polish Jews Under Soviet Rule," in *The Jews in the Soviet Satellites,* Peter Meyer, Bernard D. Weinryb, Eugene Duschinsky, and Nicolas Sylvain, eds. (Syracuse: Syracuse University Press, 1953), p. 331; and Szyja Bronsztejn, *Ludnoćś żydowska w Polsce w okresie miedzywojennym. Studium statystyczne* (Warsaw: Ossolineum, 1963), p. 114.

3. Even among high officers of the Polish Army and functionaries of the administration—that is, among those individuals who of all people should have known what was going on—there was total confusion. In Taropol, county prefect Majkowski urged the population through loudspeakers to give a friendly welcome to the entering Soviet army. Posters signed by the mayor of Stanisławów and appealing for a calm, friendly reception were put up throughout the city on the morning of 18 September. In Równe, the county prefect came out personally with a retinue of local officials to great the spearhead of the Soviet column. He thanked the Red Army profusely for bringing help to Poles locked in combat with the German invaders. In Kopyczyńce, a city official spoke from the town hall balcony: "Gentlemen, Poles, soldiers, we will beat the Germans now that the Bolsheviks are going to help us," while Red Army commanders embraced Polish officers. Soviet columns marched through Ternopol and Łuck side by side with detachments of the Polish army, each giving way to the other at intersections (Hoover Institution [HI], Polish Government Collection [PGC], 4102, 7568, 10015, 10204, 3435, 7557; Anders Collection [AC], 4307). In a conversation engraved in the memory of the mayor of Lwów, the commanding officer of the Lwów garrison, General Langner, informed him that the city would be surrendered to the Bolsheviks, who were Slavs and who would assist the Poles in their war against Germany (General Sikorski Historical Institute [GSHI], Collection 88, File B, Dr. Stanisław Ostrowski, "Lwów walczy we wrześniu 1939"). All of the preceding may have been dictated by necessity, as there were no available means to oppose the Soviets; but I would not classify such episodes as overt acts of betrayal. They genuinely bespoke confusion.

4. See, for example, the following HI, AC, 12394; PGC, 7147, 1650, 8933, 2655, 7135, 7159; or county reports in PGC, dolina, 13; kałusz, 1; nadworna, 18; bóbrka, 2; krzemieniec, 3.

5. HI, Poland. Ambasada USSR, Box 46, Stanisława Kwiatkowska.

6. See for example the following county reports from the PGC: białostocki, 3; Białystok, 3, 4; sokolski, 9; mołodeczno, 5, 9; postawy, 5; dzisna, 4; brasław, 3; prużana, 2; nadworna, 17; dubno, 3; łuck, 5; lida, 2, 3 (on the presence of Jews); szczuczyn, 1; postawy, 5; nowogrodzki, 10, 11; wilejaka, 5 (on the presence of Belorussians); mościska, 2; sambor, 6; bóbrka, 2; kowel, 7; horochów, 2; skałat, 5; luboml, 2; stryj, 20 (on the presence of Ukrainians).

7. HI, Poland. Ambassada USSR, Box 46, Stanisława Kwiatkowska; Box 47, Alićja Sierańska; PGC, 3194, 4060, 7508; nieśwież, 13; postawy, 5; wilejka, 5; sokolski, 9; kołomyja, 22; kostopol, 5.

8. Yad Vashem, 03/2309, 03/1791; drogobycz, 2; HI, PGC, Box 131, Palestinian protocol no. 187.

9. The reminiscence of one young enthusiast reveals an underlying misun-

feel, when he finally comes, the way we felt then. It is hard to find words to describe the feeling—this waiting and this happiness. We wondered how to express ourselves—to throw flowers? to sing? to organize a demonstration? How to show our great joy?" Certainly such enthusiasm must have been plainly visible, even though in any one community only a few may have been overwhelmed by such feelings. But even this young woman reports a sense of confusion. "First contacts with the Russians—I mean with the Soviet soldiers—struck us with something strange and unpleasant. We thought that every soldier was a Communist and therefore it was also obvious to us that each must be happy. So their comportment, their behavior, struck us as queer. First of all their looking after things, after material objects—watches, clothing—with so much interest and so much rapacity. We waited for them to ask about life under capitalism and to tell us what it was like in Russia. But all they wanted was to buy a watch. I noticed that they were preoccupied with worldly goods, and we were waiting for ideals" (Interview with Celina Końiska, Tel-Aviv, winter 1980).

10. Another instance of misunderstanding is found in a report of an encounter with a Soviet officer who, when asked about the prospects for emigration to Palestine, told his young interlocutor that the Soviet authorities would gladly create Palestine for Jews . . . , but "right here." "One of them, himself a Jew, said to us, 'You want to go to Palestine? Fine, l'shana Habaah Biyerushalayim—next year we shall all be in Jerusalem. The Soviets will be there too" ([Hashomer Hatzair] *Youth Amidst the Ruins: A Chronicle of Jewish Youth in the War* [New York, Scopus, 1941], pp. 88, 90).

11. I discuss this in my *Revolution from Abroad: The Soviet Conquest of Poland's Western Ukraine and Western Belorussia* (Princeton: Princeton University Press, 1988, pp. 35–45).

12. When "anarchy" began in Drohiczyn county, "everybody hoped that some pacification detachment would come—it didn't matter whether ours or foreign—and restore order." Józef Użar-Sliwiński, the military settler who wrote these words, fled to Drohiczyn, where "the Soviet authorities and the military had already arrived." Only after three weeks did he dare to return to his village (HI, Poland. Ambasada USSR, Box 47). A forrester from Dolina county recalls that he "had to leave the house and all possessions and hide with the whole family in the forest until the Soviets came" (HI, Poland. Ambasada USSR, Box 47; see also HI, PGC, 2432, 8764; AC, 1078).

13. HI, PGC, Box 131, Palestinian protocol no. 120, 123; YV, 03/666, 03/1327, 03/2148, 03/2127, 03/1323; Irena Grudzińska-Gross and Jan T. Gross, eds., *War Through Children's Eyes* (Stanford: Hoover Institution Press, 1981), doc. no. 118, 120.

14. HI, Poland. Ambasada USSR, Box 48, Barbara Lejowa.

15. For some preliminary statistics see Szymon Datner's "Zbrodnie Wehrmachtu w Polsce w czasie kampanii wrześniowej," quoted in S. Bronsztejn, *Ludność żydowska w Polsce*, p. 269.

16. Let the story recounted at the time by 22-year-old Rosa Hirsz stand in lieu of many:

> I spent a long time in the so-called neutral zone. Germans robbed me thrice. They even took a packet of needles, they took my coat and linen,

they said they needed linen for their wives and children. There were instances when Germans took clothes away from Jewesses and gave them to Polish women. I saw how Germans took all clothing from some Jews and tore it into pieces, just to harm the Jews. Young Germans were the worst. With older ones one could manage somehow and cross the border for a few pennies. I finally managed to bribe a patrol and with some other young Jews I found myself on the other side. As soon as we moved in a little, Germans alerted the bolsheviks and from both directions shots were fired at us. We hid in a ditch. Three in our group, including one young woman, were killed on the spot. Others miraculously survived. We spent two days in the ditch near the Soviet border without food or drink. As soon as we raised our heads shots would be fired. . . . We could not stand it any longer and risking our lives we crawled on all fours toward the Soviet border. [A] Soviet patrol caught us. They were quite friendly. They gave us something to eat and to drink and then "assisted us" to get over to the German side. We were ready to commit suicide. We were totally exhausted mentally and physically. We were dead tired and could not see how to extricate ourselves from our predicament. A German patrol beat us with rifle butts. They thought we were trying to get in from the Soviet side. In our presence, unashamed that a lot of people were watching, Germans raped two young Polish women and then savagely beat them. We spent another ten days in the neutral zone. We witnessed horrible mistreatment of people. We saw the arrival of a group of Jewish artists with Turkov and Ida Kamińska. They were well-dressed and must have thought they . . . [would] be left in peace when they . . . identified themselves as actors. [The] Germans ordered Ida Kamińska to strip naked. They took her precious coat, all [her] underwear, all [her] dress[es] and then when she stood completely naked a young German officer order[ed] her to act. My heart was breaking when I looked at this wild scene. I admired her comportment. With a faint smile she gave away everything, her face was pale, but she did not want to show the Germans that she was afraid. The same happened to the whole group of artists who showed up on the border. Completely naked they were allowed into the border zone. We were lucky that [the] Gestapo enforced the principle of racial purity in the border zone. Some German military were quite eager for Jewish girls whom they wanted to make happy and in exchange smuggle across the border, but they were afraid of the Gestapo. Finally we managed to get over to the Soviet side. It was at the end of the month, during a pitch dark night, when we got to Białystok by passing Soviet patrols. Even though I had no place to stay and I was constantly hungry the feeling of freedom and the return of my human dignity after weeks spent with the Germans gave me strength to bear all the discomforts. The most important was that one could freely walk the streets, Soviet bands were playing cheerful marches. Nobody was pulling Jewish beards off in the streets, and one didn't see pale, trembling people" (HI, PGC, Box 131, Palestinian protocol no. 85).

See also Palestinian protocols no. 120, 124, 182, 188; AC, 10559, 15526).
    17. As differentiated from anecdotal evidence; we can find numerous accounts indicating that there were Jews in the local militias, for example. But this

evidence, frequently the very same witnesses, would not dispute that others, non-Jews, were in the militias as well.

18. One can find these names quoted in individual depositions stored at the Hoover Institution. I studied them carefully, since they revealed interesting features of the paradigm of Soviet occupation—for instance, that frequently groups of relatives would take over enforcement of Soviet rule in individual villages or gminas. Here is a sample list, with villages drawn from several different voivodeships: three Furman brothers and their sister were in the militia and in the village committee, also the Samosenko couple (Dederkały, Krzemieniec county in Wołyń); in Żurawica (Łuck county in Wołyń), Jakub and Dymitr Maksimczuk ran the village committee; in Świsłocz (Wołkowysk county of the Białystok voivodeship), the gmina committee was headed by Piotr Kordosz, assisted by his daughter Luba and his brother Aleksander; in Chołojow (Radziechów county of Tarnopol voivodeship) a Ukrainian named Szulba and his two sons "took the power"; in Wolica Derewlańska (Kamionka Strumiłowa county of the Tarnopol voivodeship) Jan and Bazyli Baka, Jan and Teodor Szczur, and Stefan and Łać Bohonos were on the village committee; in Bratkowce (Stanisławów voivodeship), among the "activists" of the local committee were Iwan Żyrdak and his brother Jarosław and Teodor Chiczyj and Irena Kaczor, Teodor's daughter; in Wieckowice (Sambor county of the Lwów voivodeship), Michał, Grzegorz, and Jan Hołowa were in the village militia (see *Revolution from Abroad*, p. 118). For other names of local level "prominents" see also chapter 2.

19. There is yet another powerful mechanism, in my judgment, which helped to perpetuate the image of treacherously collaborating Jews. I have in mind what psychologists call a "projection mechanism." In this particular case it was triggered by events which took place in the opening weeks of the Russo-German war when local population engaged in anti-Jewish pogroms and collaborated with the Nazi occupants by identifying Jews to them.

The subject, apparently, still awaits its monograph. Let me but point out that on the basis of a single archival collection—the Ringelblum archive deposited in the Jewish Historical Institute in Warsaw—Andrzej Żbikowski recently identified 31 villages and cities (not counting rural hamlets)—namely, Bolechów, Borysław, Borczów, Brzeżany, Buczacz, Czortków, Drohobycz, Dubno, Gródek Jagielloński, Jaworów, Kołomyja, Korzec, Korycin, Kowno, Krzemieniec, Lwów, Radziłów, Sambor, Sasów, Schodnica, Sokal, Stryj, Szumsk, Tarnopol, Tłuste, Trembowla, Tuczyn, Wizna, Woronów, Zaborów, and Złoczów—where murderous pogroms took place at the time (See Andrzej Żbikowski, "Local Anti-Jewish Pogroms in the Occupied Territories of Eastern Poland, June–July 1941," the chapter following this one in the present volume.

My point is this: pogroms were not unusual in this part of Europe and people expected their intermittent occurrence. But in this instance the situation got out of hand. Nobody knew what the Nazis were up to. And as assault on the Jews promptly evolved into a slaughter and then into an all-out extermination, the indigenous population suddenly discovered that it took part in something altogether different than a pogrom. So while relaxation of moral obligations in conduct toward Jews allowed for some interpersonal violence, even an occasional killing, it certainly did not permit the wiping out of an entire community. Thus, the eventual enormity of Nazi crimes in which—without knowing what they were getting into—they participated left the local people with a horrendous burden. What could possibly alleviate their collective conscience was an image of the past according to which immediately prior to the Nazi invasion they were the victims and the Jews were willing collaborators in a murderous assault against them.

20. It was called by this name as people were supposed to pick up their certifications of Soviet citizenship, ID cards, called passports.

21. HI, AC, 12128. See also 10560, 12332, 12333, 12334; PGC, Box 131, Palestinian protocol no. 186.

22. *Khrushchev Remembers,* Strobe Talbott, ed. (Boston: Little, Brown, 1970), p. 141.

23. Chaim Hades (*sic!*) from Brześć wrote the following: "I stood long hours in line and I finally got the authorization card for departure, which was considered at the time a pot of luck. A German officer turned to a crowd of standing Jews and asked: Jews, where are you going? Don't you realize that we will kill you?" (HI, PGC, Box 131, Palestinian protocol no. 148).

24. HI, PGC, Box 588, "Obliczenie ludności polskiej deportowanej do ZSSR w latach od 1939 do 1941."

25. Simon Redlich, "Jews in General Anders' Army in the Soviet Union 1941–1942," *Soviet Jewish Affairs,* 1971, no. 2, p. 97. Klemens Nussbaum, following Anders, quotes an even smaller number of 4,000 evacuated Jews ("Jews in the Polish Army in the USSR 1943–1944," *Soviet Jewish Affairs,* 1972, no. 3, p. 95).

26. Yad Vashem, SH, 191–2131, quoted after Ben-Cion Pinchuk, *Polish Shtetl Under Soviet Rule,* in manuscript, p. 56.

27. On the eve of the 1940/41 school year, in the summer of 1940, there were 1,003 Ukrainian-language schools, 314 Polish-language schools, 7 Russian-language schools, and 20 Yiddish-language schools in the Lwów district (*Czerwony Sztandar,* 20 August 1940). Ethnically, the area was divided more or less equally into groups of Poles and Ukrainians (some 44–45 percent of the total for each nationality); the remainder, 10–12 percent, was Jewish. These numbers do not reflect the influx of refugees, predominaetly Jewish, who dramatically swelled the population of Lwów and other towns in the district. Thus 20 Yiddish-language schools among a combined total of 1,344 (i.e., about 1.5 percent) means underrepresentation by a factor of nearly 10—a result of deliberate policy, no doubt, rather than a mere oversight. And by January 1941 the total number of Yiddish-language schools in the Lwów district had further declined to 14 (*Czerwony Sztandar,* 5 January 1941).

28. Ibid., p. 68.

29. *Galed,* vols. 4–5, Tel Aviv, 1978, p. 565, quoted after Pinchuk, p. 68.

30. Of course, an insulated, inward-looking community life was a deliberately chosen and craftily practiced art of Diaspora Jews. Thus, I do not deplore here the hostility of the environment but simply point out that this sociological particularity of Jewish life turned sovietization into an especially destructive experience.

31. Ironically, in the collective memory of their neighbors, this explicitly "anti-Jewish" behavior of a small minority was misconstrued as self-serving, ingratiating behavior on the part of the entire community.

Local Anti-Jewish Pogroms in the Occupied Territories of Eastern Poland, June–July 1941

ANDRZEJ ZBIKOWSKI

When one reads the memoirs and accounts written just after World War II by Jews who had remained in the eastern part of Poland occupied by Soviet troops after 17 September 1939, one immediately notes a common feature. Almost all the authors recognize that their first war experience was the confrontation of the Jewish community with a decidedly hostile attitude on the part of the local population, which very often took a form of classical pogrom following the outbreak of war in June 1941.

This fact must awaken the natural interest of an historian who realizes that such statements were certainly not evoked by the compilers of these memoirs and interviews. In fact, the interviewers were employees of Jewish committees, preeminently the Jewish Historical Commission, and, in an emphatic majority, well disposed toward "the people's authorities." They were, accordingly, inclined to a "leftist" conception of anti-Semitism, according to which the only enemies of the Jews were the "bourgeois and fascist conservative classes of society" (the bourgeois, the clergy, the gentry), but never the "working class."

It must be stressed that experiences at the hands of the German invaders prevail in these often lengthy memoirs, while "local pogroms" are as a rule described in a dozen or so often very vague sentences. Yet a contemporary reader will be struck not only by the fact that aggression against the Jews was so widespread but also by the fact that people recalling those tragic times were astonished by their neighbors' attacks and did not feel that they had done anything to provoke such violence.

How is one to understand this phenomenon? Unfortunately, existing studies of the Holocaust are not very helpful, inasmuch as they are descriptive rather than analytical. Generally they attempt to deal with the fate of the Jews across an enormous and very differentiated territory that was captured by the Wehrmacht with lightning speed. The military offensive was then followed by mass actions of terror against Jews by the Einsatzgruppen, which advanced in the army's wake. It is the methodical and global character of this assault that commands attention. In this respect, the executioner has determined the historian's agenda, rather than the victims.

It is my view that the Jewish population living in Soviet territory became, after 22 June 1941, the victims of two tragedies. The first, but the more obscure for the majority of these Jews, was the Nazi determination to exterminate the Jewish nation; the other, more proximate, was the violent explosion of the latent hatred and hostility of local communities.

Generally, the aggression of local populations against the Jews was a result of two processes. The first consisted of a secular system of mutual references, a modern, typically interwar ideological anti-Semitism professed in various degrees by the "educated classes of society" and by the numerically dominant peasantry. The other process involved a "fresh memory," that is, events that occurred between the Jews and the Poles, Lithuanians, and Ukrainians during the Soviet occupation. This is not to say that anything happened on a scale which might justify a hostile attitude toward the Jews. Nevertheless, separate events may have seemed important enough to generalize and encode in the collective consciousness on the base of that system of local images oriented toward anti-Semitism. Thus, in order to understand the wave of aggression directed almost exclusively against Jews one must analyze Jewish–Polish, Jewish–Lithuanian, and Jewish–Ukrainian relations between September 1939 and June 1941.

The task is not simple. Sources are generally scanty, and the attitude of many researchers has reflected a nineteenth-century type of national historiography, or rather hagiography. The best available studies concern Polish–Jewish relations in the Soviet occupational zone.

Briefly and generally stated, a substantial growth of tension in Polish–Jewish relations can be traced to two phenomena: first, the common enthusiasm of the Jewish population upon the occupation of the Polish eastern territory by Soviet troops, which Poles perceived as evidence of disloyalty to the Polish state; and second, a prevalence of people of Jewish origin in the Soviet occupation apparatus, and frequent abuse of those ranks to the disadvantage of representatives of other nations.

Yet, from a certain point of view this disaffection from the Polish state and its representatives (both civil servants and the staff of municipal institutions) was understandable, given the earlier official anti-Semitism. Likewise, it was the Soviets who did not allow the Germans to seize this area; and in any case the Jewish community suffered enormous losses during the Soviet occupation, comparable with Polish losses. These considerations should balance the objections raised against the Jews.

In my opinion, these arguments have been well aired in the analysis of Polish–Jewish relations during this period, while the subject of Jewish–Ukrainian and Jewish–Lithuanian relations has been ignored. Even the recent Polish-Ukrainian dialogue leaves out consideration of the fate of the Jewish population in the occupation.

The domination of stereotypes in historical literature and its divisions along national lines can be overcome first of all by expansion to include new historical sources. For example, unpublished documents from the Ringenblum Record Office (the Oneg Szabat group from the Warsaw ghetto) are important but neglected historical sources which could explain the origin of local pogroms of the Jewish population in eastern Poland. These original reports of Jewish refugees from the towns of Vilno, Grodno, Bialystok, and Lwow were largely written in Warsaw at the turn of 1941. It is worth stressing that in these reports Jews express fears that their relations with other nations worsened during the Soviet occupation. One author noted that "the Jews related to Poles disrespectfully and often humiliated them"; another stated that the "tensions" were caused exclusively by the fact that the Jews were "striving to take over managerial positions."

Only a search of the archives will substantiate whether Jews in fact took a disproportionate share of important positions. Nevertheless, there is evidence that local communities took offense or even felt threatened by the sudden preferment of the Jewish population. The beginning of the war permitted people to act on a repressed need to "take revenge" and to "pay the Jews back" for real and imaginary wrongs.

An aggression against local Jewish societies took various forms. Victims themselves most often called these acts of enmity pogroms. Of course, that notion always had very wide meaning and covered a full gamut of unfriendly behavior, from robbery or blackmail to brutal assassination and torture. What was the scope of these "local pogroms" of June 1941? At the Record Office of the Jewish Historical Institute in Warsaw I analyzed 113 reports from a collection of "Reports of Saved Jews," composed of 4,500 units, eleven memoirs, and ten reports from the Ringenblum Record Office. (I should add that these collections are very superficially catalogued, so we can expect that still more documents will be recovered.)

My first question concerns the geographical distribution of pogroms. There were at least thirty-one pogroms in greater localities in eastern Poland that resulted in fatalities (see Table). A dozen or so reports confirm bloody pogroms in the countryside, all of them at the hands of Ukrainian peasants. Other acts of harassment and violence stopping short of murder occurred in at least twenty places.

As the table reveals, violence was most prevalent in regions with a Ukrainian population. Anti-Jewish outbreaks in the remaining territories occupied by the Soviets in 1939–40 were milder and without bloodshed, excluding events in the town of Kovno (Kaunas).

Unfortunately, using memoir materials, it is difficult to find answers to many questions. First of all, you cannot tell whether the German troops in a particular place were from military or police formations, and how that may have influenced the form of pogrom. We do know that the situation of the Jewish population was considerably better in localities occupied by Hungarian troops, where there were almost no fatalities before the Hungarian garrisons were replaced with German ones.

The most tragic events took place in several towns where Ukrainians, as well as Jews and Poles, lived, particularly the towns of Boryslaw, Brzezany, Buczacz, Czortkow, Drogobycz, Lwow, Tarnopol, Zaborow, and Zloczow. In all these localities pogroms were precipitated by the discovery of the bodies of Poles and Ukrainians who had earlier been arrested by the Soviets. All of these pogroms were very violent and bloody. The obvious question is whether the violence against the Jewish population was committed by the Ukrainians. Were other nations, also ill-disposed toward their Jewish neighbors, able to restrain any impulse to "repay" Jewish Bolsheviks for the two years of Soviet occupation?

The answer is not simple. In the memoirs archived in the Record Office of the Jewish Historical Institute I found not much information on bloody pogroms that had taken place outside the region inhabited

Anti-Jewish Pogroms That Resulted in Fatalities, Eastern Territories of Poland

Region	Population	Number of reports
1. Bolechow	Ukrainian	3
2. Boryslaw	Ukrainian	8
3. Borczow	Ukrainian	
4. Brzezany	Ukrainian	2
5. Buczacz	Ukrainian and German	2
6. Czortkow	Ukrainian and German	3
7. Drohobycz	Ukrainian	5
8. Dubno	Ukrainian and German	1
9. Grodek Jag.	Ukrainian	1
10. Jaworow	Ukrainian	1
11. Kolomyja	Ukrainian	4
12. Korzec	Ukrainian	1
13. Korycin	Belorussian	1
14. Kowno	Lithuanian	2
15. Krzemieniec	Ukrainian	1
16. Lwow	Ukrainian	23
17. Radzilow	Polish	2
18. Sambor	Ukrainian	2
19. Sasow	Ukrainian	2
20. Schodnica	Ukrainian	1
21. Sokal	Ukrainian	1
22. Stryj	Ukrainian	3
23. Szumsk	Ukrainian	2
24. Tarnopol	Ukrainian	6
25. Tluste	Ukrainian	3
26. Trembowla	Ukrainian	2
27. Tuczyn	Ukrainian	1
28. Wizna	Polish	1
29. Woronowo	Lithuanian	1
30. Zaborow	Ukrainian	1
31. Zloczow	Ukrainian and German	4

Source: Accounts and memoirs in the archives of the Jewish Institute in Warsaw.

by Ukrainians. The history of the Lithuanian pogrom in the town of Kovno (Kaunas) has been analyzed before, so I will not discuss it here.

A pogrom in the country town of Radzilow near Grajewo and bloody events in neighboring Wasocz and Jedwabno were related only by Menachem Finkelstein, whose reports were given to officials of the Jewish Committee in the town of Bialystok in 1945. The record of these interviews is a rather poor translation from the Yiddish. Finkelstein's testimony clearly indicates that several Poles from the country town of Radzilow helped the Germans look for native communists and members of the Komsomol. It was rumored that these people were armed by the Germans and terrorized the whole town for three days. Some of the author's reports raise large doubts, for example the number of victims, said to be about 1,500 people; the account of the pogrom in Jedwabno is equally dubious.

Thus the question arises, why were the Ukrainians so involved in anti-Jewish violence? The sources I analyzed do not provide a full answer. The authors, who were both witnesses to and victims of these excesses, cite the low cultural standard of their persecutors ("barbarians," "rabble," "hooligans") and a unique hatred of the Soviets who had occupied western Ukraine. The Ukrainians' delight at their sudden rescue from Soviet oppression is evident in accounts of the events in the town of Kolomyja. A spontaneous pogrom in the town after the withdrawal of Soviet troops lasted for two days. Only the firm attitude of the command of the Hungarian troops that seized the town brought events under control. As we now know, what happened is that the Hungarians and the Ukrainians agreed on an "appropriate" anti-Soviet manifestation. According to the sources, "a great round-up of Jews" took place. The Jews were driven into a marketplace (Pilsudski Square), where a monument of Joseph Stalin was being erected. The Jews were forced by the Ukrainians to destroy the monument. The same ritual was repeated in a town park, where monuments of Stalin and Lenin were destroyed. In one of these places, "for the crowd's entertainment, the Ukrainians ordered one Jew to stand on the monument and the other Jews were to shout 'You are a stupid Stalin!' " It was a sort of magical ritual.

The attitude of the Hungarian command saved the Jewish population from a pogrom in at least several localities. In the country town of Horodenka, for example, a Hungarian general recommended that a detachment of the Ukrainian "Sicz" organization be disarmed. In the town of Melnica, the Hungarian troops dispersed peasants who had come to rob Jews. The same happened in the town of Stanislawow. According to one account: "The anti-Semitic activities of Ukrainian nationalists were immediately stopped by the Hungarians. . . . The Ukrainians were very dissatisfied about this and resented them."

Exceptionally tragic was the lot of the Jewish population living in small concentrations in purely Ukrainian villages. Several reports from the quoted collection certify that these groups of Jews were put to death by their Ukrainian neighbors without any assistance from the German occupiers. Unfortunately, our informants were not able, mainly on account of their low level of education, to explain the reasons for this aggression. Surely it could not have been only jealousy about wealth and property. The pogrom in the village of Ulaszkowo near the town of Tluste followed the old Russian pattern. Peasants who came to a church fair from surrounding villages were stirred up by a sermon preached by a local Greek Catholic priest, supported by a teacher. A wave of pogroms spread to neighboring villages. Those few Jews who saved their lives escaped to the town of Tluste. In that town the pogrom quickly came to an end, thanks to the attitude of another Ukrainian priest who was assisted by a director of a Ukrainian bank and a lawyer. Bandits from the country were not allowed to enter the town, and the situation was stabilized. Alas, it seems that this priest was a glorious exception. According to some reports, in the town of Bolechow a Ukrainian priest openly urged the people to make a pogrom.

A separate question is to what extent the antipathy of local communities to their Jewish neighbors was connected with quislingism with the German invader. One of saved Jews stated that "from the very beginning, Ukrainians informed the Germans about Jews who had been employed by Soviets. Every Ukrainian pointed out Jews against whom he had a grudge. These Jews were taken prisoner and they never came back." Many accounts confirm that private and not just "ideological" motives played a role.

Jews who had been born and raised in the town of Bolechow noted that "many Ukrainians had a weapon; even teenagers were armed and looked only for an occasion to use their weapon." Another witness from the same town reported: "immediately in first days they made a pogrom, especially those who during the Soviet occupation were reputed to have been members of the Komsomol. They threw off the mask, broke into homes and dragged out Jews who only yesterday had been their colleagues."

Descriptions of attacks, murders, and robberies committed against the Jews after 22 June 1941, at the hands of both the German invaders and a considerable part of the local population, can be multiplied without limit. The hostility of the local population was not changed by the establishment of ghettos or by their later "liquidation." It can be treated as a strange phenomenon that requires further intensive study. This is demanded in memory of the victims and also by the conviction that not all witnesses of crimes were responsible for them, and so in memory of those righteous men.

The Two Ghettos in Riga, Latvia, 1941–1943

GERTRUDE SCHNEIDER

The Jews of Latvia Between World War I and World War II

For most of its history, Latvia was part of the Russian Empire. It was only between the two great wars, from 1919 to 1939, that it achieved independence. The Jewish element in Latvia greatly contributed to this long-awaited event and to the viability of the new state.

As a result, Jews had far more freedom in modern Latvia than in any of the neighboring states. Jewish life flourished. There were Jewish schools, theaters, hospitals, cultural institutions, and, best of all, an important and well-developed Zionist movement, with great emphasis on Revisionists. In fact, the Betar movement originated in Latvia, when Vladimir Jabotinsky arrived there in 1923. He remarked in one of his speeches, as an aside, that the Jews of Latvia behaved differently and looked better than Jews from other countries, perhaps because they had never been in a ghetto. (In 1914, at the start of World War I, during induction procedures, it was found that the Jews of Latvia were taller than their Polish counterparts. Military records show that their average height was 164 cm, while the average height of Polish Jews was 161 cm.)

The state of equality and freedom for Jews lasted only until 1934, when a fascist coup d'état brought back old, well-remembered restrictions. Zionist activities were severely curtailed, Jewish life deteriorated, the Jewish press was outlawed, Jewish schools were closed, and so was the Jewish theater. Latvia's Maccabi and Hakoah teams all but stopped their activities. Much of what had been out in the open now went underground, but that was not always possible, especially due to the severe economic restrictions on Jews. Thus, many Latvian Jews, disillusioned, left that formerly vibrant and distinguished community for Palestine, the United States, England, and South Africa, not realizing at the time how fortunate they were in leaving behind that doomed continent.

Russian and German Occupation of Latvia

In 1939, when the Baltic lands became part of the Russian sphere of influence, and in 1940, when they were annexed outright by the Soviet Union and rejoined Russia after a hiatus of twenty years, there were approximately 93,000 Jews in Latvia, most of whom were not too happy to be a part of the Russian Empire once again. The Jews, after all, constituted the business class, and soon, in line with their expectations and to their chagrin, they were forced to give up the factories and stores they had built up and were made part of the working class. Of course, there were some among them who greeted the Russians happily, just as Latvians did. Curiously, the Latvian people to this day forget that they had a sizable Communist Party at the time, although they often bring up their displeasure with the Jews, who, in their words, "greeted the Russians with open arms."

Almost immediately the heavy hand of the occupation made itself felt, and over a period of time almost 12,000 Jews were sent to Russia proper, some as outright arrestees, for economic and political reasons, others as deportees, while still others were permitted to go along with their relatives who had been charged with being "unreliable." Although two-thirds of these people who ended up in the farthest reaches of Siberia died of hunger, sickness, cold, and the rigors of slave labor camps, the other four or five thousand eventually came to realize that their forcible removal from Latvia had been a saving grace. In fact, shortly before the Germans actually entered Latvia in June 1941, at least a thousand Jews saw their salvation in going to Russia of their own free will, rather than waiting for what the Germans had in store for them. And not only the Germans. The Latvian Perkonkrusts, the Aizargis, as well as other, nonaffiliated civilian Latvians, wasted no time in "getting even" with the helpless Jews, who had lived on Latvian soil for centuries. In cities, towns, and villages all over Latvia, whole groups of Jews were murdered even before the arrival of the

Germans. It came as a shock to Latvian Jews, who had never thought that their erstwhile neighbors hated them with such passion.

By the time the German administration was in place and some semblance of order had been restored, the real "final solution" in Latvia could and did take its course. Einsatzgruppe A, under the command of Brigadeführer Dr. Walter Stahlecker, was in charge of eliminating Latvian Jewry from the face of the earth. (It was Stahlecker who sent a map of the Baltic States to Himmler, on which he had drawn small coffins with numbers indicating how many were still left.) He was ably assisted by mobile Einsatzkommandos led by SS and Polizeiführer Friedrich Jeckeln, the inventor of the *"Sardinenpackung,"* which meant putting the intended victims head to toe into graves and shooting them from above, rather than have them tumble down the ravines. At his trial after the war, Jeckeln told the presiding judge that "Latvians were excellent for the job of murdering Jews, since they had strong nerves for executions of that sort." It may have been that particular talent and those "strong nerves" which saw Latvian guards in almost every concentration and extermination camp as the war progressed.

Of the almost 80,000 Latvian Jews alive and present when the war between Germany and Russia started, slightly over 500 survived, making Latvia the country with the highest death rate. The summer and early fall of 1941 saw the planning and erection of ghettos in the larger cities of Latvia and the simultaneous destruction of Jews in the smaller towns and villages of Latvia, with the enthusiastic help of the Latvian Sonderkommandos which were attached to the mobile Jeckeln forces. Einsatzgruppe A was divided into several Einsatzkommandos, one in each of the larger cities. Riga had Einsatzkommando 2C, headed by Obersturmbannführer Dr. Rudolf Lange. By October 25 he had all the Jews of Riga, numbering around 30,000, contained in the ghetto, which was located in the poorest section of the city, Moskauer Vorstadt. Earlier, an expert from Germany, Dr. Heinrich Wetzel, had decreed that Latvia would be a very good place for the solution of the Jewish question. And indeed it was.

The Latvian Ghetto

As in all other ghettos in the East, the Jews, although confronted by enormous problems, tried to make the best of things. Housing was inadequate; families lived in very close proximity, sharing resources whenever possible and hoping for better times. Able-bodied men and women were assigned to work in the city of Riga, which enabled them to bring badly needed food into the starving ghetto. Although they were searched upon returning, which meant extreme punishment if something were found on them, these daring people really had no choice, but had to try again and again to alleviate the hunger in the ghetto.

The Linas Hazedek hospital served these 30,000 Jews, and there was no dearth of doctors. Medications, on the other hand, were scarce, and there was great concern about the approaching winter and the illnesses that would be sure to come in its wake. The inhabitants of the ghetto had no idea that there would be no winter for them; their days were numbered.

Schools were opened, soup kitchens were instituted, people began to get used to the grimness of their lives, and it assumed a drab kind of stability. There was the belief that the central position of Riga, with its supply line to the Russian front, would ensure the need for Jewish workers and thus be of help in the survival of the ghetto inmates. Among the younger people, though, there was doubt, and at that early date they formed a secret society called *Selbstschutz,* consisting mainly of former Betar members. Small groups of them met and practiced with weapons, all in the belief that a day would come when these skills would be needed.

On 27 November 1941, the Jews of the Riga ghetto were informed that they would be resettled further east. By the next day certain streets were to be evacuated, and they were told to be ready for the journey. Long before dawn, however, Latvian SS, led by SS Sturmbannführer Victors Arajs and other officers, and German SS, led by Rudolf Lange, started the evacuation with calculated acts of terror. They broke into apartments, they killed babies by smashing them against walls, they shot older people who were not fast enough, and they spread terror which was designed to numb and destroy the will of these victims, even before they would reach the forest where graves were waiting for them.

On that day, mindless with terror, approximately 15,000 marched into the Rumbuli Forest, guarded on all sides by a cordon of inhuman, uniformed devils, in full view of the Latvian population.

In the forest, after disrobing and handing over their valuables, the Jews were murdered by both Latvian and German Sonderkommandos. While this operation was in progress, a transport of one thousand Jews from Berlin arrived at the Skirotava Station, and Lange decreed that they should join the fate of the Latvian Jews already in the forest. Fifty young men were selected to take care of the luggage and were then brought to Jumpramuize, which was later to become the model farm Jungfernhof, and from there to a new camp, called Salaspils.

In the Latvian ghetto, meanwhile, there was great dismay; yet there were some who hoped that in spite of the excesses their fellow Jews had truly been shipped to the East. People moved closer together, both physically and spiritually. A "small" separate ghetto for younger men only was established. There were many rumors too awful to be believed by sane people, and Latvians at work told of macabre things going on in the forest.

On 8 December the carnage was repeated; this time, over 10,000 went to their deaths, and the very last Jews left the "large" ghetto in the morning of the 9th. Afterward, in a frenzy, there was a search for hidden children, and then the survivors had to clean the streets of corpses and bring them, on small sleds, to the old Jewish cemetery.

Approximately 4,500 men had survived in the newly formed ghetto, and slightly over 200 women, who were later housed on the edge of what had been the large ghetto, soon to become the German ghetto.

Jews from the Reich

Plans for the deportation of Jews from the Reich to Riga had been made as early as October, but there was no intention to keep them alive and replace the indigenous Jews. While a suggestion by Dr. Wetzel to build gas chambers was shelved, the mobile Sonderkommandos would be aided by two gas vans. During the month of November 1941, five transports, originally intended to go to Riga, were sent to Kovno instead. Thus, on 15 November a transport left Munich; on 17 November a transport left Berlin; on 22 November a transport left Frankfurt; and on 23 November one transport left Vienna and another one left Breslau. The Jews who came with the first three transports were murdered at Kovno's Fort IX on 25 November. The Jews who came with the last two transports were murdered on 29 November.

It was the sixth transport from the Reich, which had left Berlin on 27 November and whose members had been murdered together with the 15,000 Jews in the Rumbuli Forest, which earned Dr. Lange a cordial invitation to attend the famous Wannsee Conference in Berlin on 20 January 1942. He described to his attentive audience how "things were done" and how successful his methods were. Being the only one at the conference who had actually had a hand in the "final solution" earned him a promotion. It was also apparent that he had a free hand in Riga; his decisions there were law, even though he was frequently at odds with other officials.

Earlier, for instance, when on 10 December 1941 he brought the Jews from the Cologne transport into the empty ghetto, where Latvian Jews were in the process of cleaning up the evidence of the latest massacre, Lange was chided by the Generalkommissar for Latvia Brigadeführer Dr. Otto Heinrich Drechsler, because the latter had no use for more Jews in the ghetto. His interest was solely the collection of valuables left behind by the Latvian Jews. Lange, however, after being in touch with Berlin, prevailed and saw to it that subsequent transports from the Reich entered the ghetto and stayed there, for the time being.

Already during the first week of December, four transports had arrived in Riga and had been brought to Jungfernhof. They came from Nuremberg, Stuttgart, Vienna, and Hamburg. Most of the young men did not stay at Jungfernhof but were sent to Salaspils. In both camps, conditions were awful and the death rate was high. In addition, at Jungfernhof, there were sporadic selections and the old, the sick, and the very young were taken away. Then, on 26 March 1942, there was one last selection at Jungfernhof, and the camp was left with 400 strong young people who helped to make it into the model farm envisioned by Dr. Lange.

In the ghetto, the first transport from Cologne was followed by transports from Kassel, Düsseldorf, Bielefeld, and Hanover. Each such transport became a group called by the name of the city of origin; each group had an "elder" and a "labor administrator," and each group had several "police men," called the Ordnungsdienst.

The Kommandant of the ghetto, SS Obersturmführer Kurt Krause, explained that there would be more transports from the Reich. He indicated that an important factor was the ability to speak German and thus do proper work for the good of the Reich.

His explanation allayed any fears the German Jews might have had after seeing the remnants of the massacre and hearing from their Latvian brethren what had transpired. Their smugness and the fact that they occupied the very homes from which Latvian Jewish families had been taken gave rise to the myth that Latvian Jews had been murdered to make space for the German Jews. Nobody knew about the first six transports, and nobody knew that of the 4,000 Jews at Jungfernhof only 400 were still alive. The isolation of each camp was complete; there were rumors, but nothing concrete, and so the myth, in the minds of all concerned, became reality and a chasm opened between the two groups, a chasm that has never been bridged, despite later evidence of all Jews being equal and marked for death.

The Two Ghettos

Despite distrust and animosity, there was much positive interaction between the two ghettos. It must be said that the Latvian Jews were helpful and even magnanimous when they, for example, gave food to the slowly starving children of the German ghetto, who were a constant reminder of their own children who had been murdered only a few days earlier.

By the middle of January, transports from the Reich started arriving once more. They came from Theresienstadt (the group was called "Prague"), from Vienna, from Berlin, from Leipzig, and from Dortmund. At the same time, every few days, many of the young men who had just arrived were taken to Salaspils, where they were busy building a large camp. The conditions at Salaspils were such that of the 3,000 young, healthy Jews, only 300 came out of it alive, and of these no more than perhaps a hundred survived the rest of the war. Salaspils was eventually used as a prisoner-of-war camp for Russian prisoners and for gentile Latvian communists. It also had a center for "medical research," where experiments were made on Jewish orphans who were sent to Salaspils from all over Europe. They were killed, together with subsequent transports from the Reich, where no selections were made upon arrival, except for one last time, at the end of September 1942, when fifty Jews from a Berlin transport were chosen to work in a distant city. There was one survivor. Of the 20,000 Jews from Germany, Austria, and Czechoslovakia sent to Riga in the winter of 1941– 42, no more than 800 survived.

As the ghetto inmates struggled with adverse conditions during the spring and summer of 1942, there were rumors of atrocities being committed in the forest, but people did not believe it, despite the fact that the German ghetto, too, had suffered two selections, one on 5 February and one on 15 March. The first one involved only the Jews from Berlin and Vienna, but the second one involved all the groups. In order to prevent panic, Obersturmführer Gerhard Maywald, Lange's deputy, invented a clever ruse. It was announced that people were needed to work in one of the big fish canneries at a place called Dünamünde, the mouth of the river flowing through Riga. It would be easy work for the elderly, there would be food, the work would be inside, and it all seemed so logical. After all, the Baltic Sea was rich in fish, and there were canneries.

On 5 February about 1,100 Jews from Berlin and 400 Jews from Vienna were sent to "Dünamünde," and while there were misgivings, people could point to the fact that Maywald permitted some of the older people to remain in the ghetto, while adding some younger ones to those who were leaving.

(On 10 February 1942, the last transport, or rather, a small part of it, arrived in the ghetto, totally unexpected even by the commandant. After many years it became clear that both Lange and Maywald wanted to entertain the commander of the transport from Vienna, a certain Alois Brunner, who was then slated to become an aide to Eichmann and who had come to Riga to see "how it was done." At the Skirotava Station, Lange told the new arrivals that they were free to go by bus, since the ghetto was quite far and it was 42 degrees below zero. He added that those who went by bus could prepare a place in the ghetto for those who walked. He was very polite and convincing.

No more than 300 preferred walking; the other 700 hundred relied on the buses, never to be seen again. My father, my mother, my younger sister, and I were among those who walked, mainly because my father decreed we had to and we obeyed. He was adamant and serious and totally out of character. In later years, I have often wondered what prompted this unusual behavior. Since he died on the day Buchenwald, his last camp, was liberated, I never got the chance to ask him.)

The selection on 15 March was different. Two thousand people, mainly families with small children or older persons who had not been working, were notified by the groups' employment offices that they, too, were to make ready to leave for Duenamuende. There were, in addition, many who volunteered, either to go along with their families or because it seemed to them that anything would be better than the dismal ghetto.

Thus, on Sunday almost 2,500 Jews left the ghetto, feeling reassured by the fact that physicians and "elders" were made part of the transport. On Monday and Tuesday, however, events occurred which shattered the complacency of the remaining Reichsjuden. The same vans in which the 2,500 had left, returned to the ghetto, filled with clothing and personal items, milk bottles, pocketbooks, shoes, all of it seemingly taken off in a hurry. This cargo was delivered to a building on the Tin Place, and a Kommando of older women was assembled, women who had to sort the clothing, look for valuables, and put order into chaos. The women recognized many of the items, some found things belonging to friends and relatives, and now the German ghetto knew not only that the Latvian Jews had been correct about the disaster but also that they, too, were meant for slaughter and were evidently just as expendable as the "Ostjuden."

Nevertheless, life went on. The trauma subsided, conditions stabilized, and the two ghettos somehow "found each other," since the young men had been taken away from the German ghetto and the Latvian ghetto was essentially a society of men. Romance thrived, love songs were composed and sung, there were concerts given in the German ghetto, some of which featured Latvian artists, there were other cultural ties, and there were Onek Shabbat meetings of the young, organized by the Latvian Jewish police, most of whom were Betarim. Schools had been opened earlier, and for a while, during spring and summer of 1942, everyone thought that the worst was over, that willingness to work would buy survival, and that the war would have to end.

October 1942 reminded everyone how vulnerable they really were.

Resistance

All along, during the momentous events occurring in the winter, spring, and summer, some of the men in the Latvian ghetto had practiced their shooting, had brought in more weapons from the various depots in the city, and had slowly prepared themselves for an eventual uprising. They had nothing to lose, and since they never doubted that they were doomed, they felt that they would not go to their slaughter as their families had done. They were unencumbered, and they wanted to take some of the hated enemies along with them, so that future generations should know that Jews, beaten and powerless, had taken matters into their own hands and had fought back.

In early October, the leadership of the Latvian ghetto held an important meeting, during which it became apparent that many of the

Selbstschutz members were against a general uprising and opted for joining the partisans in the eastern part of Latvia. On 4 October, eleven men left the ghetto in a van prepared by an outside "friend." Unfortunately, he had betrayed them. Only ten kilometers outside Riga, on an obscure road, they ran into an ambush; they returned the fire, killing several of the SS men, but of the Jews only two returned to the ghetto, where one died after a few days. The other one was arrested, tortured, and eventually executed, after having told the Germans all they wanted to know.

During the next few weeks all was quiet, but the Germans had made their plans. After several meetings between the authorities and the forty-one Latvian Jewish police, the Germans struck. On Saturday, 31 October, early in the morning, the forty-one were asked to come to the Kommandantur on Ludzas Iela. They did so, suspecting nothing. While they were held in the courtyard, a large contingent of SS entered the ghetto, burst into houses, and chased the Latvian Jews in the direction of the gate, where about 300 of the older men were selected and taken to the central jail. They were murdered there a few days later.

At 8 A.M., the forty-one men were marched toward the Tin Place. Finally realizing that they were doomed, their chief of police called out that they should scatter and save themselves. Alas, it was too late. The SS opened fire, and the forty-one were no more. One of the SS men was killed by a stray bullet, but that was no consolation.

Subsequently, the Latvian ghetto was no longer autonomous. The Latvian Jews had to turn over their money, and they were administered by the authorities of the German ghetto. Furthermore, since the German Jews were not involved in the plans for an uprising, nor were they touched during the carnage, some of the Latvian Jews, distrustful and not too fond of their German brethren, thought that the plans for the uprising had been disclosed to the SS by the girlfriends of the Latvian Jews. Their conclusions were illogical and dreadfully wrong, but the stigma of betrayal persisted. Later on, when German Jewish police were used by the SS to look for hidden weapons in the Latvian ghetto, the erroneous beliefs intensified.

Gradual Liquidation of the Two Ghettos

The second winter in the Riga ghetto was as harsh and hopeless as the first one had been, with one exception: it was evident that the Germans were losing the war. Work details going to the city every day, busy in the various hospitals and supply depots, heard and saw things that fed their hope of a quick end to the war. Newspapers were smuggled into the ghetto, but what they said was obviously propaganda. Despite all these hopeful signs, there was no let-up in the murder of Jews or their destruction through hard work.

In line with the latter policies, the summer of 1943 saw a gradual reduction in the ghetto's population. Little by little, Jews were sent to the peatbogs of Latvia, and a new camp was built in what had been the most expensive section of Riga. The camp was called Kaiserwald and was administered by criminal and political prisoners. In July, the transfer from the ghetto to the new camp began. Over a period of several months, both the Latvian and the German Jews had to face this new horror. It was a real concentration camp, complete with separate barracks for men and women, endless roll calls, terrible food, and the constant torment meted out by the German prisoners who lorded it over the Jews.

Then, on 2 November 1943, after some of the remaining work details had left the ghetto for the day in the usual manner, once more, for the last time, large contingents of SS entered the now ghostly ghetto. All of the older people, all of the sick whose very appearance gave them away, and all of the remaining children were selected and sent to Auschwitz.

It was a logical choice. The forests around Riga were just too busy, for the grisly task of digging up the corpses and burning them on pyres had begun during the summer, in an effort to obscure the crimes against humanity which had been committed there.

Jewish prisoners, shackled together, had to do this macabre work and were replaced every few weeks by a "fresh" batch of workers. That was why these 2,800 ghetto inmates were sent to the most efficient slaughterhouse; of them, only two men survived. They had gone along to be together with their families, but were selected for work, together with some 300 others, upon arrival.

Kaiserwald and its numerous satellite camps now became "home" to the remnants of the two ghettos; they numbered less than 8,000 and the death rate was high, especially during the winter. The dwindling labor force was augmented by transports which came from Kovno, Vilno, Libau, Siauliai, Dvinsk, and finally, in May 1944, from Auschwitz. One day, like an apparition, there they came, Hungarian and

Slovakian Jewish women, with shorn heads, clad in shapeless gray shifts, totally bewildered and visibly unhappy. Only two weeks earlier they had been in their own apartments and had thought themselves safe from the conflagration which engulfed Eastern Europe. From Kaiserwald they were sent to the labor camps, and they died like flies; they could not withstand the hardships, and the hunger, and the hard work, all of which the Latvian and German Jews had become used to. The Hungarian women had no time to become tough and hardened, and they wasted away before the eyes of friend and foe alike.

Then, suddenly, in late summer of 1944, there was real hope of deliverance. On clear days one could see smoke over the cities in the distance. The Soviet army was approaching. Freedom seemed so near—just around the corner.

Alas, the Germans were reluctant to let go of their victims. After a last selection on Latvian soil, done differently in every one of the camps, the Jews were brought to the forest and murdered there. The clean-up of corpses was left unfinished, and those who were deemed fit were taken across the Baltic Sea to Stutthof, an extermination and concentration camp not far from Gdansk.

With the exception of a few Jews who went into hiding, the whole country was finally *Judenrein.*

On 14 October, Soviet forces entered Riga. Among the soldiers there were Jews who had originally come from Riga and who hoped to find some of their friends or, better yet, some of their relatives. All they found were the graves in the Rumbuli Forest, in the Bikernieku Forest, in Salaspils, and in every place where their fellow Jews had been imprisoned, had been worked to death, had been starved, and had been murdered.

The once thriving community of Latvian Jews was no more. Gone also were the thousands and thousands of Jews from Germany, Austria, Czechoslovakia, Poland, Lithuania, and Hungary. The Germans and their Latvian collaborators had done their work well. The destruction was complete.

The survivors who later came out of Stutthof after being decimated during the last winter and the death marches were totally shattered when they comprehended the extent of the tragedy. There was no more hope to find loved ones; most were all alone. In the case of the Latvian Jews, they could not forgive the Latvians with whom they had lived side by side for centuries and who had turned on them with such hatred, such cruelty, and such abandon. Thus, very few of the survivors returned to their former homes, and the Jewish community in Latvia at this time consists of those who survived the rigors of the war in Russia and others who had never been Latvian Jews but moved to that republic in the postwar years.

The Jews from the Reich who survived have never forgotten the deportation either, nor have they forgotten the Latvian guards and civilians who treated them in such an abominable way. In fact, in every camp to which they had been sent upon their return to Germany, they were sure to find Latvian guards, the most famous "export" of Latvia.

To quote SS Unterscharführer Franz Suchomel, of Treblinka, while speaking to Claude Lanzmann, the creator of Shoah, "when the victims were made ready for the gas, there was a special detail.... We called them hellhounds.... The Ukrainian guards were bad, ... but the Latvians were the worst."

The Physical and Metaphysical Dimensions of the Extermination of the Jews in Lithuania

ZVI KOLITZ

The first passage of the 56th Psalm summarizes in words unsurpassed for tenderness and heartbreak the essence of what we feel about the life and death of the Jewish tribe in Lithuania. "A eulogy"—that is how we interpret here the *Lemnatzeah*—"A eulogy for a silenced dove far away." The metaphor of the dove, and even more so of the silenced dove, stands not only for gentleness, but for inwardness; it stands, in other words, for what Nietzsche refers to as "the delicate shudder which light feet in spiritual matters send into every muscle" ("The Twilight of the Gods"). It was not in vain that Nietzsche himself embraced the dove metaphor in his statement that "the thoughts that shape the world come on dove's feet." That is exactly how the *Mussar* (Ethicist) thought of Lithuania came into the Jewish world—on dove's feet—and that is also why it remained little known within Jewry, not to say in the non-Jewish world.

Lithuania itself—here we mean Christian Lithuania—knew nothing of what most characterized the distinctiveness of Lithuanian Jewry, some of whose finest young men, and they numbered in the thousands, regarded character-improvement, in the midst of a world swept by the tides of a morally neutral science, as the only way to heal the widening rift between life and the spirit. The Lithuanians could enumerate with great exactness, as they do in the *Encyclopaedia Lithuanica,* for example, the exceedingly high percentages of Jews in the free professions between the two wars, without mentioning at all the fact that when

Lithuania gained its independence from tsarist Russia right after World War I, it was so poor in resources for advanced education that the medical and legal skills of Jewish professionals were absolutely indispensable. Thus the government saw fit to grant cultural autonomy to the Jewish community and even had a Minister for Jewish Affairs. If most stores in the Lithuanian towns and villages were closed on the Sabbaths, it was the storekeepers and their families who on Mondays and Thursdays, the accepted market days, attracted the peasants from the various rural areas who came to sell their agricultural products to mostly Jewish customers. Lacking heavy industry or natural resources, Lithuania was agriculturally self-sufficient.

With the emergence, between the wars, of a Lithuanian educated class, competition developed with a better educated class of Lithuanian Jews whose representation in the free professions far exceeded their proportion in the general population. What is so astonishing is that the Lithuanians who speak of the high cultural level of the Lithuanian Jews never mention their universally recognized high ethical level. The Lithuanian Torah-academies shaped a world view which was based on the thought that character-improvement is man's contribution not only to his own perfected self, but to the perfection of the world as a whole. Gedalyahu Alon, a magnificent product of the Lithuanian Mussar Yeshiva in Slobodka, summarized it as follows: "One rule applies to all commandments and to all good deeds: any defect or sparing of oneself is a destruction of worlds." "Man's every deed is eternity." "Our Rabbis said: there are three commandments for which a man must allow himself to be killed rather than transgress them. But the Halaha states that in every aspect of our service to G. and man, we must be prepared to lay down our lives." The meaning of the Rabbinic injunction that a man should bear his friend's burden along with him is: total identification with him. If a man did not totally identify with his friend, he was considered among the shedders of blood. The Halaha, therefore, is to be as it was according to Ben-Petorah, who ruled (see Baba Metzia 62a): Two men were traveling in a wilderness and only one had a flask of water. If both would drink both would die. If one would drink he could reach inhabited land. It is better that both drink and die rather than that one drink and watch his friend die. The Halaha is not according to Rabbi Akiba, who ruled that "your life takes precedence over your friend's life."

"Once again," Gedalyahu Alon comments, "acute tension. But it is counteracted by every shadow of a good thought in the mind and by even the slightest manifestation of kindness—the central point of the creation of the world, the source of man's nourishment."

Alon was speaking about the centrality of kindness. In Lithuanian Yiddish there was a very special word for it, a word that defies translation: *eidelkeit.* It is not refinement, not even fineness. It includes those, but goes beyond them. *"Gan Eden,"* paradise, is, literally translated, "the garden of *eidelkeit,"* *Adinut,* the ultimate and highest rung of spiritual perfection. Thus Rabbi Haim of Volozhin states that eternity begins right here, in this world, and that, to quote the Zohar, "Man wears in eternity the garments he had woven for himself all his life."

In the Lithuanian Mussar Yeshivoth this was paradigmatic. The idea, or ideal, was the man who justifies mankind by completing himself—a complimentary and redeeming instance of man, constantly involved in self-creation, for whose sake one can stoutly maintain his belief in mankind; but because of whom, and on account of whom one must be doubly careful lest the powers that oppose him—the powers of "De-creation"—are doubly eager to take him on.

The powers of de-creation, or evil, in the world, were never underestimated in the Mussar literature. Evil was not depicted as just a psychophysionomic force, but as a metaphysical one. Rabbi Israel Salanter, the founder of the Lithuanian Mussar movement which produced some of the finest spirits in Jewry for almost a century and a half, dared to speak of a metaphysical evil. That is why in the Lithuanian Mussar literature, evil, metaphysical evil, was taken very seriously—so seriously, in fact, that some of the Mussar teachers were accused by their opponents of lacking that joy of life which typified Hasidism, for example. It is not in vain that the Litvak to this day is associated in the Jewish mind not only with learning and *midoth,* but with an unmistakable streak of sadness. It took a world war with its fifty million victims to cause a godless philosopher like Jean-Paul Sartre, for example, to embrace the despair that comes with the realization of the almost tangible power of evil in the world. "We have been taught, " he writes (in *What Is Literature?),* "to take evil seriously." "Whoever heard entire blocks screaming knows the unredeemable reality of evil."

Mussar never thought evil was unredeemable, but dangerously elusive. Reason itself may deceive us, for it almost invariably resorts to rationalizations and self-righteousness. Character perfection cannot be achieved by reason alone, but by an understanding heart—that is what

King Solomon prayed for, *Lev Shomea*—and that is what the Mussar movement held up as its banner. The Mussar movement, contrary to Hasidism, was always elitist, but so great was the shudder that "light feet in spiritual matters send into every muscle," that every branch of Lithuanian Jewry, secular and religious alike, was imbued with *eidelkeit*. *Eidelkeit* in Lithuania was understood not only as a moral or religious but an ontological category. The opposite of *eidelkeit* was *"grobkeit," "Timtum Halev,"* and *grobkeit* was something against which an education to ingenuity, even intellect, provided no cure whatsoever.

We are told time and again by historians of the Shoah that in Lithuania, where the extermination of the Jewish community was almost total, it was the Lithuanian intelligentsia that was in charge of the slaughter. We also know that some of the most vicious madmen in Nazi Germany were scientists. Forty-six percent of German physicians and 38 percent of lawyers were active members of the Nazi Party. That we know. But Nazi Germany had six years of relentless racist indoctrination before its hordes were unleashed for genocide. How are we to understand that Lithuania, with no such indoctrination, but with what is referred to as a regular education, produced such monsters? To keep on saying, as we do, "We shall never forget" is meaningless as long as we keep on talking about the evil without a major effort to identify the true nature of an education that proved no deterrent to evil and that was already at work in Germany and other lands from the second part of the nineteenth century. Erich Kahler, a German Jewish historian and social thinker, spoke (in *The Jews Among the Nations*) of a "progressive overcivilized dehumanization" which the German Jews refused to recognize for what it was. This is an astonishing insight into the nature of a malaise that still haunts our educational system and that was almost totally overlooked by those who were to become its first victims.

It was not overlooked, however, by the Lithuanian Mussarists, who kept on insisting that a bias—*neghiah*—is not eliminated by more ingenuity or even by more education; on the contrary, ingenuity and soulless intellect may infuse bias with greater authority. "We must admit," writes Rabbi Eliyahu Dessler, one of Lithuania's last Mussar luminaries, "that the intellect is powerless to produce reliable results in any moral problem. An approach to youth can be made only insofar as the heart is cleansed of bias. And since bias is caused by character defects, these must be eliminated and replaced by a strong, burning desire for truth and integrity."

In Lithuania, it was the bias of the Lithuanians, particularly the educated Lithuanians, that was responsible for indiscriminate slaughter, unparalleled for savagery, a slaughter which in the few months between June and December 1941 destroyed 200 Jewish communities and murdered more than 150,000 Jews. The bias of the Lithuanians was threefold: sociopolitical, cultural, and religious.

In Germany, the Jews were accused of trying to be too much like the Germans; in Lithuania of being too little like the Lithuanians, of keeping themselves too much apart. The sociopolitical bias may have fed itself on awareness of the cultural superiority of the Jews. Was that the reason why in Lithuania, more than anywhere else in Nazi-dominated Europe, the extermination campaign was directed not only against Jews as Jews, but against whatever and whoever, in persons or in institutions, was distinctly Jewish? Rabbi Ephraim Oshri, the last surviving Rav of the Ghetto in Slobodka, is not the only one who has stressed that it was the men and women of the Jewish intellectual, cultural, religious, and spiritual elite whom the Nazi Lithuanians eliminated before the rest. As a matter of fact, the Lithuanians began the mass murder of Jews in Slobodka, the small suburb of Kaunas where the world-famous Mussar Yeshivah "Knesset Israel" was located. The Lithuanians did not wait for the Germans to unleash the slaughter. By the time the Germans arrived, many thousands of Jews were dead already, among them 800 Jews in Slobodka alone.

Some aspects of the Shoah in Lithuania, presided over by members of the Lithuanian intelligentsia, were of what we may call a distinctly metaphysical nature. It is one thing to burn bodies, but to burn books—as the Nazis did at the outset of their rule—is clearly a form of metaphysical revenge, for it bespeaks an attempt, conscious or unconscious, as was the case with the original autos-da-fé, to set fire to the spirit. To my knowledge, book burnings, excepting Germany before the war, took place *only* in Lithuania. In Lithuania, where there were hardly any illiterate Jews, the anger of literate Lithuanians at the abundance of books among the people of the book expressed itself in what I must regard as a metaphysical, and hence irresistible, urge to burn them in public.

These book-burning ceremonies took place in several communities. I shall confine myself to one location only, Yurburg, not far from the

German border on the one side and of the Ghetto of Shavel, or Šiauliai, on the other. Thousands of books were piled up in the marketplace. Then the Holy Scrolls, the *sifrei-Torah,* were ordered to be brought from the local prayer houses. The books and the Torahs went up in flames in the presence, we are told, of the city elders, the local intelligentsia, SS men, Lithuanian "activists," and the mayor. Jews, prior to their execution, were forced to dance around the fire. The frenzied hatred of Jewish books and Torah scrolls was matched only by the frenzied hatred of religious Jews, something which belies the well-known argument of embarrassed Lithuanians that their countrymen under the Nazis were reacting, or overreacting, to the excesses of Jewish communists during the Soviet occupation of Lithuania. Did the Lithuanians not know—and we deal here, after all, with educated Lithuanians, alas!—that the Jewish community in Lithuania, particularly the religious one, had for years regarded the *Evsektsiia,* the Jewish section of the Communist Party in Russia, as an abomination? But metaphysical evil is precisely an evil that feeds itself on its own self-sufficiency. Exactly as there is good for good's sake, there is evil for evil's sake.

The diabolic fervor displayed by Lithuanians in their swift campaign of genocide of the Jewish tribe in Lithuania defies anything we know about the limits of human cruelty. Here is a state in which cruelty becomes as limitless and unfathomable as its extreme opposite, which is supernatural goodness. It is one thing, as an example, to condemn two Jews, as was the case in the ghetto of Šiauliai, to hang for smuggling some bread to the starving ghetto, but to decree that the hanging must be carried out by other ghetto-Jews goes beyond the limits of human cruelty and touches upon the diabolically metaphysical. Baudelaire knew exactly what he was talking about when he said that the neatest trick Satan played upon man was to convince him that he does not exist. The order, which was complied with, belongs to the realm of supernatural evil. The pleadings of the condemned to let them be hanged by anybody but their fellow Jews makes one think of Theodor Adorno's famous line that no poetry should be written after Auschwitz. No drama could be written after those Siauliai hangings!

In my Lithuanian birthplace of Alytus, a provincial capital where my father served as rabbi between the wars, the rabbi who followed him was ordered by the local Lithuanian activist leader, Aleynis, to be brought before him, for he wanted to kill him himself. The old, sick rabbi was thrown face down into a ditch in front of Aleynis. Aleynis ordered that he be turned over so that he could face him and shoot him in the eyes, which he did.

And let us make no mistake about it: these metaphysical evils were not exceptions. The Shoah in Lithuania was one of the cruelest and meanest on record. The Nazis knew exactly what they were doing when they singled out Lithuanians and Ukrainians for special assassination-squads which they activated in other lands.

The other bias, as said, was sociopolitical. We must recount its genealogy. On 15 June 1940 the Soviet army assumed control of Lithuania. Following the takeover, the Soviets deported many thousands of Lithuanians, Jews and non-Jews, to Siberia as "enemies of the people." In this mass deportation were included, according to Dov Levin's reliable figures, 7,000 Jews, that is to say, about 3 percent of the Jewish population which swelled at the outset of the war to about 200,000. Only 1 percent of the non-Jewish population was deported. In the Lithuanian encyclopedia published in Chicago after the war, there is, however, no mention of deportation of Jews, but there is mention of the important role which Jews played in the subjugation and deportation of Lithuanians. There is no doubt that the Jewish communists in Lithuania, whose number was estimated at 900 out of a total of 2,500, were very active in expropriating properties and in the choice of the deportees. They were helped by Jewish members of the NKVD, who arrived together with the Red Army following the Molotov–Ribbentrop treaty, which assigned Lithuania to the Soviets. The Jewish members of the NKVD—imbued with the self-hating spirit of the *Evsektsiia*, which made Jews shudder with disgust long before the war—undoubtedly treated anybody they regarded as socially undesirable, Jew and Gentile alike, as "an enemy of the people." Lithuanians, however, many of whom have themselves collaborated with the Soviets, remember to this day what Jewish communists, whether Lithuanian or Russian, have done to Lithuanians, but completely overlook what Lithuanians have done to the Jews. The impression was given, and rumors were spread, that Soviet Russia was a Jewish power and that the communists were trying to take over Lithuania as a part of a Jewish conspiracy, whose center was in Moscow, to take over the world. It is not mentioned that (according to Dov Levin's reliable figures) 83 percent of the commercial enterprises and 57 percent of the factories that were nationalized after the Soviet takeover belonged to Jews. Nor is it recalled that the communists abolished the Hebrew educational system, one of the finest in the world, and closed down the great Torah centers of Slobodka, Tels, and Kelem.

But that is not all. Contrary to the claim of many Lithuanian apologists that Jews occupied most of the leading positions under the Soviet regime, Leib Garfunkel asserts that the Soviets did all they could to appoint ethnic Lithuanians, even Lithuanians known for their former fascist ties, like the minister of justice in the communist regime, to high positions in the government. It was to such Lithuanian "traitors," as they were referred to by the pro-Nazi Lithuanian "activist movement" centered in Berlin, that the famous promise was made in a proclamation issued on 16 March 1941: on the day of reckoning only those Lithuanian "traitors" could hope for forgiveness who could prove that they killed at least one Jew.

That was three months before the attack on Russia. We shall never know how many communist Lithuanians, so as to qualify for mercy, killed at least one Jew. We do know that leaders of the Lithuanian community in the United States boasted that their fellow Lithuanians back home had eliminated the Soviet regime in Lithuania even before the entry of the German army. That they did, except that, since the Soviets retreated without waiting for the Germans, the Lithuanians chose to describe the remaining Jews, not the retreating Russians, as the regime they defeated. Units of Lithuanian anti-communist partisans, the *siaulistai,* as they were called (there were no Lithuanian anti-Nazi partisans), emerged from the woods even before the Germans arrived, and devoured like beasts of prey every Jewish community in the land. This metaphor, apt in itself, recalls also the warning of the great Rav Soloveichik: "It is either the Divine Image or a beast of prey." The Lithuanians, let it be said without hesitation, chose the side of the beast.

The role of the church in Lithuania during the Shoah was, at best, ambiguous. There can be no doubt that the absence of an unequivocal papal condemnation of the excesses caused many a Lithuanian Catholic to assume what many have suspected all along: that in the mind of Pius XII, a former papal nuncio in Berlin, the German attack on Marxist-atheist Russia overshadowed in importance the violence against the Jews. Yet there were a few churchmen who paid dearly for protesting the horror. One priest by the name of Kazimiras Pulaikis was executed in the Ninth Fort for his fearless sermons that warned: "A Divine punishment will come upon people who murder the innocent." However, we know of another priest by the name of Yankauskas, who was in charge of a Lithuanian assassination squad. A leading Lithuanian churchman, Bishop Valencius, at a time when a good part of Lithuanian Jews were either dead or dying, noted in his diary: "While there have been regrettable excesses in the treatment of the Jews, one must admit that there is some truth in what Hitler maintains in *Mein Kampf* about the Marxist Jewish venom which is poisoning the nations."

A lethal bias is couched here in subtle terms of a seemingly balanced, objective approach. The few outstanding examples of sacred *subjectivity* notwithstanding, we must regard the church in Lithuania as mostly *objective* about evil.

Some say that there were no righteous gentiles in Lithuania, but there were, though fewer even than in Poland, and less often among the clergy or the so-called "educated classes" than among the peasants. Because the crimes the Lithuanians perpetrated against the Jews were so heinous, the shame that the very few righteous among them give expression to is especially moving. Ana Shimaite speaks with a profound sense of shame and sorrow about the impression created among Jews that "the Lithuanians have no heart," though she admits that those who did were few. "A shame and a curse on you, you scum of the earth," cried out Professor Mironas in an article published in Kaunas in 1945. "You who in the mornings, following your disgusting night orgies, got dressed in your best and went to church. . . . To my sorrow I admit that the stain of the great shame is embedded in me, too, for in the midst of all the unspeakable cruelties I did not cry out my passionate protest. Great is my shame that I was a guilty bystander and was not put to death for a just cause. In those horrifying days we had so many villains and so few brave souls. Alas!"

In Lithuania, writes Avraham Kariv, the inspired author of one of the most moving eulogies on Lithuanian Jewry, "the hordes of the ultimate Nazi vulgarity encountered its most implacable enemy, the standard bearers of *eidelkeit.*" And who are the standard bearers of *eidelkeit* if not the bearers of the *Image?* In Lithuania, the Divine Image seemed to infuriate the beast of prey. One is almost compelled to raise the question, at the risk of exposing oneself to mystical terrors, whether it was by accident that Slobodka, where the Mussar movement had its great, nay greatest citadel, was also the place where the Lithuanian Nazis murdered 800 Jews even before the arrival of the Germans. The powers of de-creation appear to be doubly eager and doubly able, when darkness sets in, to attack the pure and the sacred in their midst.

Thus Nachmanides, after visiting Jerusalem for the first time early in the twelfth century, wrote back home to Spain that that which was most sacred suffered the greatest destruction. That is what happened in Lithuania. In the last stages of the Lithuanian Jewish experience, the few surviving luminaries of the Lithuanian Mussar movement began to feel, in their loneliness and abandonment, an increasing sense of responsibility for the world. That, after all, was Mussar's main theme: every man, with his deeds, creates and de-creates worlds. With the terrifying proliferation of de-creation in the world, Reb Nahum Yanushker, as Pessach Markus tells us in his remarkable account of the last days of Slobodka, managed to gather together—illegally, we assume, for it must have been during the last days of communist rule— some students of the Slobodka Yeshiva and asked them: "If evil is so widespread, who will keep the world going if not Slobodka?"

The students noticed something above his open shirt collar: Reb Nahum was wearing a shroud under his clothes. It is not clear whether he expected death by the Lithuanians, by the communists, or by the approaching Germans. But he expected death. His last words to his students were simple: "Remember to tell the world what a fine and decent life the Jews lived in here." The word he used for "fine" was *eidel.*

When we think of what we lost in the Shoah, not only of how many but of how they were lost, we are bound to conclude that the only thing that can still be saved from extinction is what we least speak about and perhaps what we least understand: the notion of *eidelkeit* as an ontological, not only moral or religious, category.

"Remember to tell the world what a fine and decent life the Jews lived in here."

That goes beyond remembering the dead. It speaks of a way of life that may take a lifetime to create, for man was created, in the words of Rav Soloveichik, to create himself.

Part 4

Sources for Study of the Holocaust in the Soviet Union

The Jewish Population Losses of the USSR from the Holocaust

A Demographic Approach

SERGEI MAKSUDOV

The problem of evaluating the Jewish population losses in the USSR (pre-1939 frontiers)—the currently accepted number is around 700,000 victims—is extremely complex. Raul Hilberg and other authors who examined data on the activities of the Einsatzgruppen arrived at a figure of about 700,000.[1] Nora Levin estimates the losses at 1,050,000 (including the Baltic states), or 800,000 (pre-1939 borders).[2] The estimate by Lestchinsky in 1946, which was revised by the Yad Vashem bulletin in 1955, was 1,500,000.[3] All these estimates are very approximate.

In this work an attempt is made to arrive at a more precise figure on the basis of new demographic data.

The difficulties encountered in studying this problem stem from the large number of complex processes that affected the Jewish population. There are three groups of problems.

A. *The problem of determining the Jewish population in the occupied territories:*

1. the annexation of the Baltic states and the western parts of Ukraine, Belorussia, and Moldavia; the evacuation of populations from the newly annexed lands to the east, as well as arrests and Red Army mobilization;

2. the reevacuation from the east to the west, both of the west's original inhabitants and of new settlers, as well as the permanent resettling of western populations in eastern regions;

3. emigration from the western, and to a lesser extent the eastern, parts of the USSR to Poland after the war.

B. *The accuracy of demographic data:*

4. numbers of Jews by age and sex before and after the war;

5. the birth and mortality rates in the war years and thereafter;

6. the assimilation of Jews into the Russian population as a result of mixed marriages between 1939 and 1958.

C. *Estimating the losses not caused by Holocaust:*

7. losses from Stalin's repressions of 1939–53;

8. the higher mortality rate of civilian populations during the war years in all territories;

9. losses sustained at the front;

10. civilian casualties.

All of these factors resulted in changes in the size of the Jewish population and have a direct bearing on any evaluation of the overall population losses. A method for computing the losses, taking all of the above factors into account, relies on an analysis of the 1939 and 1959 censuses with respect to sex and age and utilizes materials concerning the demography of the USSR which have become available in recent times.[4]

The Population of the Territories Annexed in 1939

The Baltic states, Bessarabia, and the eastern areas of Poland contained about 2,000,000 Jews. They, among other peoples, were partially deported to Soviet concentration camps in the east in 1940–41; thereafter, those who were able evacuated voluntarily to escape the advancing Germans. Some of the men were mobilized into the Red Army (several dozens of thousands). The total number of Jews who came from the west to the eastern territories of the Soviet Union during the war amounted to about 500,000. Practically all who remained in German-occupied territory were exterminated. After the war the migrants returned to the western areas, and some went as far as Poland. A much smaller part remained in the evacuation areas of western Siberia, the Urals, the Volga region, and Central Asia.

The 1959 census counted 67,000 Jews in the Baltics, 95,000 in Moldavia, 95,000 in western Ukraine, and about 10,000 in western Belorussia. It is certain that, by and large, they were original inhabitants of these areas who had returned from the east.

The percentage of new arrivals—people who had not previously lived on those lands—can be approximated by using the Kaliningrad region (formerly Königsberg) as a model. The 1959 census showed 4,250 Jews, about 0.7 percent, residing in the Kaliningrad region; obviously it is impossible for any of them to have been original inhabitants.[5] Since there were around 3,000,000 new arrivals to the west by 1959, one can deduce that the number of Jewish new arrivals from the east in western territories was about 20,000.

In order to evaluate the number of Jews from western territories who remained in Siberia and other eastern areas, one can utilize the native-language data from the 1959 census. Ten to twelve percent of the Jews who were long-standing residents of the Russian Republic (i.e., the regions of Moscow, Leningrad, Briansk, Rostov, etc.) had kept Yiddish as their native language. For the Jews of the Chernovtsy area, further to the west, this number was as high as 50 percent. However, the proportion of Yiddish speakers among Jews in the areas of Kuibyshev and Saratov, and in Tataria and Bashkiria, was as high as 15–20 percent, whereas it should have been about the same or lower than the proportion in the Russian Republic (i.e., 10–12 percent). This unusually high number can be explained by the fact that several thousand western Jews remained in these eastern areas after the war. It is evident that even more Jews remained in the eastern parts of Ukraine and Belorussia, especially in the capitals of Kiev and Minsk, thus raising the proportion of Yiddish-speaking Jews; in Kiev the figure was as high as 30 percent. In sum, the total number of western Jews who did not return home and remained within the boundaries of the USSR can be estimated at 50,000–60,000.

All in all, the 1959 census puts the population of Jews then living in the territories annexed in 1939–40 at 267,000. Similarly, according to the 1959 census, the total Jewish population was 2,226,000; those born within the pre-1939 boundaries of the USSR numbered 1,916,000 (including 1,723,000 Ashkenazy from territories within the pre-1939 frontiers).

Jewish Population Losses During the War

The size of the USSR's Jewish population according to the 1937 census was 2,669,147, of which 773,976 resided in Russia, 1,470,484 in Ukraine, 363,217 in Belorussia, 40,620 in Azerbaidzhan and Georgia, and an insignificant number in the other republics.[6] The size of the

Jewish population according to the 1939 census—in other words, two years after the census of 1937—was 3,028,500. The growth of the population by 359,000 in two years (170,000–180,000 per year) reflects an annual growth rate of 6 percent—a rate that cannot possibly occur as a result of natural processes. Such a rate can only bear witness to some discrepancies in the statistical data or in the ethnic self-identification of census participants. Nevertheless, although 6 percent is excessive, one is safe in assuming some growth in the Jewish population over this period. A more believable growth rate can be deduced by comparing the 1926 and 1939 censuses, which give Jewish population figures of 2,600,000 and 3,028,500, respectively. This amounts to a growth rate of 43,000 per year, or roughly 1.3 percent. One can also assume a similar rate for 1939–41, which in a period of 2.5 years would add another 90,000 Jews to the population by the beginning of the war. All in all, this means that by 22 June 1941, the Jewish population contained within the pre-1939 borders of the USSR can be estimated at about 3,120,000.

The Jewish population (Ashkenazy) in 1939 amounted to 2,903,000. The calculations show that by the beginning of 1944, with the birth rate that existed at the time,[7] the population numbered 2,890,000. According to the census of 1959, the figure for the Jewish population (Ashkenazy from territories within the pre-1939 frontiers) was 1,723,000. Using these data in conjunction with a generational count of men and women for the period in question, we can derive similar data for 1944.

This is done with the help of mortality rate tables for the Soviet population that were recently developed by the Central Statistical Administration.[8] Throughout this process it is important to remember that for the 1944–59 period, Jews had a lower mortality rate than the overall Soviet population. This was because Jews resided in cities and were also relatively healthier due to phenomenally high mortality rates among the sick, old, and weak during the war. The completed analysis indicates that in 1944 the Jewish population numbered about 1,668,000, diminishing during the war to 1,222,000 people (see Table).

Wartime Jewish Population Losses Not Caused by the Holocaust

Contemporary estimates put the losses of the Red Army on the German front at 7,000,000 killed in action and 3,500,000 dead in German

Jewish Population (Ashkenazy) by Sex and Age in 1939 and 1959, and Losses of Jewish Population in the USSR in 1944

(thousands, pre-1939 frontiers)

Age	1939 M	1939 F	1944(a) M	1944(a) F	1944(b) M	1944(b) F	Losses M	Losses F	1959 M	1959 F
0–4	121.8	116.0	83.0	80.0	42.4	41.1	40.6	38.9	44.2	41.5
5–9	104.4	101.5	112.1	107.9	67.6	66.1	44.5	41.8	49.1	46.7
10–14	142.1	139.2	101.6	99.6	60.1	58.0	41.5	41.6	57.2	54.0
15–19	121.8	121.8	139.1	137.0	70.2	81.5	68.9	55.5	38.0	38.1
20–24	101.5	113.1	118.3	119.3	61.1	79.1	57.2	40.2	64.3	63.9
25–29	139.2	159.5	98.2	110.5	55.0	74.3	43.2	36.2	56.5	56.0
30–34	136.3	153.7	134.2	155.6	79.4	102.6	54.8	53.0	64.8	78.1
35–39	110.2	153.7	131.6	149.4	78.8	101.6	52.8	47.8	56.5	75.3
40–44	104.4	116.0	104.2	148.9	61.6	93.9	42.6	55.0	50.0	70.2
45–49	75.4	78.3	97.2	111.9	64.1	69.5	33.1	42.4	70.4	95.9
50–54	63.8	66.7	68.5	74.9	47.1	43.8	21.4	31.1	67.2	93.7
55–59	49.3	58.0	56.2	62.9	34.6	34.6	21.6	28.3	49.5	84.8
60–64	40.6	55.1	41.8	53.7	21.3	23.5	20.5	30.2	47.3	60.8
65–69	31.9	43.5	32.8	49.0	11.4	15.0	21.4	34.0	31.1	35.8
CT. 70	37.7	46.4	5.0	66.0	9.5	19.2	35.5	46.8	34.7	47.4
Total	1,380.4	1,522.5	1,323.8	1,526.6	764.2	903.8	599.6	622.8	780.8	942.2

Sources: 1939 and 1959 census data from the archives of the Central Statistical Administration of the USSR (excluding Jews from Central Asia and the Caucasus). The figure from the 1959 census does not cover the Jewish population from the western regions (and their children).

Note: 1944(a) is calculated from 1939; 1944(b) is calculated from 1959. Losses = the difference between 1944(a) and 1944(b).

captivity.[9] Considering that Jews comprised roughly 1.5 percent of the country's population, one can assume that out of the 7,000,000, 1.5 percent were Jewish. In fact this number is likely to be even lower, since the Jewish population, as compared to the population as a whole, had a larger percentage of elderly, who were ineligible for the battle front, and a higher concentration of various specialists who could not be replaced on the home front. All in all, this means that roughly 90,000 Jews were killed in action and roughly 70,000 more died as prisoners of war.

During the war years civilians perished as a result of military tactics such as bombing population centers; of German actions on occupied territories; and of higher mortality rates caused by poor nutrition and lack of medical care. Those who died from the higher mortality rates, induced by a lower quality of life, numbered about 5,000,000. Of these, 2 percent, or 100,000, were Jewish.

However, as far as the occupied territories are concerned, losses among the Jewish population do not correlate to, and should not be considered as part of, the losses of the population as a whole. In these territories Jews were killed, solely because they were Jews, at the very beginning of the war, and thus they were not affected by the later sickness and famine of the war years. One also cannot consider as normal the deaths of Jewish prisoners of war. They also died specifically because they were Jewish and not as a result of the poor conditions facing the prisoner-of-war population as a whole.

Consequently, losses among the Jewish population not connected with direct extermination of Jews by the Germans amount to about 250,000. This figure breaks down to 90,000 killed in action, 100,000 who died as a result of higher mortality rates among civilians in unoccupied territories, 40,000 killed due to military actions directed against civilians, and 20,000 who died from Stalin's repressions in labor camps and prisons. These 250,000 comprise approximately 12 percent of the average numbers of Jewish population during this period. This is the same percentage of losses as for the population of the whole country (25 million losses out of a population of 190 million).

Thus, losses of the Jewish population of the pre-1939 Soviet Union, suffered as a direct consequence of the German policy of extermination, amount to about *one million* (970,000). This includes only the direct physical extermination of prisoners of war and civilians.

This estimate is larger than those of other scholars. The reason for that is that we are able to calculate more precisely the Jewish population in 1944. In addition, we took into account the entire population of the western region which remained within the territory of the country after the war.

Notes

1. Raul Hilberg, *The Destruction of the European Jews* (New York: Holmes and Meier, 1985), vol. 1; Abraham Edelheit Hershel, ed., *Bibliography of Holocaust Literature* (Boulder: Westview Press, 1986); "SS Statistics on the Final Solution of the Jewish Question, March 23, 1943" (prepared by Richard Korherr, head of the Statistics Department in Himmler's office), No. 5194, in Yad Vashem, *Documents on the Holocaust*, pp. 332–34).

2. Nora Levin, *The Holocaust: The Destruction of European Jewry, 1933–1945* (New York: Schocken Books, 1973), pp. 715–18.

3. Nora Levin, *The Holocaust Years: The Nazi Destruction of European Jewry, 1933–1945* (Melbourne, FL: Krieger, 1990), p. 345.

4. *Itogi vsesoiuznoi perepisi naseleniia 1959 goda* (Moscow: TsSU, 1962–

63), vols. SSSR, RSFSR, USSR, BSSR. Unpublished archival materials on the censuses of 1939 and 1959 were kindly given to me by Dr. Darsky.

5. *Itogi vsesoiuznoi perepisi naseleniia 1959 goda* (Moscow: TsSU, 1963), vol. RSFSR, p. 312.

6. *Perepis' naseleniia SSSR 1937.* Istoriia i materialy. Ekspress informatsiia. Istoriia statistiky, vols. 3–5, Part 2 (Moscow: Goskomstat, 1990).

7. The 1959 census shows the number of Jews born in 1939–43 to be 90,000; those born in 1944–48 to be 131,000; those born in 1949–53 to be 112,000; and those born in 1954–58 to be 101,000. These numbers are surprising because they seem to indicate that the birth rate among Jews was higher during the war years than during the mid-1950s. This, of course, is erroneous. The solution is found in the assimilation of children from mixed marriages, which increased during the 1940s and 1950s. Nevertheless, the data do show that even during the worst of times the birth rate never went below 1–1.5 percent per year. The prewar mortality rate of Jews was about 1.5 percent. This means that from the standpoint of normal demographic development, the population numbers decreased approximately 0.5 percent per year, 60,000 during the period 1941–45 (30,000 during the period 1941–43).

8. *Istoriia naseleniia SSSR 1920–1959.* Ekspress informatsiia. Istoriia statistiky, vols. 3–5, Part 1 (Moscow: Goskomstat, 1990).

9. See ibid. and S. Maksudov, *Losses Suffered by the Population of the USSR 1918–1958* (London: Merlin Press, 1981), pp. 220–76.

Captured Nazi Documents on the Destruction of Jews in the Soviet Union

LUCJAN DOBROSZYCKI

During the war, as territories were liberated from German control, and then as a result of the total defeat and unconditional surrender of Germany in 1945, all records generated in the Third Reich, from top to bottom, were seized by the Allies. Most of them were quickly made public, not years after they had lost their immediacy, but shortly after the events in question. Indeed, no other period in contemporary history has been as well documented and as accessible to researchers as the Nazi years. Suffice it to say that there are many millions of pages of such documents in the U.S. National Archives in Alexandria, Virginia, which holds more than 30,000 rolls of microfilm. The published catalogue of these microfilms consists of nearly 100 volumes.[1]

The Nazis kept very careful and exact records of their ideas, observations, plans, and deeds. When they killed people, they also counted, and in some instances, photographed them.[2] In the Nazi files, besides official documents, there are also many private accounts written not simply out of obligation but for pleasure, in great detail, and with characteristic precision and accuracy.[3]

There is a notion that the Germans destroyed records in order to wipe out traces of their crimes; here and there many documents were indeed destroyed, in accordance with orders from above or as a last-minute effort by individuals acting on their own initiative. As a rule, however, the German documents were left intact, for until the very last month of the war, the Nazis simply did not believe that they were going to be defeated. Hans Frank's diary, a daily account of events taking place in occupied Poland from October 1939 until January 17, 1945, consists of forty-one volumes in folio. Fleeing Poland before the advancing Red Army, Frank's people dragged these huge volumes with them to Germany where they fell into the hands of the Americans.[4] Today's Frank's diary is one of the most important records of the German order in Poland and the destruction of the Polish Jews.

By now the basic documents seized by the Western Allies have been published. These include, first of all, documents gathered by the International Military Tribunal (IMT) in Nuremberg for the trial of the major war criminals and for subsequent trials. We thus have at our disposal:

(a)   the 42-volume set, the Blue Series, of the official records of the trial in English, French, and German. At least seventeen of the forty-two volumes consist of documents; the rest concern the trial proceedings themselves;[5]

(b)   the 15-volume set of twelve separate trials, the so-called Green Series.[6] They include, among others, the cases of the RSHA (the Reich Main Security Office), the High Command, the Einsatzgruppen, and Oswald Pohl, who had been head of the WVHA (the Economic Office of the SS).

(c)   the 13-volume set titled the *Nazi Conspiracy and Aggression,* better known as the Red Series, which is the largest single collection of IMT documents in English translation.[7]

There are also thirty-nine volumes of typewritten or mimeographed transcripts of the IMT documents and proceedings in Russian.[8] For over four decades, however, the Soviet Union treated these as military secrets. They have not yet been made public.

In addition to the official IMT records, dozens of anthologies that include Nazi records have been published in the West. Among these are:

—eighteen volumes compiled by the late John Mendelsohn;[9]
—the 23-volume set edited by Henry Friedlander and Sybil Milton;[10]
—*Documents of Destruction,* edited by Raul Hilberg;[11]
—*The Holocaust Reader,* edited by the late Lucy Dawidowicz;[12] and
—*Nazism 1919–1945: A History in Documents and Eyewitness Accounts,* edited by Noakes and Pridham.[13]

From the beginning it was obvious that the Red Army had captured a large, if not the largest, portion of the German records as it pushed the occupier out of Eastern Europe, including the Baltic republics. Most importantly, the Red Army captured Berlin, Königsberg, and Vienna, in addition to the territories of eastern Germany. However, no one, aside from a few selected people in the Soviet Union, knew what the Red Army had taken or where the records were kept. Catalogues or lists of holdings were never published. There was even great concern whether the captured German records were being preserved at all. In 1948 Hugh Gibson observed that

> When the Russians occupied Berlin in 1945 they went through the German official archives with more vigor than discrimination, shipped some material to Russia, destroyed some, and left the rest scattered underfoot. They often followed a system that is difficult to understand —emptying papers on the floor and shipping the filing cabinets that had contained them.[14]

I remember well a discussion among historians that took place in Warsaw in the late 1950s. It was long after Stalin's death, but his ghost still haunted Eastern Europe. Wondering what one might find if someday the Soviet archives were to open their doors, one brilliant scholar quipped, "I am afraid that we might find nothing but piles of *Pravda* and *Izvestiia.*"

Fortunately, this prediction turned out to be wrong, as the recent disclosures about the Katyn massacre and the Erlich–Alter case indicate. Indeed, the compilation and preservation of files is one of the major functions of a bureaucratic, centralized, totalitarian state. It never occurs to the officials of such a state that their regime might not last forever and that the files that had been so laboriously collected might one day be seen by undesirable people. This first happened at the Twentieth Communist Party Congress in Moscow in 1956, when Nikita Khrushchev cited many documents from the Soviet archives detailing Stalin's crimes. During Khrushchev's brief rule seven volumes of the Nuremberg records were published, in addition to a few anthologies of documents from the Nazi occupation of parts of the Soviet Union. At the same time, a portion of Goebbels's diaries, until that point considered lost, was sold by the Soviet Union to a Western publisher.[15]

To be sure, discussion of the Jewish Holocaust would remain taboo in the Soviet Union for another two decades. Only with the advent of glasnost and perestroika in the late 1980s were the archives that contained Holocaust records made accessible. For the first time, foreign historians and archivists in Jewish history were given permission to inspect Nazi files kept in the Soviet Union.

As a result of the efforts of a joint project undertaken by Yad Vashem in Jerusalem and the United States Holocaust Memorial Museum in Washington, along with other Western institutions, we now have at our disposal inventories from a dozen Soviet archives. Among these are:

—the Central State Archives of the October Revolution in Minsk;
—the Central State Historical Archives in Riga;
—the Central State Archive of Lithuania in Vilnius;
—the State Jewish Museum in Vilnius;
—the oblast archives in Lvov, Kharkov, and Minsk;
—the Archives of the October Revolution in Moscow;
—the Minsk Museum of the Great Patriotic War;
—the Kiev Central State Archive of the October Revolution.

Also of great interest to historians are the materials and proceedings of the investigations into Nazi crimes that were conducted during the war and shortly afterward by Soviet authorities in the territories they liberated. Regardless of what one might think of the way the Soviets conducted the investigations, the files of the Archive of the State Commission to Investigate German-Fascist Crimes in the Occupied Territories should not be overlooked.

According to Yitzhak Arad, the chairman of Yad Vashem, the microfilming of selected records is already in progress in Moscow. A substantial anthology in Russian entitled *Unichtozhenie evreev SSSR v gody nemetskoi okkupatsii (1941–1944)* was published in Jerusalem in 1991. I was told by its editor that the volume would also be published in Moscow.

A separate agreement was signed between the YIVO Institute for Jewish Research in New York and the Central Administration of the Lithuanian Archives of the Government of the Lithuanian Republic in Vilnius. The agreement primarily concerns documents on the history of Jews in Lithuania proper, among them the hundreds of files which before World War II were the property of the Vilna YIVO. According to the signed agreement, the YIVO Institute in New York will also be allowed to microfilm the captured Nazi records.[16]

I have not yet seen the documents.[17] However, if I can judge from hundreds of inventory descriptions, the captured German records kept in the Soviet Union's archives are of singular value for study of the fate of the Jewish population in the occupied territories in Ukraine, Belorussia, the Baltic republics, and Transnistria. The records are from larger towns and cities that had a substantial Jewish population as well as from villages and even hamlets with just a hundred or fewer Jewish families. A few entries from the many inventories will give the reader a better idea of what the archives hold:

1. monthly reports about the creation of the ghettos in Riga and Daneburg (Dvinsk); Jewish work camps around Riga; deportations of Jews;
2. the census in Kharkov, which includes Jews, listed, separated, and broken down by gender, December 20, 1941;
3. Jewish resettlements in Galicia, 1941–42;
4. statistics on Jews in the Province of Tarnopol, November 1942;
   —minutes of the Judenräte in Zimna Woda and Rudno, from November 1941, their respective populations being 336 and 195;
   —inventory of Jewish firms and property;
   —deportation of Jews from Limanowa in July 1941;
   —Jewish objects catalogued for the museum;
   —Judaica-Hebraica items sent by the *Einsatzstab Rosenberg* to the Institute in Frankfurt;
   —list of Jews in the ghettos of Transnistria;
   —lists of Jewish specialists and students;
   —lists of Jews deported;
   —list of Jews by locations in Transnistria;
   —list of Jews in Linbasovca Region; tables with names, gender, number of children;
   —list of Jews in Bershad village who were deported by 20 April 1942;
   —Jews and the Judenräte in Drogobycz;
5. the Jewish census in Vilna;
   —treatment of people in mixed marriages, October 1941;
   —persons shot in Ponary;
   —receipts for clothing, from Ponary.

Although few people realized it at the time, in the second half of 1941 the Nazis' "Final Solution of the Jewish Problem" entered a new phase, one of direct genocide. This occurred at the moment when, after attacking Russia, the Germans were literally intoxicated with their initial victories and believed that they were on the threshold of a thousand-year Reich. The killing of human beings at once assumed forms and dimensions unprecedented in history. Mass executions by firing squads or gas vehicles were carried out by mobile killing units at the rear of the German troops as they advanced deeply into the Soviet Union. In the course of barely six months, from the middle of June to the end of December 1941, they murdered about half a million Jews.

It is always difficult to find the beginning in history. The Nazi files captured by the Soviet Union will be of great help in this endeavor. They will open up new opportunities for the next generation of students of the history of the Shoah.

Notes

1. See *Guides to German Records Microfilmed at Alexandria, Virginia* (Washington, DC: National Archives and Records Service, 1957).
2. For examples see Sybil Milton and Andrzej Wirth, eds., *The Stroop Report: The Jewish Quarter of Warsaw Is No More!* (New York: Pantheon, 1986); and *The Auschwitz Album* (New York: The Beate Klarsfeld Foundation, 1980).
3. See the letters of SS Obersturmführer Karl Kretschmer (SK4a) from the Nazi-occupied territories in the Soviet Union, to "My Dear Soska," to "Dear Sonja, dear children," to "Beloved wife, dear children," to "Dear Mutti, dear children," in Ernst Klee, Willi Dressen, and Volker Riess, eds., *"The Good Old Days": The Holocaust as Seen by Its Perpetrators and Bystanders* (New York, 1991).
4. Lucjan Dobroszycki et al., *Okupacja i Ruch Oporu w Dzienniku Hansa Franka, 1939–1945* [The Nazi Occupation and Polish Resistance in Hans Frank's Diary] (Warsaw, 1970), vol. 1, p. 10.
5. *Trial of the Major War Criminals Before the International Military Tribunal. Official Text* (Nuremberg, Government Printing Office, 1947–1949), 42 vols.
6. *Trials of War Criminals Before the Nuremberg Military Tribunals under Control Council Law No. 10* (Washington, DC: Government Printing Office, 1949–1953), 15 vols.
7. *Nazi Conspiracy and Aggression* (Washington, DC: Government Printing Office, 1946), 13 vols.
8. Jacob Robinson and Philip Friedman, *Guide to Jewish History Under Nazi Impact* (New York: Yad Vashem and YIVO, 1960), p. 192.
9. John Mendelsohn, ed., *The Holocaust: Selected Documents in Eighteen Volumes* (New York, 1981).
10. Sybil Milton and Henry Friedlander, eds., *Archives of the Holocaust. An*

International Collection of Selected Documents (New York, 1990–91).

11. Raul Hilberg, ed., *Documents of Destruction: Germany and Jewry, 1933–1945* (Chicago, 1971).

12. Lucy Dawidowicz, ed., *The Holocaust Reader* (New York, 1976).

13. J. Noakes and G. Pridham, *Nazism 1919–1945: A History in Documents and Eyewitness Accounts* (New York, 1975), vols. 1–2.

14. Louis P. Lochner, trans., *The Goebbels Diaries, 1942–1943* (New York, 1948), p. v.

15. Peter Stadelmayer, "The Story of the 1945 Goebbels Diaries," in Hugh Trevor-Roper, ed., *Final Entries 1945: The Diaries of Joseph Goebbels* (New York, 1978), pp. xxxv–xli; some 1,600 glass plates containing the microfiche of Goebbels diaries were discovered in Moscow in March 1992 by a German historian, Elke Frohlich of the Institute of Contemporary History in Munich, as reported in *The New York Times,* 13 July 1992, p. 8.

16. The agreement between YIVO and the Lithuanian State Archives was signed at the outset of perestroika in the Soviet Union. After Lithuania gained independence however, the project came to a halt. It is to be hoped that YIVO will soon hear from Vilnius that the microfilming of the massive Jewish collection and the captured German records in the Lithuanian State Archives will begin.

17. Soon after the Yeshiva University conference, in May 1992, I had an opportunity, while at Yad Vashem in Jerusalem, to examine quite a large number of captured Nazi records from the former Soviet archives. In addition, thanks to the kindness and help of Brewster Chamberlin, the Director of Archives at the United States Holocaust Memorial Museum in Washington, DC, I obtained photocopies of some requested Nazi records which the museum, like Yad Vashem, obtained from the archives of the former Soviet Union. Although I am aware that I have seen just a tiny fragment of the records, nevertheless there is no question in my mind that the records in the former Soviet archives are indeed of tremendous value.

"Yizker-Bikher" as Sources on Jewish Communities in Soviet Belorussia and Soviet Ukraine During the Holocaust

ROBERT MOSES SHAPIRO

Among the more than 450 *yizker-bikher,* or memorial books, published to commemorate East European Jewish communities destroyed during the Second World War,[1] there are twenty-one about communities within the pre-1939 boundaries of Soviet Belorussia and Soviet Ukraine.[2] The memorial books comprise a collective response to the Holocaust by survivors and emigrants who undertook to assemble a variety of historical accounts, documents, testimonies, and memoirs about their hometowns. Typically, most of the memorial books were published by and for the members of *landsmanshaftn,* the mutual aid societies formed in America, Israel, and elsewhere by Jewish emigrants from various East European towns. The editors and authors of the memorial books were usually not professional writers, but were amateurs driven to preserve for future generations images of the world from which they had come. As a result, the quality of the memorial books varies widely, and there is a great emphasis on the prewar history of communities. Most of the *yizker-bikher* were published in Hebrew or Yiddish, often bilingually, while some also have sections in English and other languages. In addition to surveys of the history of a community from its founding to the Holocaust period, the memorial books usually include sections focusing on the array of Jewish communal and educational institutions as well as prominent Jewish personalities and social, religious, political, and youth movements in the town. The adjacent non-Jewish population, society, and culture tend to be referred to only briefly. Often the books include materials about neighboring towns. Sections dealing with the period of the Second World War include both firsthand accounts and secondary sources, often together with partial lists of the dead. The books frequently contain photographs of town scenes, individuals, and groups, as well as maps of the region or the town itself. About 85 percent of the *yizker-bikher* are about localities within the pre-1939 boundaries of Poland. This paper examines the twenty-one memorial books for localities that were already under Soviet rule before the war.

On the eve of the Holocaust, Soviet Belorussia had about 375,000 Jews and Soviet Ukraine about 1.5 million, altogether about two-thirds of Soviet Jewry.[3] Yet only a small number of memorial books have been devoted to communities within the two republics. The editors of the Dnepropetrovsk (Ekaterinoslav) memorial book explained the overall dearth of books about communities on Soviet territory as being due to the failure of corresponding *landsmanshaftn* to develop in Israel, while the societies that existed in America declined during the interwar decades with the restriction of immigration. Moreover, access to source materials in the Soviet Union was impeded for political reasons during the Cold War.[4] While a wave of Polish Jews emigrated to America and Israel in the years after 1945 and revived *landsmanshaftn*, substantial Soviet Jewish emigration did not occur until the 1970s.

Still, there were efforts in the immediate postwar years to commemorate some Soviet Jewish communities. The Hebrew memorial periodical *Yalkut Volin*[5] was published from 1945 in then Palestine by the Federation of Volhynian Associations. Each issue of *Yalkut Volin* included a variety of articles, memoirs, and testimonies about Jewish communities within the boundaries of historic Volhynia, a portion of which had remained part of Soviet Ukraine after the 1920 Polish–Soviet War. An entire issue in 1951 was devoted to Berdichev, which otherwise has not had its own book.[6] Three years earlier, in 1948, the second volume of The Rav Kuk Institute memorial series about destroyed Jewish communities included chapters on Gomel in Belorussia and Nemirov and Odessa in Ukraine.[7]

Aside from the aforementioned items, between 1946 and 1985 some twenty-one *yizker-bikher* appeared about Jewish communities within the pre-1939 boundaries of Soviet Belorussia and Soviet Ukraine.[8] Thirteen were published in Israel, seven in the United States, and one in Argentina. Most are collective works published by *landsmanshaftn*, although the books for Bershad, Teplik, and Ternovka are by single authors.[9] Eight are entirely in Hebrew, four entirely in Yiddish, while six contain both Hebrew and Yiddish. Five have English sections and only one or two are partially in Russian.[10] In the cases of Kiev (Babi Yar), Vitebsk, and Yustingrad, each locality has had two memorial books (one published in Israel, the other in New York), with much material in common. One two-volume memorial book, *Yidn in ukrayne* (New York, 1961–67), was intended to commemorate Ukrainian Jewry as a whole. Most of the other *yizker-bikher* being considered in this chapter concentrate on a single community, although the books for Bobruisk, Husiatyn, Kamenets-Podolskiy, Koidanovo, Zvhil (Novograd-Volynskiy), Slutsk, Vitebsk, and Yampol include sections dealing with numerous neighboring towns. Thus, the twenty-one memorial books and the items about Berdichev, Gomel, Nemirov, and Odessa together provide information about nearly one hundred localities. The communities described ranged in size from small towns with less than 2,000 souls to Kiev and Odessa with more than 175,000 Jews each in 1939. While far from including all the Jewish communities in Belorussia and Ukraine, the memorial books under consideration do embrace localities which included about a third of all the Jews who had lived in both republics.

Paradoxically, although the *yizker-bikher* were inspired by the destruction inflicted on Jewish communities during the Second World War, these memorial books actually devote relatively little space to the Holocaust. With the exception of the Babi Yar books, the memorial books focus much more attention on earlier periods, especially before the First World War. In many, if not most, instances, editors and authors had themselves emigrated before 1914 or during the first years of the Soviet regime. The editors of these memorial books were generally anxious to preserve accounts of the multifaceted former Jewish way of life in their hometowns. For example, neither of the two published volumes of *Yidn in ukrayne* includes any chapters on the Holocaust period; presumably the Catastrophe would have been the theme of a projected third volume. The two-volume Teplik book, published in Argentina in 1946–50, concludes its account in about 1920, when its author emigrated. Nor does the Stavishtsh book have anything to say directly about the Second World War period. Instead, it describes the community until the civil war and pogroms of 1919. Thus, the Stavishtsh book is closer to the interwar memorial books for Proskurov and Felshtin, although one of its initiators explained that his motivation to publish a book about Stavishtsh arose from the most recent destruction and a visit to the new State of Israel.[11]

Even editors of this group of memorial books who wanted to include more Holocaust material encountered a dearth of eyewitness testimonies or other materials about the events under the German occupation. This compelled editors and writers to devote only a tiny portion of their books to the Holocaust. For example, of sixty-six double-columned pages on Berdichev, only three recall the German occupation, while the Husiatyn book gives no details on the fate of the town's 1,800 Jews, except for a list of about 200 names of murdered Jews collected and submitted by a *landsman* residing in Gorki.[12] The editors of the Kamenets-Podolskiy book expressed regret at being able to include material on only ten of the 137 communities in the region of Podolia. Efforts to obtain material from emigrants from most Podolian localities were to no avail, leaving the editors of the Kamenets book to hope that people from neighboring towns would be moved to gather material for another memorial book.[13] The editor of the Yampol book rued his inability to find any documents or photographs from the Holocaust period, leaving him unable to pinpoint even the exact day of the community's death.[14]

An important source of information about the fate of a town's Jews was letters from survivors, often themselves repatriates from the Soviet east, writing to relatives and acquaintances in Israel or America. In the case of Koidenovo, one of the *landsmanshaft*'s leaders in New York wrote a letter addressed to "Jews in Koidenovo" in care of the postmaster. A reply from a childhood acquaintance revealed that there were only nine Jews left in the town in 1946 after 1,600 Jews had been killed by the Germans. Hoping to find and aid more survivors, the Koidenover *landsmanshaft* formed a society to aid survivors, eventually locating 460 in the displaced persons camps.[15] The Koidenovo book also includes extracts from more than a score of letters from survivors, including a couple who had managed to evade death with the other ghetto inhabitants on 21 October 1941 and fled to the forests.[16] Letters from survivors are also to be found in the books for Babi Yar, Berdichev, Gomel, Husiatyn, Nemirov, Slutsk, and Zvhil. Unfortunately, the letters are often poorly edited, generally without dates or names. The Slutsk book includes Leah Flaysher's letter, written in Slutsk on 19 February 1946, in reply to a letter from a former Slutsker in New York which reached her after nine months' delay. Flaysher listed relatives who had survived and the many who had been killed on 8 February 1943, with the rest of Slutsk's Jews.[17] An undated letter by Fanye Levovitsh in the town of Luban, near Slutsk, described the fate of Jews during the war in detail, with special regard to relatives and friends. She told of a visit to the mass grave of a thousand Luban Jews and noted that only fourteen Jews remained in Luban. She concluded, "Perhaps it seems to you that this is exaggerated; I swear to you that the pure truth is even more bitter."[18]

Some of the memorial books included eyewitness testimonies gathered systematically by the Jewish historical commissions in liberated Poland and in the displaced persons camps in Germany shortly after the war. The Slutsk book presents the testimony of seventeen-year-old Daniel Mlodinov, who had been interviewed in Bialystok in May 1945. Mlodinov gave a detailed account of the arrival of the Germans, the treatment meted out to Jews, the establishment of two ghettos, and the mass shootings in October 1941 and May and November 1942. Mlodinov recalled how on 8 November 1942, as Lithuanians and Germans liquidated the Slutsk ghetto, a group of ten Jews opened fire on the Germans with concealed weapons. The teenager was one of the few who managed to flee and hide in the forest. There are differences between the Yiddish text and the Hebrew translation of Mlodinov's testimony, which are symptomatic of defective editing and translation to be found in many memorial books.[19]

Most of the *yizker-bikher* devote less than ten pages and often as little as two or three pages to the events of the Holocaust. In the foreword to the 1957 Vitebsk book, its editor admitted that the Second World War period was far from thoroughly discussed. He assumed that much material was yet to be found among the Vitebskers scattered across Russia and other countries. Still, the single chapter dealing with the destruction of Vitebsk Jewry was written by one of the most capable historians of the Catastrophe, Dr. Philip Friedman.[20] Friedman observed that memorial books' sections about the Nazi period were compiled mostly on the basis of eyewitness testimonies and memoirs of surviving Jews, as well as poetry and other documents. But such materials were not available about Vitebsk, nor was he able to locate a

Jewish survivor from occupied Vitebsk. A search of the press in various languages produced a single article about Vitebsk by the Soviet Yiddish writer David Bergelson, in the Moscow *Eynikeyt* of 5 September 1942. A search of the captured materials assembled for the Nuremberg trials of the Einsatzgruppen did produce some relevant documents about the killing of Vitebsk Jews in October 1941. Very valuable for Friedman were memoirs published in Russian in a Paris periodical by a non-Jewish Latvian socialist who witnessed the slaughter in Vitebsk.[21]

The editors and authors of these memorial books made relatively little use of German documents. Aside from Friedman, who wrote about Vitebsk, Rabbi Dr. Tsvi Harkavi sought and found information among the captured *Einsatzgruppen* reports to detail the fate of over 50,000 Jews killed in Dnepropetrovsk beginning on 13/14 October 1941.[22] Writing about Bobruisk, Yehuda Slutski quoted from a 1941 German intelligence report in which a German unit justified a special action in which 5,281 Jews were shot in an effort to end Jewish resistance.[23] The English section of the Slutsk book presents an unusual German document in which the German civil administrator in Slutsk wrote to his superiors to protest the chaotic brutality, looting, and indiscriminate killing of useful skilled Jews in October 1941 by a unit of German police with Lithuanian partisans. There follows the text of an angry letter from Wilhelm Kube, commissioner general in Minsk, calling for prosecution of the entire staff of officers of the police unit involved.[24]

A number of survivors' accounts in the memorial books describe the initial period of confusion after the German invasion in June 1941, for example in Shpola, Slutsk, and Zvhil.[25] In many instances, those who survived had managed to flee eastward to Soviet-held territory and could recount the final fate of the local Jews only on the basis of hearsay, ruins, and mass graves. The editor of the Yampol book was unable to find any documents about the town during the Holocaust, but he did publish an account by a former resident of a nearby town, describing his family's panicky flight through Yampol at the time of the German invasion in 1941. Some Jews decided to remain in Yampol because they saw no difference between the threats of the German SS and the Soviet NKVD.[26]

Most memorial books were printed in small editions and were rarely reprinted. An exception was the Ternovka book, first published in

1970 and reissued in a second, expanded edition in 1972. Its single author wrote on the basis of his own recollections and stories heard from other Ternovka natives. The brief account of the 27 May 1942 slaughter of the town's Jews was apparently based on the testimony of an unnamed individual who was the only Jew to escape both the Germans and hostile local gentiles who killed other escaped Jews.[27]

The 1972 Yustingrad book in Hebrew was reissued in facsimile within the 1983 Yustingrad volume, which also included a partial English translation. The original Yustingrad book was the result of a class project undertaken in 1965/66 by a group of twelve-year-olds at a kibbutz secondary school in Israel. While such projects were undertaken at scores of Israeli secondary schools in the wake of the Eichmann trial, only a few were published.[28] The children's research concentrated on contacts with emigrants from the town, including the former kibbutz director who edited the school project into book form in 1972. Like a number of other books, the 1972 volume expatiates more broadly about the pogroms of 1919–20 than about the final catastrophe, only mentioning two physicians who visited the town immediately after the war and twenty years later and did not find any Jews.[29] The American 1983 Yustingrad book does not add any more information about the Holocaust period.

The community of Zvhil (Novograd-Volynskiy) was memorialized in an unusual double volume published in 1962 in Israel, consisting of separate Hebrew and Yiddish sections. The Yiddish section has its own title page dated 1957, suggesting that the editors had to wait five years until enough money was raised to publish the Yiddish memorial book together with the Hebrew version. Much of the material in the Hebrew section seems to have been translated from the Yiddish section. Both sections devote only about twenty-five pages to the Nazi period.[30] Of great interest are the memoirs of Moshe Gildnman, famous as the partisan leader "Uncle Misha," who describes Zvhil in the years of Soviet rule before and after German occupation. Gildnman's accounts focus on the partisan struggle against the Germans and note the persistence of violent hatred for surviving Jews after the German defeat, even among Russian and Ukrainian Soviet officials.[31] The most extensive accounts of Jewish partisans are to be found in the Minsk book's second volume.

The return of surviving Jews from the east or from the forests is described in several of the memorial books. For example, in June

1946, Red Army soldier Chaim Kuntser visited Slutsk before returning to his nearby hometown of Pahost for the first time, but found that no other Pahost Jews had survived. Kuntser did recognize his father's cow, which he reclaimed at gunpoint from a Belorussian.[32] An anonymous account in the Kamenets book tells of the return of a surviving former *gabbay* or trustee of the Tailors' Synagogue, which had been closed by the Soviets before the war. Dozens of Torah scrolls, hidden away years earlier to avoid state confiscation, had survived the German occupation and were now distributed among Jewish prayer groups formed by survivors in nearby towns.[33] The Shpola book presents an account of the first Yom Kippur prayers held there after the liberation, when there were virtually no local Jews, only about eighty men and women from other towns who gathered to pray: "We had no holiday prayerbooks; the cantor read the prayers slowly and we repeated after him with bitter weeping."[34]

The massive, bilingual Hebrew and Yiddish Bobruisk book was edited by the professional historian Yehuda Slutski, who composed a major historical monograph about the town from its medieval origins until after the Second World War.[35] For the few pages dealing with the Holocaust period, Slutski made use of a number of Russian memoirs by former partisans, as well as articles from the Moscow *Pravda* and the Yiddish *Eynikeyt* and some captured German documents referring to the slaughter of the city's Jews in November 1941.[36] Several of the Jewish testimonies and press reports are reprinted in full in the book.[37] Of particular interest is an interview with "The Partisan Granny" from the Moscow *Eynikeyt* of 16 April 1946, in which the elderly Khasye Berkovitsh recounted how she joined the partisans in August 1941 and served the war effort by cooking, washing, mending clothing, nursing the wounded, and occasionally entering area villages to gather information for the unit.[38]

The most impressive of the memorial books in regard to depicting the Holocaust period is about Minsk. Its first volume, dealing with the period until 1917, appeared in 1975. The second Minsk volume was published a decade later and was devoted to the half-century since 1917. Most of the second volume consists of memoirs and testimonies by eyewitnesses, scores of whom were interviewed during the early 1970s by David Cohen, who worked with the cooperation of the Oral History Division of the Institute for Contemporary Jewry at the Hebrew University in Jerusalem.[39] Cohen interviewed both veteran residents of Israel, who had left Minsk in the first years of the Soviet regime, and members of the new wave of Soviet emigration after the 1967 Six-Day War. In addition to selections from Cohen's interviews, there are also extracts and translations of previously published memoirs, such as that of Sofia Sadovskaya, which originally appeared in a Russian anthology published in Minsk in 1970.[40] Haim Baram, born Heinz Behrendt in Berlin, recalls being incarcerated in the special ghetto established at Minsk for German Jews, about which he also testified at the Eichmann trial in 1961.[41] Curiously, even though the Minsk book focuses on the underground and partisan struggle by Minsk Jews, none of the memoirs of Hersh Smolar, the Polish Jewish Communist who was a leader of the underground, are included.[42]

Yet even the Minsk memorial book ultimately devotes less than half of its second volume to the Holocaust. The only memorial books that focus almost entirely on the period of the Second World War are the Babi Yar books. Instead of being called the Kiev memorial books, they are simply named after the site of the mass killing on the city's outskirts. There is no discussion of the pre-Soviet history of Kiev Jewry, nor of Jewish life during the interwar decades. Jewish life after the Second World War is briefly referred to in the context of suppression of attempts to commemorate the Jewish dead at Babi Yar. The 1983 Babi Yar book is quite unusual, in that it has a major segment in Russian, having been initiated by recent Soviet Jewish emigrants with the purpose of publishing a list of thousands of names of Jews who perished at Babi Yar. The lack of any accounts of Kiev's pre-Soviet history in the 1983 Babi Yar book is symptomatic of the uprooting of historical knowledge among Soviet Jewry.

In general, it can be said that the more than a score of *yizker-bikher* dedicated to Jewish communities within the prewar limits of Soviet Belorussia and Soviet Ukraine are valuable sources about the history and Jewish way of life in those places until the start of the Soviet regime. Some of the books include information about Jewish life under the Soviets. However, with the exceptions of Minsk and Kiev (Babi Yar), the memorial books present relatively little material about the Catastrophe under German occupation. This material generally consists of a handful of survivors' testimonies, brief memoirs, some letters written in the aftermath of liberation, and reprinted articles from the Soviet Russian and Yiddish press. Rarely is there recourse to captured German documents, such as those assembled for the Nuremberg trials.

Editors encountered practical obstacles in obtaining materials about the Holocaust period in their towns from which there were few available survivors. Ultimately, the editorial decision to devote less space to the Holocaust reflected a desire to preserve the record of the life of the destroyed communities in preference to recounting details of their final torments and deaths.

Notes

1. On the memorial books in general, see Zachary M. Baker, "Memorial Books as Sources for Family History," *Toledot,* vol. 3, no. 2–3 (fall 1979–winter 1980), pp. 3–7; Jack Kugelmass and Jonathan Boyarin, eds., *From a Ruined Garden: The Memorial Books of Polish Jewry* (New York, 1983), pp. 1–19; Zachary M. Baker, "Bibliography of Eastern European Memorial Books," in ibid., pp. 223–64; Abraham Wein, " 'Memorial Books' as a Source for Research into the History of Jewish Communities in Europe," *Yad Vashem Studies,* vol. 9, ed. Livia Rothkirchen (Jerusalem, 1973), pp. 255–72.

2. See the appended bibliography. Zachary M. Baker has counted a total of 145 memorial books for localities within the present boundaries of Ukraine, of which only fifteen are for places that were within pre-1939 Soviet Ukraine. Letter to Robert Moses Shapiro, 25 September 1991.

3. Population figures given in this paper are based on census data and estimates in *Encyclopedia Judaica* (Jerusalem, 1972) and in the relevant memorial books.

4. Yekaterinoslav book, p. 6. Also quoted by in Z.M. Baker, "Memorial Books as Sources for Family History," p. 5.

5. See appended bibliography, under Volhynia.

6. See appended bibliography, under Berdichev. Other Soviet Ukrainian communities were also commemorated with individual articles and testimonies in various issues, e.g., Zhitomir in *Yalkut Volin,* 1950, no. 7, pp. 9–12; and no. 10, pp. 7–8. The thirty issues of *Yalkut Volin* which appeared through 1978 have not as yet been indexed.

7. See the appended bibliography.

8. A third Babi Yar memorial book was reportedly published in Russian in Israel in summer 1991; I have not yet seen it.

9. The Shpola book is largely by a single author, although it also includes some memoirs by others.

10. I have not had access to a copy of the 1981 Babi Yar book published in Jerusalem and so do not know what languages it includes, although I would expect Hebrew and Russian.

11. Stavishtsh book, pp. 21–26.

12. Husiatyn book, pp. 130–32.

13. Kamenets-Podolskiy book, pp. 11–13.

14. Yampol book, p. 4.

15. Koidenovo book, pp. 11–14.

16. Ibid., pp. 239, 249–58.

17. Slutsk book, p. 387.

18. Slutsk book, pp. 456–58.

19. Slutsk book, Hebrew translation, pp. 143–44; Yiddish version, pp. 381–82. The original testimony is to be found at Yad Vashem Archives, M 11/317.

20. Vitebsk book (1956), pp. 603–26; Vitebsk book (1957), cols. 439–52.

21. Iv. Ivanov, "Iz nedavnevo proshlovo," *Sotsialistitsheskii vestnik* (Paris–New York), 1950, no. 1–2, pp. 26–27; and no. 3, pp. 49–50.

22. Ekaterinoslav book, pp. 89–92.

23. Bobruisk book, p. 108, note 53.

24. Slutsk book, pp. x–xv reproducing documents presented at Nuremberg trials and published in *Nazi Conspiracy and Aggression* (Washington, D.C.: U.S. Government Printing Office, 1946), vol. 3, p. 785.

25. Shpola book, pp. 275–77; Slutsk book, pp. 376–77; Zvhil book, Hebrew pp. 302–3.

26. Yampol book, pp. 76–78.

27. Ternovka book, pp. 100–102.

28. The project was undertaken by the children of Kibbutz Mashabei Sadeh and was the 68th such booklet produced to commemorate destroyed Jewish communities. Yustingrad book (1983), p. 197. Another such project resulted in an anthology about Lodz, Poland: *Kovets le-zekher kehilat lodz* (Tel Aviv, [1965/66]).

29. Yustingrad book (1983), pp. 57–58.

30. Zvhil book, Hebrew pp. 281–306, Yiddish pp. 200–27.

31. Zvhil book, Hebrew pp. 286–92.

32. Slutsk book, pp. 469–71.

33. Kamenets-Podolskiy book, pp. 64–65.

34. Shpola book, pp. 280–81.

35. Bobruisk book, pp. 19–112 (Hebrew), pp. 113–220 (Yiddish).

36. Bobruisk book, pp. 106–12.

37. Ibid., pp. 727–37.

38. Ibid., pp. 734–37.

39. Minsk (1985), Part II, pp. 267–416, deals with the Holocaust period, while Part III, pp. 417–64, deals with the postwar period and the attempt to revive Jewish life in Minsk.

40. Minsk (1985), pp. 350–56.

41. Ibid., pp. 336–49.

42. E.g., Hersh Smolar, *Fun minsker geto* (Warsaw, 1946).

Bibliography of Memorial Books for Jewish Communities in Soviet Belorussia and Soviet Ukraine

Key to Symbols:
(B) = Located in Belorussian SSR. before 1939.
(U) = Located in Ukrainian SSR before 1939.
 * = Indicates that the translated title was supplied by the work itself.

This bibliography is based on Baker, "Bibliography of Eastern European Memorial Books," pp. 223–64.

Babi Yar (U). *Babi Yar.* Ed.: Yefraim Bauch. Jerusalem, Jewish Agency [?], 1981. [No copy of this book is at the Library of Congress or YIVO.]

Babi Yar (U). *Yizker-bukh fun di umgekumene yidn in Babi-Yar* [The Babi Yar book of remembrance*]. Eds.: Joseph Vinokurov, Shimon Kipnis, Nora Levin. Philadelphia, Publishing House of Peace, 1982. 202, 82 pp., illus., ports. (Yiddish, Russian, English)

Berdichev (U). Special Berdichev issue of *Yalkut Volin; osef zikhronot u-teudot* [Anthology of Volhynia; collection of memoirs and documents], Tel Aviv, vol. 2, nos. 12–13, Nisan 5711 [1951], ed. Barukh Kru (Krupnik). 66 pp. (Hebrew)

Bershad (U). *Be-tsel ayara* [Bershad*]. [By] Nahman Huberman. Jerusalem, Encyclopedia of the Jewish Diaspora, 1956. 247 pp., port. (Hebrew)

Bobruisk (B). *Bobruisk; sefer zikaron le-kehilat Bobruisk u-venoteha* [Memorial book of the community of Bobruisk and its surroundings]. Ed.: Y. Slutski. Tel Aviv, Former Residents of Bobruisk in Israel and the U.S.A., 1967, 2 vols., 871 pp. , ports., map, facsims. (Hebrew, Yiddish)

Dnepropetrovsk (U) see Yekaterinoslav

Dzerzhinsk (B) see Koidanovo

Ekaterinoslav (U) see Yekaterinoslav.

Felshtin (U). *Felshtin; zamlbukh lekoved tsum ondenk fun di Felshtiner kedoyshim* [Felshtin; collection in memory of the martyrs of Felshtin]. New York, First Felshtiner Progressive Benevolent Association, 1937. 670 pp., illus. (Yiddish, English)

Gomel (U). "Homel" by Yalag Kahanovits, in *Arim ve-imahot be-yisrael; matsevat kodesh le-kehilot yisrael she-nehrevu be-yedei aritsim u-temeim be-milhemet ha-olam ha-aharona* [Towns and mother-cities in Israel; memorial of the Jewish communities which were destroyed ...]. Ed.: Y.L. Fishman (Maimon). Jerusalem, Mossad ha-Rav Kuk, vol. 2, 1948, pp. 187–269. (Hebrew)

Homel (U) see Gomel

Husiatyn (U). *Husiatyn; Podoler Gubernye* [Husiatyn; Podolia-Ukraine*]. Ed.: B. Diamond. New York, Former Residents of Husiatyn in America, 1968. 146, [40], 123 pp., ports. (Yiddish, English)

Kamenets-Podolskiy (U). *Kamenets-Podolsk u-sevivata* [Kamenets-Podolsk and its surroundings]. Eds.: A. Rosen, Ch. Sarig, Y. Bernstein. Tel Aviv, Association of Former Residents of Kamenets-Podolsk and Its Surroundings in Israel, 1965. 263 pp., ports., facsims. (Hebrew)

Kiev (U) see Babi Yar

Koidanovo (B). *Koydenov; zamlbukh tsum ondenk fun di Koydenover kedoyshim* [Koidanov; memorial volume of the martyrs of Koidanov]. Ed.: A. Raisen. New York, United Koidanover Association, 1955. 216, 207 pp., ports., facsims. (Yiddish)

Minsk (B). *Minsk; ir ve-em* [Minsk, Jewish mother city; memorial anthology*]. Ed.: Shlomo Even-Shoshan. Israel, Minsk Society, Ghetto Fighters House, ha-Kibbutz ha-Meuhad, 1975, vol. 1, 692 pp.; 1985, vol. 2, 504 pp., illus. (Hebrew)

Nemirov (U). "Nemirov" by Yohanan Pogrebinski, in *Arim ve-imahot be-yisrael; matsevat kodesh le-kehilot yisrael she-nehrevu be-yedei aritsim u-temeim be-milhemet ha-olam ha-aharona* [Towns and mother-cities in Israel; memorial of the Jewish communities which were destroyed ...]. Ed.: Y.L. Fishman (Maimon). Jerusalem, Mossad ha-Rav Kuk, vol. 2, 1948, pp. 270–83. (Hebrew)

Novograd-Volynskiy (U). *Zvhil-Novogradvolinsk.* Eds.: A. Uri, M. Bone. Tel Aviv, Association of Former Residents of Zvhil and the Environment, 1962. 354, 232, 16 pp., ports. (Hebrew, Yiddish, English)

Odessa (U). "Odessa" by Barukh Shohetman, in *Arim ve-imahot be-yisrael; matsevat kodesh le-kehilot yisrael she-nehrevu be-yedei aritsim u-temeim be-milhemet ha-olam ha-aharona* [Towns and mother-cities in Israel; memorial of the Jewish communities which were destroyed ...]. Ed.: Y.L. Fishman (Maimon). Jerusalem, Mossad ha-Rav Kuk, vol. 2, 1948, pp. 58–108. (Hebrew)

Proskurov (U). *Khurbn Proskurov; tsum ondenkn fun di heylige neshomes vos zaynen umgekumn in der shreklikher shkhite, vos iz ongefirt gevorn durkh di haydamakes* [The destruction of Proskurov; in memory of the sacred souls who perished during the terrible slaughter of the Haidamaks]. New York, 1924. 111 pp., illus. (Yiddish, Hebrew)

Shpola (U). *Shpola; masekhet hayei yehudim ba-ayara* [Shpola; a picture of Jewish life in the town]. [By] David Cohen. [Haifa], Association of Former Residents of Shpola (Ukraine) in Israel, 1965. 307 pp., ports. (Hebrew)

Slutsk (B). *Pinkas Slutsk u-venoteha* [Slutsk and vicinity memorial book*]. Eds.: N. Chinitz and Sh. Nachmani. Tel Aviv, Yizkor-Book Committee, 1962. 450 pp., ports., maps, facsims. (Hebrew, Yiddish, English)

Stavische (U). *Stavisht.* Ed.: A. Weissman. Tel Aviv, The Stavisht Society, New York, 1961. 252 columns, ports. (Hebrew, Yiddish)

Stavishtsh (U) see Stavische

Teplik (U). *Teplik, mayn shtetele; kapitln fun fuftsik yor lebn* [My town Teplik; chapters from fifty years of life]. [By] Valentin Chernovetzky. Buenos Aires, El Magazine Argentino, 1946–50, 2 vols., illus. (Yiddish)

Ternovka (U). *Ayaratenu Ternovka; pirkei zikaron u-matseva* [Our town Ternovka; chapters of remembrance and a monument]. [By] G. Bar-Zvi. Tel Aviv, Ternovka Society, 1972. 103 pp., illus. (Hebrew)

Ukraine (U). *Yidn in Ukraine* [Jews in the Ukraine*]. Eds. M. Osherovitch, J. Lestchinsky et al. New York, Association for the Commemoration of the Ukrainian Jews, 1961–67. 2 vols., 342 pp., ports., maps, facsims. (Yiddish)

Vitebsk (B). *Sefer Vitebsk* [Memorial book of Vitebsk]. Ed.: B. Krupnik. Tel Aviv, Former Residents of Vitebsk and Surroundings in Israel, 1957. 508 columns, ports., facsims. (Hebrew)

Vitebsk (B). *Vitebsk amol; geshikhte, zikhroynes, khurbn* [Vitebsk in the past; history, memoirs, destruction]. Eds.: G. Aronson, J. Lestchinsky, A. Kihn. New York, 1956. 644 pp., ports. (Yiddish)

Volhynia (U). *Yalkut Volin; osef zikhronot u-teudot* [Anthology of Volhynia; collection of memoirs and documents]. Tel Aviv and New York, Former Residents of Volhynia in Israel and America, 1945–1978, 5 vols. (Hebrew, Yiddish) [Nominally a quarterly, thirty issues appeared through 1978. Only in Hebrew until no. 30 in 1970, when Yiddish also began to be used.]

Yampol (U). *Ayara be-lehavot; pinkas Yampola, pelekh Volyn* [Town in flames; book of Yampola, district Volhynia]. Ed.: L. Gelman. Jerusalem, Commemoration Committee for the Town with the Assistance of Yad Vashem and the World Jewish Congress, 1963. [154] pp. (Hebrew, Yiddish)

Yekaterinoslav (U). *Sefer Yekaterinoslav-Dnepropetrovsk* [Memorial book of Yekaterinoslav-Dnepropetrovsk]. Eds.: Tsvi Harkavi, Yaakov Goldbort. Jerusalem–Tel Aviv, Yekaterinoslav-Dnepropetrovsk Society, 1973. 167 pp., illus. (Hebrew)

Yustingrad (U). *Sokolievka/Justingrad: A century of struggle and suffering in a Ukrainian shtetl, as recounted by survivors to its scattered descendants.* Eds.: Leo Miller and Diana F. Miller. New York, A Logvin book, Loewenthal Press, 1983. 202 pp., facsims., illus., maps, ports. (English, Hebrew, Yiddish) [Includes facsimile and translation of 1972 Mashabei Sadeh edition.]

Yustingrad (U). *Yustingrad-Sokolivka; ayara she-nihreva* [Yustingrad-Sokolivka; a town that was destroyed]. Kibbutz Mashabei Sadeh, 1972. 63, [17] pp., ports., map, illus. (Hebrew)

Zvhil (U) see Novograd-Volynskiy

Polish Jewish Officers Who Were Killed in Katyn

An Ongoing Investigation in Light of Documents Recently Released by the USSR

SIMON SCHOCHET

Katyn is a tragic chapter in the history of Poland. The officers who died there were murdered without regard to their faith, race, or occupation. They were massacred for the sole reasons that they wore the uniforms of their country and had tried to defend their fatherland in the capacity of soldiers of their nation. My attempt to classify and identify the Polish officers of Jewish faith was conceived in the spirit of attesting to this specific horror which befell the nation. An additional factor was to expand our knowledge of the history of the Polish Jews as well as to honor these brave men who, in most instances, have not been survived by any relatives because of the tragic events of World War II, and thus for the most part were relegated to oblivion.

My first study of the Jews in Katyn was, after years of research, published in 1988 in *Niepodleglosc,* a yearly publication about modern Polish history issued under the auspices of the Pilsudski Institute in New York and London.[1] It was then published in English in a revised version, under the auspices of Yeshiva University in 1989.[2] The study concentrated only on the camp in Kozielsk where bodies had been found, and the main sources used in the research were the German list, *Amtliches Material zum Massenmord von Katyn* and the more accruate and revised *Lista Katynska*, by Adam Moszynski.[3]

In addition, documents available at the time in the West, memoirs, and personal and written interviews were utilized. The methodology used was to check the given names of the victims, as given names had distinctive differences based on Polish and Jewish traditions. Other criteria used were the family names. These posed great difficulty, as many Slavs and especially many Germans sometimes used these names as well. Family names that had Hebrew roots were a positive sign used to identify the bearer as Jewish. Using these criteria, but without having any contact with Polish historians or access to sources in the Soviet Union and Poland, in this pioneer study, I was able to identify 262 Jewish officers who had perished in Kozielsk and stipulated that there might be an equal number who had perished in the camp at Starobielsk. The camp at Ostaszkow was not considered in this study because of the small number of available names and because the population in this camp consisted of policemen, border guards, and other nonmilitary forces, among which it was assumed that there were few if any Jews.

Shortly after the first publication of my study in *Niepodleglosc* and by Yeshiva University, my findings were widely quoted and referred to in many periodicals and newspapers (among them, *Nowy Dziennik, The New York Times,* and *L'Express*).[4] In addition, Radio Free Europe broadcast an interview in which I appealed to listeners in Poland who might have information about the Jewish officers who were in Katyn to contact me with any data they might be able to provide. As a result, I was able to obtain additional information about these men, as well as photographs, and was thus able to identify an additional twenty-eight officers of the Jewish faith who had perished in Kozielsk. Among the photographs received were six of the chief rabbi of the Polish Armed Forces, Rabbi Boruch Steinberg.[5] These photographs, all taken in the 1930s, show the rabbi in Polish military uniform. One very interesting photo shows the rabbi celebrating the Passover seder; at the table are high-ranking officers of various faiths and representatives of the Warsaw City Government and leaders of the Jewish community.

After the Russians admitted that the Soviet secret police had been responsible for the massacre at Katyn and Soviet President Mikhail Gorbachev handed over hitherto unknown documents to Polish President Wojciech Jaruzelski on 13 April 1990, I was able to correspond freely with historians in Poland who had researched the events at Katyn. The courage, dedication, and sacrifices of these historians, who struggled to compile and record the historical data through the long years of Communist rule in Poland, is admirable. Many of them had been interrogated, many of their homes had been searched, and some of them were even imprisoned because of their pursuits.

The Katyn Institute, founded in Krakow, Poland, in 1978, was a clandestine organization which published thirty illegal bulletins about the Katyn massacre that were distributed by the underground. The June 1980 issue was dedicated to the memory of Major Steinberg and his many coreligionists who were soldiers and officers in the Polish Army and his comrades-in-arms. In this issue it was estimated that among the approximately 14,500 Polish Army prisoners in the Katyn camps, 15 percent were Jews. A sample death roll bearing Polish-Jewish names was listed, and it was stated that it had not been possible to identify others as being Jewish as they had Polish-sounding names. This sample list contains 129 names from the camp in Kozielsk, 94 from the camp in Starobielsk, and 5 from the camp in Ostaszkow, making a total of 228 Jewish names.[6]

In August 1990, knowing that the Russian documents were now in the hands of the Polish historians, and with their kind permission and consent, I went to Poland to study these documents and to discuss details pertaining to my research. The documents that I have seen are very selective, especially those relating to orders and the execution of orders by the NKVD in connection with the establishment and administration of the POW camps in Ostaszkow, Kozielsk, and Starobielsk.

The Russian NKVD lists are quite extensive as to the number and names of the prisoners. The lists are 10 to 20 percent longer than the *Lista Katnyska* of Moszynski as far as Kozielsk and Starobielsk are concerned. The list of Ostaszkow is markedly longer, as the Russians listed 6,287 prisoners there as against 1,260 listed by Moszynski. These listings are still far from complete, as they do not list any prisoners who died or were sent elsewhere before April 1, 1940. No reports about those men are available (for example, what happened to Rabbi Major Steinberg and the chaplains from Starobielsk, whom we know were sent out from that camp before Christmas of 1939). The Russian lists number about 100 names each and are difficult to read, as they are photostats of original typewritten pages. (All the documents President Gorbachev gave to President Jaruzielski were also photocopies.) The names written on the NKVD transport lists are in many instances russified in their spelling and thus must be properly checked against the correct Polish names listed by Moszynski and other sources and then corroborated. Despite all these shortcomings and discrepancies, the Russian lists provide information which was not available before, namely, not only the name and given name but also the father's name. This last piece of information is of great help in identifying the Jewish officers since, as a rule, the majority of these officers came from an acculturated Polish background and thus had commonly used Polish first names. Their fathers, however, very often retained their Jewish first names, and these names indicate that officers were of the Jewish faith. Take, for example, Laufer Adolf Dawid, or Sinchowicz Anatol Sziepsjelewicz. Having just the names and given names, there would not be any justification in even contemplating their classification as Jews. In the first instance the name might indicate someone of German origin and in the second, someone of strictly Polish origin. However, the listing of the father's names clearly identifies these individuals as being Jewish, since Dawid and Szieps (Szeps) were distinctively Jewish names.

In Lodz, I saw one of the most impressive collections of materials relating to Katyn. In the collection there is a highly detailed and computerized list of Katyn victims who came from the city of Lodz and its environs. The monies needed to compile this list and the ongoing research have come solely from the donations of about 600 members of the Association of the Families of the Victims of Katyn from Lodz.

Colonel Zygmunt Gaul, a researcher and archivist of the Lodz Chapter of the Association of Katyn Families, drew my attention to an NKVD transportation list from Starobielsk (No. 052/3), dated 27 April 1940 and signed by Chochlov, an NKVD lieutenant. Among the 100 prisoners' names which appear on the list, about 30 are Jewish names. In general, the lists are not written in alphabetical order, and these Jewish names are scattered among the others. This unusually large group of Jews on one lists poses various questions as to why there were proportionately so many.

There is evidence that the NKVD officers in charge of the death transports had some authority to remove some prisoners' names from the lists. An incident attesting to this is cited by Professor Janusz Zawodny in his book *Katyn*, in which one of the NKVD officers, Pieta Pszeniczny, removed the name of Air Force Lieutenant Jan Mintow-Czyza from a list from Kozielsk after he realized that as children they had known one another and had even played together.[7] He had him sent instead to a camp in Grazovec.

It seems likely to me that prisoners in all three camps may have been preclassified according to their prewar membership in various so-called counterrevolutionary organizations. A directive from Lavrenty P. Beria dated 8 October 1939 orders the creation of a special departmental network of agents to detect and classify and to watch closely the Polish POWs as to their past affiliations and their present political sentiments.[8] The list of the prewar Polish organizations deemed subversive is a lengthy one and includes not only political and military ones but professional ones as well. For example, the Union of Polish Lawyers appeared on the list. Among the various associations, Zionist groups are included. Thus, it may be possible that the Jewish officers on the list were known to be members or sympathizers of the Polish Zionist movements. If this assumption is correct, a detailed analysis of the transport lists must be made in order to determine whether the NKVD grouped prisoners according to their past organizational affiliations or purported sympathies.

An additional question was posed in regard to the Jewish POWs taken by the Soviets and their attitude and consideration in regard to sending them back to the Germans. There is little doubt that the Russian authorities were informed about the fate of the Polish Jewish military men who were taken prisoner by the Germans. Their immediate segregation from non-Jewish soldiers and the ensuing high casualties they suffered after their capture has been well documented by Polish historian Szymon Datner.[9] It must, however, be noted that about 300 Jewish officers who were sometimes segregated and at times given unduly harsh treatment did survive with their non-Jewish colleagues in the German POW officers' camps.

Based on my research, there is no evidence that the Russians gave any consideration to the future fate of Jewish Polish POWs when handing them over to the Germans. As proof, there are documents in the Central State Archives of the Soviet Army dated mid-October 1939, which concern the accord reached by the Germans and Soviets about an exchange of POWs on the basis of their prewar residences.[10] Accordingly, 20,000 Polish POWs, ethnic Belorussians and Ukrainians were to be handed over by the Germans to the Russians while those born in Poland, primarily in those areas which had been annexed into the German Reich, were to be sent back into German military hands. Many Polish soldiers, the majority of them Jews, feared persecution by the Nazis and petitioned camp authorities to be allowed to stay in the Soviet Union. A plea to this effect is recorded among the documents. It is the petition of a Jewish Polish soldier, M. Maszkowicz, a tailor by profession who had lived in Warsaw since 1905.[11]

These applications for nonreturn were denied by Moscow as being unsound, and an order was given from Moscow by Major P. Soprunenko of the NKVD, who was in charge of POW affairs.[12] He ordered the camp commanders to return the prisoners to the areas annexed by the Third Reich, with the very probable result that the majority of those of the Jewish faith met with death. According to the documents, 42,292 such prisoners were ceded by the Russians to the Germans between 24 October and 23 November 1940, as reported by historians N. Lebedeva and A. Chubarian of the Institute of German History, USSR Academy of Sciences.[13]

It is still unknown whether the Soviet authorities classified the prisoners according to their nationalities or religions. There is, however, one document of 1 March 1940, signed Major Soprunenko, which lists Polish officers who had formerly lived in the eastern part of Poland (at that time part of Belorussia and the USSR). This document does categorize the prisoners into six national groupings, one of them being Jewish.[14]

It would be an impossible task, in my opinion, to identify correctly the exact number and names of the Jewish officers who were murdered in Katyn. We still lack full documentation, and, as stated before, because of the decimation of the Polish Jews, there are few descendants of families of these victims who are still alive to testify to their faith.

In 1991 the Polish newspaper *Folks-Sztyme,* a publication of the Social and Cultural Association of Jews in Poland, published two issues in which a partial list of names of Jews killed in Katyn was given as 145: 88 from Kozielsk and 57 from Starobielsk. Based on an explanation of the researcher, Marian Fuchs, who had prepared this list, further publication of the names had to be abandoned because of the difficulties of obtaining sufficient documentation and because of the time needed to search out archival sources.[15] However, taking all these factors into consideration and based on my own years of research into this subject as well as my many exchanges with historians who are expert on the subject of Katyn, and with the full understanding that these figures are subject to revision and correction, to the best of my belief and estimates, at least 700 and perhaps as many as 800 Jews were killed in all the camps at Katyn. Almost all of these were officers, but there were also some civilians among them who were members of other formations. Among the officers, the majority of Jews in Katyn were reserve officers who had been mobilized prior to 1 September 1939. The largest group was medical doctors, followed by lawyers, engineers, pharmacists, and dentists. The vast majority of the Jewish officers held the rank of second or first lieutenant. In my estimation, the highest ranking among them was a colonel, Jan Wladyslaw Nelken, a prominent psychiatrist whose personal notes dating from the time of his imprisonment were recently discovered in Krakow among the papers of a Polish physician who worked for the Germans and had hidden these documents, found on the slain officer's body in Katyn.[16]

I should like to quote, with their permission, the opinions of two eminent researchers. One, Professor Janusz Zawodny, estimates that at least 800 Jews were in Katyn. He bases his estimate on the statistical percentage of the Jewish population in Poland prior to 1939 as well as the number of Jewish university graduates. Professor Zawodny estimates that out of approximately 800 medical doctors in all three camps, about 400 were of the Jewish faith. I tend to concur with this number, as, based on the last census of 1931, 55.5 percent of all physicians in Poland were Jews.[17] Furthermore, during my visit in connection with my research, I met with Dr. Med. Edmund Wiliamski of Lodz, who is in charge of setting up a commemorative plaque to honor the physicians associated with one hospital in that city who were killed in Katyn. The committee chose only those doctors who worked in the hospital in Moscickiego, as representative of all the physicians killed. This had been a state hospital, to which, as was well known, Jewish physicians had difficulty in obtaining appointments after 1935, and so were mostly in private practice or in Jewish or privately run hospitals. Among the seventeen doctors listed, Dr. Wiliamski has identified seven as having been of Jewish origin.

In Poland, Mgr. Ing. Jedrzej Tucholski of the Independent Historical Committee to Research the Crime of Katyn is regarded as a foremost researcher on the victims of Katyn. His recently published book, *Mord w Katyniu* (The Murder in Katyn), lists all the names of the prisoners in the three camps based on the available (to date) Russian records.[18] These records are also reprinted in their original form in the Russian language. Tucholski is a member of a special Polish commission set up to visit the sites of the graves of former prisoners of Starobielsk which are located in the vicinity of Kharkiv in Ukraine. Analyses to pinpoint the possible sites of these graves are being done in part by an American aerial photo reconnaissance expert, Waclaw Godziemba-Maliszewski.[19] He uses German Luftwaffe intelligence photographs of the Ukrainian, Belorussian, and Russian terrain which were made during World War II.

I had the honor of spending some time with Tucholski and discussing the matter of my research on the Jews in Katyn. Tucholski, based on his research of the Polish and Russian material, including the estimates given in the report of the Polish Red Cross, members of which were present during the German exhumation of the bodies in Kozielsk in 1943, told me that at least 600, and perhaps as many as 800, Jews were in all the camps in Katyn. Also, according to Tucholski, who has examined the files of the police officers who were in Ostaszkow, there were at least several Jews among them. Although up until 1939, the Polish police force in the independent Poland of the time did not as a rule have Jews in its ranks, Jews did occupy certain administrative, legal, and technical posts in various police departments.

The classification of 5,033 policemen who were in Ostaszkow must be carefully examined in light of the documents found by a Russian researcher at the Institute of General History, Natalia Lebedeva. In her paper "The Katyn Tragedy," published in Moscow in the July 1990 issue of *International Affairs,* she cites a report from the chief of the first section of the NKVD, Tishkov, in which he requests the release of the bulk of those classified as police, since many so classified were reservists made up of workers and peasants who had been attached to this group because of age and had, in truth, never served in the police force at all. This request was turned down by the leadership of the NKVD.[20] It is fair to assume that in this group there were also a number of Jews.

The *Military History Review* published by the Historical Institute of the Polish Ministry of Defense has brought out, since 1990, five issues in which there is a section devoted to Pro Memoria, a listing of a selection of officers killed in Katyn.[21] The detailed biographies, at times accompanied by a photograph of the person described, were taken from pre–World War II officers' files called *teczki oficerskie.* These files are almost intact and are stored at the Polish Military Archives in Rembatow near Warsaw. They survived the war because the German Gestapo used them as an information tool to obtain intelligence details about the former Polish officers and their families during the occupation of Poland. Among the biographical data is sometimes listed a note of the officer's religious affiliation or that of his parents. As of this writing, I was able to find fourteen officers whose religion or that of his parents was listed as Jewish.

In testimony given before a Select Committee investigation of the Katyn forest massacre and published in Washington in 1952, two witnesses, Marian Gawiak and George Grabicki, stated that among the prisoners in Katyn there were a few rabbis.[22] I have been unable to identify the other rabbis on any of the available lists. The most authoritative book, *Wspomnienia Jenca z Kozielska* (The Memoirs of a Prisoner from Kozielsk), written by Father Zdzislaw Peszkowski in 1989, lists thirty-two clergymen, mostly army chaplains, among them only one rabbi, Rabbi Steinberg.[23] Father Peszkowski, who miraculously escaped death in Kozielsk, relates that organized prayers were strictly forbidden at the camp by the prison authorities and that the inmates observed a three-minute period of silence every evening at 9 P.M. "This silence was observed by all: believers and non-believers alike, Catholics and Jews."[24]

After my return from Poland, my new research about the number of Jewish officers killed in Katyn was printed in the Polish-language *Przeglad Polski,* the weekend supplement of *Nowy Dziennik,* published in New York. The same article was reprinted in the Russian-language daily *Novoe Russkoe Slovo.*[25] In addition to the text of these two articles, two prewar photographs of Rabbi Boruch Steinberg were featured. One of the photographs showed the rabbi at a seder and the other, taken in a temple, shows the rabbi surrounded by high-ranking Polish officers of all faiths.

The first monument to the victims of Katyn was erected in 1976 in London and bears a cross, a Star of David, and a crescent, the symbols of the religions of the victims who were murdered there. In Poland at this time, commemorations for the dead and monuments are being erected to honor the victims. In Gdansk, in the St. Brigitte church, the monument is adorned with these same religious symbols. In Krakow, in the heart of the city between the Market Square and Wawel, a large wooden cross serves as a reminder of Katyn. In Lodz, a strikingly simple monument is adorned with the "Virtuti Militari."

The tragedy at Katyn is part of Polish history. An integral part of this history encompasses the history of the Jewish people who lived there. Military graves are often marked by the religious symbols of the fallen. This is the case at the Monte Cassino cemetery, where the Polish soldiers killed there are buried. Many of these graves are marked by Mogen Davids. There are no mecevas or Jewish symbols on the graves at Katyn for the 700 or more Polish Jews—a sizable number of the most educated members of the Polish Jewish prewar community who took part in the defense of their country and were brutally murdered along with their comrades in arms. Let us commemorate them, pray for them, and bless their memory.

Notes

1. Simon Schochet, "Polscy Oficerowie Pochodzenia Zydowskiego—Jency Katynia Na Tle Walk O Niepodleglosc (Proba Identyfikacji)," *Niepodleglosc*, vol. 21 (New York–London: Institut Jozefa Pilsudskiego, 1988), pp. 152–65.

2. Simon Schochet, *An Attempt to Identify the Polish Jewish Officers Who Were Prisoners in Katyn*, Working Papers in Holocaust Studies II, Holocaust Studies Program, Yeshiva University (New York, March 1988).

3. *Amtliches Material zum Massenmord von Katyn* (Berlin, 1943); and Adam Moszynski, *Lista Katynska. Jency obozow Kozielsk, Ostaszkow, Starobielsk, Zaginieni we Rosji Sowieckiej* (London, 1982).

4. Editorial, "Zydzi w Katyniu," *Nowy Dziennik* (New York), 18–19 March 1989; Editorial Page letter, *The New York Times*, 29 March 1989, p. A22; and Michel Legris, "Katyn: Le Jour Ou Les Russes Avoueront. . . ," *L'Express* (Paris), 19 January 1990, p. 52.

5. Photographs of Rabbi Steinberg were obtained from his niece, Mrs. Henrietta Kelly, LLB, of London. Her father was Rabbi Meir Steinberg, the chief Jewish Chaplain of the Polish Forces headed by General Wladyslaw Anders who fought along with the English and Allied Forces in World War II.

6. *Instytut Katynski w Polsce*, Bulletin No. 16 (Warsaw, June 1980), edited by Andrzej Kostrzewski.

7. Janusz K. Zawodny, *Katyn* (Paris: Editions spotkania, 1989), pp. 120–21.

8. See Natalia Lebedeva, "The Katyn Tragedy," *International Affairs* (Moscow), July 1990, p. 100.

9. Szymon Datner, *Zbrodnie Wehrmachtu Na Jencach Wojennychw Drugiej Wojnie Swiatowej* (Warsaw, 1964), pp. 224–25.

10. Lebedeva, "Katyn Tragedy," p. 101.

11. Ibid., p. 102.

12. P. Soprunenko, Major of the NKVD of the USSR, was chief of the Directorate for Prisoners of War Affairs (DAPOW), which was set up on 19 September 1939 (see Lebedeva, "Katyn Tragedy"). The rank of major in the NKVD was equivalent to that of brigadier general in the Soviet Army. Despite the fact that the writer has seen many documents pertaining to Katyn which were signed by Soprunenko, no full first name was found. To date, Russian historians have not listed his full name in their papers about Katyn. Information as to the first names

of other NKVD officers mentioned in this paper (Chochlov and Tishkov) are also unavailable.

13. See Lebedeva, "Katyn Tragedy," p. 102.

14. Plk. Dr. Marek Tarczynski, "Dokumenty Katynskie," *Wojskowy Przeglad Historyczny, Rok XXXV* (Warsaw, 1990), Lipiec-Grudzien no. 3–4 (133–4), p. 318.

15. *Foks-Sztyme* (Warsaw), Organ Towarzystwa Spoleczno Kulturalnego Zydow w Polsce, nos. 1–2 (4–11 January 1991) and nos. 3–4 (18–25 January 1991).

16. Stanislaw Jankowski, "Odnaleziono Katynskie Dokumenty," *Nowy Dziennik–Przeglad Polski* (New York), 9 May 1991, p. 1.

17. *Maly Rocznik Statystyczny 1939 Naklad Glownego Urzedu Statystycznego.* (Warsaw, 1939), p. 33.

18. Jedrzej Tucholski, *Mord w Katyniu* (Warsaw: Instytut Wydawniczy Pax, 1991).

19. Waclaw Godziemba-Maliszewski is the founder of The Society for Aero-Historical Research located in Bethel, Connecticut, in the United States.

20. Lebedeva, "Katyn Tragedy," p. 103.

21. "Pro Memoria" in *Wojskowy Przeglad Historyczny Ministerstwo Obrony Narodowej.* (Instytut Historyczny, Warsaw), 1990–91.

22. *Hearings Before the Select Committee to Conduct an Investigation of the Facts, Evidence and Circumstances of the Katyn Forest Massacre.* 1–2 Session 1951–1952 (Washington, 1952).

23. Ksiadz Zdzislaw Peszkowski, *Wspomnienia Jenca z Kozielska* (Warsaw: Wydawnictwo Archidiecezji, Warszawskiej, 1989), p. 82.

24. Ibid., p. 20.

25. Simon Schochet, "Proba Okreslenia Tozsamosci Polskich Oficerow Pochodzenia Zydowskiego—Jencow Obozow Sowieckich," *Nowy Dziennik–Przeglad Polski* (New York), 21 November 1990, pp. 2–3; Simon Schochet, "Rassledovanie Daleko Ne Zakoncheno," *Novoe Russkoe Slovo* (New York), 29 November 1990, p. 7.

About the Contributors

Mordechai Altshuler is Professor of Contemporary Jewry and Head of the Centre for Research and Documentation of East European Jewry at the Hebrew University, Jerusalem. He is the author of *Soviet Jewry Since the Second World War: Population and Social Structure* (1987) and *The Jews of the Eastern Caucasus* (1990).

Lucjan Dobroszycki is Senior Research Associate at the YIVO Institute and Eli and Diana Zborowski Professor of Interdisciplinary Holocaust Studies at Yeshiva University. He is the author of many books and articles and edited *The Chronicle of the Lodz Ghetto* (1984), which has appeared in Polish, English, and German.

David Engel teaches modern Jewish history at New York University and is the editor of *Gal-Ed: Studies on the History of Polish Jewry*. He is the author of *In the Shadow of Auchswitz: The Polish Government in Exile and the Jews, 1939–1942* (1987) and *Facing a Holocaust: The Polish Government in Exile and the Jews, 1943–1945* (1993).

Zvi Gitelman is Professor of Political Science and Tisch Professor of Judaic Studies at the University of Michigan. He is the author or editor of eight books, including *Developments in Soviet and Post-Soviet Politics* (1992), *The Quest for Utopia: Jewish Political Ideas and Institutions Through the Ages* (1992), and *A Century of Ambivalence: The Jews in Russia and the Soviet Union, 1881 to the Present* (1988).

Jan T. Gross is Professor of Politics at New York University. He is the author of *Polish Society under German Occupation: General-gouvernement, 1939–1944* (1979) and *Revolution from Abroad: The*

Soviet Conquest of Poland's Western Ukraine and Western Belorussia (1988).

Jeffrey S. Gurock is Libby M. Klaperman Professor of Jewish History and Coordinator of Holocaust Programming at Yeshiva University. He is the editor of the English-language edition of S. Huberband's *Kiddush Ha-Shem: Jewish Religious and Cultural Life in Poland during the Holocaust* (1988).

Lukasz Hirszowicz is Editor-in-chief of *East European Jewish Affairs* (formerly *Soviet Jewish Affairs*). He is the author of numerous studies about the Middle East and Jewish affairs in Central and Eastern Europe.

Zvi Kolitz is Special Lecturer in Jewish Studies at Yeshiva University. He is the author of *Yossel Rakover Speaks to God,* which has been translated into fourteen languages, and was co-producer of the Tony Award–winning production of "The Deputy."

William Korey is Director of International Policy Research for B'nai B'rith. He has taught at City University of New York, Columbia University, Brooklyn College, Yeshiva University, and YIVO. He is the author of *Glasnost and Anti-Semitism* (1991), *Helsinki and Human Rights* (1983), *The Soviet Cage: Anti-Semitism in Russia* (1973), and *The Key to Human Rights Implementation* (1968).

Sergei Maksudov is a Fellow at the Harvard Russian Research Center and teaches in the Slavic Department at Harvard University. He is the author of *Losses of Population in the USSR* (1989) and *Unheard Voices: Documents of Smolensk Archive* (1987) and is the editor of *On Sakharov* (1981).

Rafael Medoff is Visiting Scholar at the Melton Center for Jewish Studies at Ohio State University and Assistant Professor of Religion at Denison University. He is author of *The Deafening Silence: American Jewish Leaders and the Holocaust* (1987). His essays have appeared in *American Jewish History, Studies in Zionism,* and *Holocaust Studies Annual.*

Dalia Ofer is Senior Lecturer, Institute of Contemporary Jewry, School of Education, Hebrew University. She is the author of *Escaping the Holocaust: Illegal Immigration to the Land of Israel, 1939–1944* (1990) and *Hamosh Shelo Hushlam: Parashat Kladovo Sabac 1939–1942* (1992).

Dr. Gertrude Schneider has taught and has held administrative positions at the Graduate School of the City University of New York. She is the editor of *Latvian Jewish Courier* and is the author of *Journey into Terror: Story of the Riga Ghetto* (1979), *Muted Voices: Jewish Survivors of Latvia Remember* (1987), and *The Unfinished Road: Jewish Survivors of Latvia Look Back* (1991).

Simon Schochet received his Ph.D. in history from the University of Munich and is the author of *Feldafing* (1982). He has taught Modern European history at Miami University, Ohio and is a member of the Pilsudski Institute.

Robert Moses Shapiro is Assistant Professor of Jewish History at Yeshiva University. He is the author of "Coup de Kehila: The Agudas Israel's Seizure of Power in Lodz, 1928," in *Proceedings of the 10th World Congress of Jewish Studies* (1990); "Jacob Shatzky, Historian of Warsaw Jewry," in *The Jews of Warsaw* (1991); "Samorzad żydowskit w Polsce: Łodz, 1914–1939," in *Dzieje Żydow w Łodzi 1820–1944* (1991), and "Aspects of Jewish Self-government in Łodz 1914–1934," in *Poliv* (1991).

Andrzej Zbikowski is a Research Associate of the Jewish Historical Institute in Warsaw and the author of studies on the history of the Jews in Poland during the nineteenth century and during the Holocaust.

Index

Adamovich, Ales, 58
Akhromeev, Sergei, 22
Alexianu, Gheorghe, 141, 149
Aleynis (Lithuanian activist leader),
    200–201
Alon, Gedalyahu, 196–97
Altshuler, Mordechai, 6
Alytus (Lithuania), 200
Ambartsumian, S., 34
Anders, Wladyslaw, 122
"Anne Frank" (poem by Aron
    Vergelis), 54
Anti-Semitism, 16
  as explanation for Soviet
      historiography on Holocaust,
      17, 20
  in occupied territories, 174
  in Odessa, 138
  in Romania, 133–34
  See also Pogroms.
Anti-Zionist Committee of the Soviet
    Public, 37
Antonescu, Ion, 133, 137, 149
Arabiej, Lidzija, 50, 52
Arad, Yitzhak, 22, 218
Arajs, Victors, 184
The Ascent (film), 58
Askoldov, Aleksandr (Soviet film
    director), 57

Babi Yar (film), 58
Babi Yar massacre, 11, 46, 52, 62–64,
    98, 226, 231
  commemoration of, in Ukraine, 22,
      23
  controversy over, 8–9

Babi Yar massacre *(continued)*
  Soviet anti-Zionism and, 37
Babi Yar monument, 8, 15, 61, 68–
    74
Babi Yar (novel by Anatoly
    Kuznetsov), 9, 17, 48–49, 67–
    68
"Babi Yar" (poem by Yevgeny
    Yevtushenko), 8–9, 17, 61, 65–
    67
Baltic countries. *See* Estonia; Latvia;
    Lithuania
Baram, Haim, 231
Begun, Yosef, 71
Beliaev, Igor, 37
Belorussia, 35–36
  evacuation from, 81, 97
  Soviet historiography on Jews in,
      10
  war crime trials in, 43
  yizker-bikher on Jews in, 224–32
Belzec, 44, 45
Ben-Gurion, David, 112, 114
Benvenisti, Beno, 148–49
Ben-Zvi, Yitzhak, 121–22
Berdichev (Ukraine), 225, 226
Bergelson, David, 228
Beria, Lavrenty P., 241
Berkovitsh, Khasye, 230
Bershad, 225
Bessarabia, 133, 139, 150*n. 1*
Betar movement, 181
Bezymensky, Lev, 32
Bialystok (Poland), 175
Bikernieku Forest (Latvia), 192
Biltmore program, 115–16

Ukraine *(continued)*
  Smirnov's treatment of persecution
    of Jews in, 12
  war crime trials in, 43–44
  yizker-bikher on Jews in, 224–32
  See also Babi Yar massacre;
    Transnistria.
Ukrainians, 46, 176–79
Ulaszkowo (Poland), 179
The Unconquered (film), 57
Uzar-Sliwinski, Jozef, 168*n. 12*

Vabalas, Romualdas, 57
Valencius, Bishop, 203
Vergasov, Ilya, 50–51
Vergelis, Aron, 54
Vershihora, Petro, 50
Vilno, 175
Vitebsk, 225, 227–28
Vlasov, A.V., 65
Volhynia, 224
Volkogonov, Dmitrii, 21–22
Volksdeutsche, 134, 137–38
Volksdeutsche Mittelstelle (VOMI),
    137–38, 151*n. 8*
VOMI. *See* Volksdeutsche Mittelstelle.
Voznesenskii, Andrei, 49–50

Wannsee Conference, 36, 185–86
War crime trials, Soviet reporting on,
    38–47
  attacks on "bourgeois nationalism,"
    46–47
  in Baltic countries, 40–42
  in Belorussia and Ukraine, 42–43
  in RSFSR, 44–46
  in West, 38–39
Warsaw, 26*n. 38*, 143
Weizmann, Chaim, 105–8, 117
West, Binyamin, 121
Western territories
  anti-Jewish pogroms in, 173–79
  evacuation and escape of Jews
    from, 77–78, 80, 84–87, 92–97
  Jewish population losses in, 208–9,
    211–12
  plight of Jews under Soviet rule in,
    155–66
  reactions to Red Army's occupation
    of, 4–5

Western territories *(continued)*
  See also Estonia; Latvia; Lithuania;
    Poland; Romania.
Wetzel, Heinrich, 183, 185
What Keeps the World Going
    (Itskhokas Meras), 49
Wiesenthal, Simon, 32
Wiliamski, Edmund, 243
World War II, Soviet regime's
    treatment of, 18

Yad Vashem Institute (Jerusalem), 22,
    152*n. 20*, 207, 218
Yalkut Volin (periodical), 224
Yampol, 226, 228
Yankauskas (priest), 202–3
Yanushker, Reb Nahum, 204
Yazov, Dmitri, 22
Yegorov, Akelsei, 69–70
Yevtushenko, Yevgeny, 8–9, 17, 61,
    65–67, 70
Yiddish language, 164, 209
Yiddish literature and poetry,
    Holocaust in Soviet, 51–55
Yishuv leadership, 111–24
YIVO Institute for Jewish Research,
    218–19
Yizker-bikher, 223–32
Yuntofsky, Shimon, 71
Yurburg (Lithuania), 199–200
Yustingrad, 225, 229

Zaborow (Poland), 176
Zakliavicius, V., 57
Zawodny, Janusz, 239, 243
Zionism and Zionist movement, 241
  in Latvia, 181
  Soviet anti-Zionist campaign, 19–20,
    37, 46
  Soviet support for aims of, 105–8
  in Transnistrian ghettos, 147–48
  and Yishuv leadership's view of role
    of Soviet Union, 114–24
Zivs, Samuil, 71
Zloczow (Poland), 176
Zvhil, 225, 226, 229